LAND OF GRASS AND SKY
AND SKY

a naturalist's prairie journey

MARY TAYLOR YOUNG

EarthTales P

WESTCLIFFE PUBLISH
www.westcliffepublishers.co...

D1005344

About the Author

Mary Taylor Young is an award-winning nature writer, biologist, and naturalist. She is the author of nine books, six under the name Mary Taylor Gray. Mary's column, "Words on Birds," has appeared in Denver's *Rocky Mountain News* since 1993. She lives in Castle Rock, Colorado, with her husband and daughter.

Also by Mary Taylor Young

Colorado Wildlife Viewing Guide Revised
Falcon Press, 2000

On the Trail of Colorado Critters: Wildlife-Watching for Kids
Co-published by Denver Museum of Nature & Science and
Westcliffe Publishers, 2000

Written as Mary Taylor Gray:
Watchable Birds of California
Mountain Press, 1999

The Guide to Colorado Birds
Westcliffe Publishers, 1998

Watchable Birds of the Southwest
Mountain Press, 1995

Dodos, Birds of Prey and Other Male Species
Fulcrum Publishing, 1994

Colorado Wildlife Viewing Guide
Falcon Press, 1992

Watchable Birds of the Rocky Mountains
Mountain Press, 1992

International Standard Book Number: 1-56579-431-1

Text copyright: Mary Taylor Young, 2002. All rights reserved.
Illustrations copyright: Richard K. Young, 2002. All rights reserved.

Copy Editor: Kate Hawthorne
Managing Editor: Jenna Samelson
Designer: Carol Pando
Production Manager: Craig Keyzer

Published by:
Westcliffe Publishers, Inc.
EarthTales Press
P.O. Box 1261
Englewood, CO 80150
www.westcliffepublishers.com

Printed in the USA by Versa Press, Inc.

No portion of this book, whether text or illustrations, may be reproduced in any form, including electronically, without the express written permission of the publisher.

Library of Congress Cataloging-in-Publication Data:
Young, Mary Taylor, 1955-
    Land of grass and sky : a naturalist's prairie journey / by Mary Taylor Young.
        p. cm.
    ISBN 1-56579-431-1
    1. Prairie ecology--Great Plains--Anecdotes. 2. Young, Mary Taylor, 1955- I. Title.

QH104.5.G73 Y68 2002
577.4'0978--dc21

                                                                    2001059205

For more information about other fine books and calendars from Westcliffe Publishers, please contact your local bookstore, call us at 1-800-523-3692, write for our free color catalog, or visit us on the Web at **www.westcliffepublishers.com**.

Acknowledgments

For their guidance, knowledge, stories, advice, companionship, and support, I thank the many people who helped me with this book, some without even knowing it. For graciously sharing their reminiscences, I thank Gene and Judy Vick. For access to the Sand Creek site, and for his perspectives, thanks to Bill Dawson. For teaching me about prairie plants, thanks to Carl Mackey. For emotional support, endless reading, companionship on prairie journeys, and help in countless other ways, I thank my sister, Sally Taylor, and my husband, Rick Young, whose marvelous artwork enlivens the book. For helping me to rediscover family roots on the Kansas prairie, I thank my mother, Patty Taylor, and aunt, Betty Collard, neither of whom lived to see this book in print. Thanks also to my late neighbor, Morris Pierce, for telling me much of the history of my Denver farmhouse.

Many thanks to: Diane Spickert for help on Rocky Mountain geology; Denver Museum of Nature and Science's Russ Graham for information on the Age of Mammals; Betsy Baldwin for advice on cultivating a backyard prairie; Donald Worster for insight into the Dust Bowl; John Pape for information on prairie dogs as disease vectors; Laird and Colleen Cometsevah and Arlie Rhoads for sharing with me a bit of the Cheyenne culture; and Will Morton for restoring the Kit Carson County Carousel for all of us. Thank you to Max Gartenberg for his efforts on my behalf, and to Derek Lawrence for his continued support. For an outstanding editing job, thanks to Kate Hawthorne. And for bringing these words to print, I thank John Fielder and Linda Doyle.

To Cody and Margo, who journeyed with me.

Contents

Introduction:

Beyond Ding-Dong Daddyville

N ext stop Dumas!" Dad called out to us over the singing-tire hum of our Chevrolet Impala as it rolled along the endless Texas highway. It was the early 1960s and our family was on its annual summer voyage across the Western prairie toward Colorado. I was a child of about seven, imprisoned in the backseat between my two big sisters. As the youngest, I was always relegated to the middle, conned or bullied despite my whining protests into this least desirable of seats. To make things worse, the car lacked air conditioning, and I squirmed in my tiny space like a salamander on a hot plate, my bare legs sticking to the vinyl seat.

Dad was an Army officer, then stationed at Fort Sam Houston in San Antonio, Texas. Each summer we made a pilgrimage to the cool, high world of the Colorado Rockies, to my grandparents' cabin next door to Rocky Mountain National Park. The Cabin, as the family called it, implying it was the only and the best cabin in the world, was a marvelous old place dating from the 1930s that had a ponderosa pine growing up through the kitchen. Visited by emerald hummingbirds, with a million-dollar view of Longs Peak out the living room window, that wonderful cabin in the mountains was our Mecca. But like all worthy journeyers, we had to earn our visit to Eden—by crossing the heat-shimmered purgatory of the shortgrass prairie. Up we came out of Texas, traversing the Oklahoma panhandle before making the hot, dry run across eastern Colorado.

Miserable is the only way to describe those family road trips. Wedged between my sisters in the backseat of the Chevy, I had a choice of two views—the backs of my parents' heads or, if I sat forward a bit, the boring brown land whizzing past the windows. There was such a sameness to it I had a panicky feeling we were passing the same stretch of land over and over, caught in an episode of *The Twilight Zone.* If anyone had talked to me then of the ethereal beauty of the prairie and its spiritual lessons, I would have advised them to sit down on a cactus and think it over.

We had already used up the best diversion for trip boredom—food. Working our way through the cooler, we devoured fried chicken, apples, Cokes, homemade chocolate chip cookies, and slices of buttered bread sprinkled with sugar. Lunch over, we tossed our trash and chicken bones out the windows without a thought (this being before Lady Bird Johnson's Keep America Beautiful program changed an entire country's conscience about littering). We never looked back as our detritus crashed to the asphalt and blew away across those open plains. This barren country, after all, was a wasteland that a little trash wouldn't hurt. Now all we had left to look forward to was a stop in Dumas, Texas.

The passage of time is a relative thing, especially for a seven-year-old, and to me those trips took at least 14 years. By the time we reached Dumas, a rough halfway point on our journey, we were all ready for even the tamest diversion. This little burg on the plains was hardly a garden spot, but it had one trick up its sleeve. Back about the time The Cabin was new, a silly little song put Dumas on the map for its 15 minutes of fame. My father, a veritable storehouse of such Americana, knew all the words. Over successive summers, he had managed to build up Dumas and its song in our minds into something to get excited about. (The appeal of our stopover was bolstered by a guaranteed ice-cream cone once we hit town.)

As we got closer, I squinted out the window, my eyes straining across the sameness of dry grass and sagebrush, scarcely noticing the occasional zigzagging jackrabbit spooked by our car. I wanted to be the first to see the billboard on the edge of town announcing our arrival at Dumas.

Finally, the Dumas billboard shimmered vaguely in the distance, remarkable in this landscape as the only thing taller than knee height. A cartoon of a barbershop quartet holding canes and dressed in striped seersucker jackets and straw boater hats proclaimed, "The Ding-Dong Daddies of Dumas Welcome You!"

"Okay, girls," Dad called over his shoulder and the three of us sat up expectantly, casting off our heat-and-highway lethargy. Following his lead we broke into a robust though off-key chorus of the Dumas theme song—"I'm a Ding-Dong Daddy from Dumas (Yeah!)…and you oughta see me Du-mas stuff!"

That was prairie to me in my childhood: the Ding-Dong Daddies prancing across a bare stage. The Daddies were the only thing I found even vaguely interesting in what seemed otherwise a great void. It would be many years before I saw prairie differently, before I found the depth and vibrancy beneath this brown-on-brown still life. Only when I learned to look close, to see with more than my eyes, to listen to silence, did I discover the fullness of this empty landscape, and of myself. This book is the chronicle of my prairie journey, a trip beyond Ding-Dong Daddyville. I traveled by foot and on horseback, but in the end, my true odyssey was a journey of the spirit.

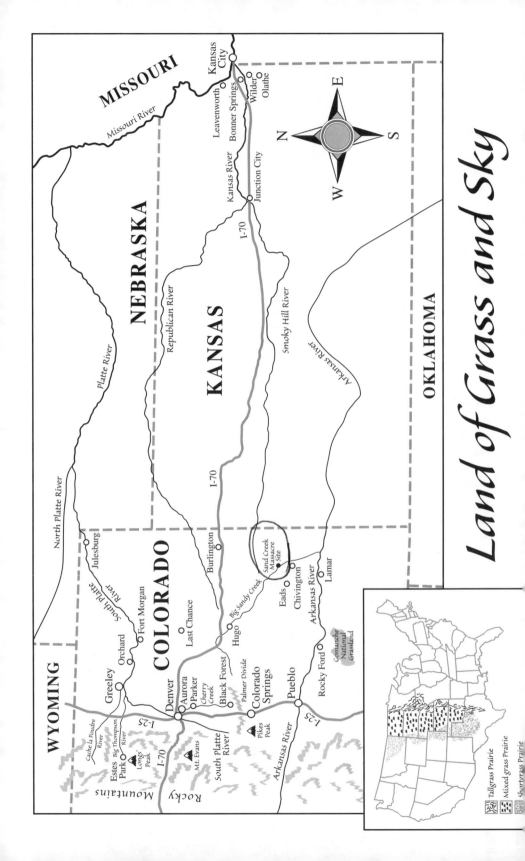

Land of Grass and Sky

Chapter 1:
Pronghorn

Maybe it's my contrary nature that makes me love a landscape despised by others. Or, if not despised, then unappreciated. This place called ugly, barren, worthless must appeal to the lover-of-waifs somewhere in my soul. Attachment to a place rarely happens at a single moment, but if I were to pick a time when my kinship with the prairie began, I suppose it would be one summer morning in the middle of the 1980s. I awoke to a quiet house just before the sun lit the eastern horizon like amber tea spilled from the pot. The house was still, yet I had a sense of excitement, of change brewing.

I padded downstairs in bare feet and an oversized bathrobe. Cody, the Chesapeake Bay Retriever, greeted me with his morning smile, the loose skin of his bulbous muzzle wrinkling to show his teeth in what the uninitiated might think was a snarl but what I knew was an expression of greeting and love. I stroked his silky head, laid my face on his. His brown fur always smelled to me like fresh-baked cookies. I patted his broad back, his shoulders as sturdy as boulders.

I brewed a pot of coffee and poured some in my favorite cup, the Valentine's mug, cherry red with white hearts incised deeply into it. Stepping out onto the deck, I felt the wood smooth and cool beneath my feet. The air embraced me, sharp and chill even on this midsummer morning. I lowered myself gingerly into a lawn chair, hurrying to tuck my robe around my bare legs to protect against the eye-opening touch of the cold metal. Cody followed silently, lying down beside me on the deck, my guardian. Margo, my sweet mixed-breed dog, an orphan adopted six years earlier from the Denver Dumb Friends League animal shelter, joined us, her silky white coat soft and glowing. The shadow of the house at this early hour lay across me like a cloak. I pulled my knees up and encircled them with my arms, my coffee cup held out before me in two hands like an alms bowl.

On the western horizon, the aristocratic profile of the Front Range of the Rocky Mountains lay like a movie star in the golden light of morning. Pikes Peak marked the border of my south view, Longs Peak my north. A swath of open country—mostly ranchland with a few buds of suburban development—stretched like an apron from the scenery right up to my backyard. My new housing development sat self-consciously surrounded by prairie, the outpost of a colonizing people—Jamestown on the Platte. I was a homesteader of a new sort, floating on a raft of urbanization amid a sea of openness. Like the palisades of a fort, a six-foot cedar fence divided my too-green lawn from a colony of prairie dogs scurrying about amid yucca and wild grasses. Other than the few stick trees we'd planted hoping to grow a spot of shade, the land around held no cover taller than a rabbitbrush. Above the landscape, a red-tailed hawk rowed upward on broad wings, climbing into a blue void.

I can sit here as long as I like this morning, I remembered. Since I'd sold my business, I was a woman of leisure. No need to hurry to shower and dress; I had nowhere to be this morning. No one, really, to report to. Even this house wouldn't offer me a home for too much longer. It was up for sale, and once a new buyer surfaced, I'd be free to move anywhere I liked. This summer had also seen the end of my marriage, by mutual consent and with minimum fuss. That part of my life did not bear further examination; it had been put to rest.

Marriage ended, business sold, house about to follow—I should have felt scared or sad, I suppose, but I shivered with excitement. I felt poised at the beginning of a journey, one taken by anyone who has started life over. I didn't know yet where I would go. It was as if my bags were packed and I'd hitched up the horses, but I didn't know which way to point their heads.

I'd lived on the High Plains, the high elevation prairie of Colorado that spreads from Kansas to the Rocky Mountains, for more than a dozen years, longer than I'd lived anywhere else. Growing up in an Army family that moved constantly, I was always stumped when anyone asked me where I was from. *Where am I from?* I wondered. Like the show-biz baby born in a stage trunk, I was born in an Army footlocker. I was only six months old when I first moved. I counted up the places we'd lived—Virginia, Kansas, Texas, Germany, Virginia (again) and Texas (again). Ten homes by the time I graduated from high school, not counting the temporary quarters we'd spent a week or a month in when we first arrived at a new post. Ten moves in 17 years. And the number of schools? My fingers ticked off the roll call—eight different schools between kindergarten and high-school graduation. Colorado was the first place that wasn't just a stopover on the way to somewhere else for me. I'd come to Colorado State University, then moved after graduation to Denver and a real job. A few years later, I married and moved to Parker, a one-time ranching town that was beginning to attract city folk but was still far enough out to the southeast that it didn't yet qualify as a suburb.

I can go anywhere I want now, I thought. Like everyone who lives in the urban Front Range corridor of Colorado, I'd always wanted to move to the mountains. The lush valley of the Yampa River in northwestern Colorado, maybe. Ski Steamboat in winter, backpack in the Mount Zirkel Wilderness in summer. The sale of my business allowed me the luxury of a career change. I had always written, for personal pleasure and fulfillment. My plan now was to give it a shot full-time, try to earn a living at writing. I would turn from the pragmatic world of business back to my passion—animals and nature. I had my degree in Zoology from CSU, where I had focused on animal behavior, specifically, the behavior and life history of coyotes. I thought back to my days working in the university's Animal Behavior Lab, where I hand-reared two litters of coyote pups for a graduate student who was studying how coyotes learned.

The goal of the research was to discover ways to keep coyotes away from sheep without killing the wily predators. Even after so many years, the names of the first litter that I raised to adulthood ran through my mind like a chant—Fera, Zemi, Chainy, Melo, Chama, Charo. They had taught me so much about the nature of wild creatures, the independent spirit captivity would never conquer. Henry Beston's beautiful prose from *The Outermost House* came to my mind: "They are not brethren, they are not underlings; they are other nations, caught with ourselves in the net of life and time." One day I hoped to write as eloquently, but at this moment, I wasn't sure how I would find my way down that path.

By noon the open country would recline in a torpor, beaten into submission by an oppressive sun—a barren-seeming land with nowhere to hide. But now, in early morning, the prairie lay at its best, rich in hues of amber, sage, and smoky blue. How rarely had I taken the time to enjoy its beauty.

Beyond the fence, I noticed movement close to the ground. The prairie dogs were already up and busy, loping about their village. Having prairie dogs as neighbors is like living next door to a colony of quaint country folk with their own ways, keeping to themselves within their community as modern life surrounds them. They rise early, tend their fields, then sit on their front porches and socialize with the neighbors. Prairie dogs are fastidious homeowners—the yards around their burrows clipped free of vegetation and swept smooth by the brush of many furry bodies. As I watched, one 'dog stopped to inspect a plant growing near its burrow. Gripping the flower in tiny hands, it sat upright and began to nibble, a farmer testing a green wheat stalk.

A car door slammed in the garage next door—the neighbor off for work. Both humans and prairie dogs go to work early, but if it were snowing and dark instead of sunny and nice, my neighbor would still be heading to the office while the 'dogs would be wisely underground, snug and dry. And while prairie dogs watch out for their neighbors, sounding off whenever danger approaches, we humans scarcely know those who live next door.

A volley of chirping alarm barks sounded from the prairie-dog town, announcing that a redtail was now cruising right overhead. Intrigued, I walked across the lawn to where the fence demarked my territory from the rough and grizzled landscape of the prairie. Cody and Margo padded after me; patrolling this perimeter was one of their main jobs. In bare feet I couldn't cross the frontier, guarded as it was by prickly pear cactus, but I peered through the gaps between the uprights of the fence. I spied a coyote trotting casually through the rounded mounds of the prairie dog village. All the 'dogs had tumbled down into the safety of their burrows, but I still heard the muffled, hollow barks of the sentinels coming from within the tunnels.

Grabbing the collars of my two dogs, I moved to the back gate and pushed against it for a better view. The gate groaned as if pained at exposing itself to the ungroomed land beyond. The gate's protest alerted the coyote; she froze, turning her dog face to look straight at me. Her eyes were a yellow-green, luminous and intelligent. We stood gazing eye-to-eye across this frontier—city meeting prairie, human meeting wild—each in frank appraisal of the other. What did she make of me? Was she afraid of me, standing there in my bathrobe, guarded by my big dogs? But then I realized I was the one with the dogs and the palisade fence.

She turned, dismissing me, and moved off in a drifting trot. Caught in the morning light, her silvery figure receded into the landscape like a silken wave ebbing out to sea. She trod a path I could not see. For a moment she stopped on a far rise. Did she look back at me? Did I catch a glint of challenge or invitation in the luminous eyes?

The coffee in my cup was cold. I turned back to the house and stepped into the kitchen just as the phone rang. My sister's voice greeted me: "Come into Denver and meet me for lunch."

A few hours later my silver Mazda RX-7 slipped along through rolling country of pastures and prairie, a gray-green carpet of grasses swept by the vigilant shadows of hunting hawks. The car was sleek and trim, low to the ground, curve-hugging, and I relished the feeling of freedom and energy it brought me. The road coursed through a series of dipsy-doos that were irresistible to a sports-car driver on a cool morning. Rushing up one rise in the road, I sensed motion to my right. Just on the other side of the wire fence, so close it seemed I might reach out and touch them, ran a band of pronghorn, their legs reaching and folding in a long-strided gallop, their horned heads bobbing slightly forward and back with each surging stride. I glanced at my speedometer—47 miles per hour—yet the animals kept pace with me effortlessly. They were the color of autumn grass, their sides shaded tawny above and pale below. From a distance this pattern helps mask them, erasing their profile so their forms blend with the horizontals of the prairie landscape. But as they ran beside me, I thought the swath of amber on their flanks must endow them with the gift of speed, like the lightning bolts Indian warriors painted on the sides of their ponies. The pronghorn never turned their heads to look at me. Their doe-eyes saw me well enough in the peripheral field of vision, but they remained princely and aloof. Acknowledging my presence was beneath them. We headed westward together—neck and neck—racing for the mountains.

I knew these animals. I had often seen this trim band feeding or resting in the open country to the north or south of the road. They looked too exotic for the Colorado prairie; with their curved horns and sleek bodies they seemed like creatures born to the African savanna. I'd made a game of spotting them, picking out their tan-and-white shapes from the dun-colored landscape. Sometimes they lay half-hidden in the grass, at others they stepped along in single file—a nomadic band on the move. Often their handsomely marked figures were quite distant and challenging to make out, but sometimes they stood close enough for me to note the elegant lines of their necks and their graceful horns.

Last fall my sister and I had tried to get a closer look at the pronghorn band. We found them lying in a fold between two grassy hillocks, perhaps a quarter mile distant. Parking by the side of the road, we fixed them in our binoculars. Like a wizard's trick, their vague shapes resolved sharply into distinct animals. Eight deer-like heads pointed our direction, all aligned exactly parallel as if oriented by an invisible compass. Eight pairs of great dark eyes regarded us, unblinking. We sat in uneasy truce with these serene animals, watching them through the car window. They accepted our presence until we decided to get closer. We opened the car doors and stepped out of the vehicle, a gross violation of the neutral zone. As soon as our upright figures emerged from the amorphous shape of the car, the buck jumped to his feet, stamped, and led his does off across the prairie. "Wait, come back," we wanted to call out to them. "We're sorry, we won't come any closer." But we stood helpless as they evaporated, melting into the landscape. Pronghorn brook no violations of protocol. We had allowed a special moment to blow away in the wind.

Now here the pronghorn were again, running along beside my car. Up a hill we ran, reaching the crest, then spilling down together, never lessening our speed, then caught again by the earth and carried up the next rise. I was flying with them, endowed with their grace and power. They flowed in a line alongside me, all tan-and-brown motion, their upright heads proudly bearing the smooth horns.

I was driving a bit too fast for that narrow country road. We topped a small rise, and suddenly there they were directly ahead, slipping one after another under the fence and darting across the road. One, two, three, four.... Like quicksilver their pale forms flashed across in front of me. I was dazzled by them, but fortunately my driver's reflexes still functioned and I slammed on the brakes. The Mazda fish-tailed precariously, skittering gravel and sand. Finally the car came to a stop on the shoulder as the last of the pronghorn darted across the road and sped off. Like forms from a dream, they sifted away from me, never looking back. My last glimpse was of their flashing white rumps disappearing into the prairie.

My pulse drummed in my head and I gasped for breath. What a near miss! I'd come close to having a major accident. The car sat askew on the shoulder where it had screeched to a stop. I gripped the steering wheel with white-knuckled hands, staring out at the quiet grassland into which the pronghorn had vanished. My moment of danger had happened so quickly, in a rush, and now all was quiet again. The grasses stirred gently, showing no evidence of the pronghorn's passage. A Kiowa legend came to my mind, about a sacred mountain opening to accept the last of the wild buffalo then closing back again to protect them and keep them safe within.

The coyote this morning, now the pronghorn. They had followed some hidden trail into the open country, vanishing in plain sight. The prairie gazed back at me, hinting of secrets I might share. Even as I prepared to move away from it, back to the city, I glimpsed the hidden face, serene and enigmatic, of this land with a Buddha smile.

Chapter 2:
Plains Cottonwood

The Realtor's voice sounded scratchy over her car phone: "I've got a showing of the house set for 9 a.m. tomorrow." Joanne was businesslike and not prone to companionable chatting. "It's best if you're out of the house." Realizing that sounded a bit cold, she laughed and her voice softened a little, "Showings just go better when the owners aren't hovering around." Joanne had made me paint the kitchen but other than that she thought the house "showed well" and should sell quickly. I'd just as soon not be there as prospective buyers tramped around my home, critically assessing its design, amenities and decor. And while docile Margo was no problem, I couldn't very well leave Cody there. I'd had no luck explaining to that 105-pound guardian, who took his mission extremely seriously, that in this case it was okay to let strangers into the house when I wasn't around.

Banished from our home, the three of us headed out on the prairie, the dogs on the scent of unseen creatures, me seeking wildflowers and native plants. I'd always enjoyed poking around in the open country around the house, had become pretty familiar with the native plants and wildlife of the High Plains. Exploring what others would call waste land had been my weekend outlet, my connection to the natural world after a week spent in an office. Now I turned that way again.

At loose on the prairie, having left our home behind and not knowing where we might land, either today or in the coming months, Cody, Margo and I were temporary nomads. The song of a meadowlark spilled suddenly out in the sunshine, the notes dancing across the open space of sky and land, the voice of the prairie. I had once met an elderly woman whose family had homesteaded in eastern Colorado. "As kids," she said, "we used to think the meadowlark was calling *Gee-whiz-whillikers* and *Yes, I am a pretty-little-bird*." I spied the singing lark perched atop the dry stalk of a yucca, its head tossed back, its open bill making a V against the blue sky.

We started in the direction I'd seen the coyote travel behind the house, but following the track of that wild and wary dog wasn't easy. The open country is a fool-me landscape. It appears a uniform gray-green, but on close inspection offers a pantry of colors, textures and scents. Even the names of the prairie plants sing—buffalo grass, needle and thread, pasque flower, bitterbrush, prairie smoke, blanket flower, goatsbeard.

Around us the tall stalks of woolly mullein stood at attention, dotting the grassland like ranks of troops. In brittle death the dry stalks are much more intriguing than when they're green and alive. I couldn't resist the urge to break them down and launch them like javelins. I became a Paleolithic huntress; Cody the dog was my prey. Fleet of foot I chased after him, coiled back my arm, hurled my spear. The lance flew straight and true, kept on course by the tight dried flowers like fletching along the upper third of the shaft. But this lance's flight was soft and barely tapped Cody's side. He looked at me with patient tolerance. Playing hunter-gatherer again, are we?

I realized the air had filled with a spicy, sensual perfume, and I tilted my head up like a fox scenting the breeze. Ah, sage! Just brushing against sagebrush is enough for the plant to release its fragrance. Now that I've trampled it, the scent of sagebrush follows me around like a friendly old dog. Where most scented plants offer fragrance through their flowers, throwing in the added seduction of a brightly colored blossom, the scent of sagebrush comes from its leaves and stems. Many shortgrass prairie plants are rough to the touch or downright prickly, but the blue-green foliage of fringed sage is soft and fragrant, like the embrace of a grandmother.

Sagebrush, nicknamed sage, often confuses people. Occasionally, Western novelists have their characters spice food with sage growing wild on the range. But the fragrant sagebrush of the West is not the same as the sage used in cooking. The culinary herb we use to flavor stuffing and meats is of the genus *Salvia*, a member of the mint family. Our wild Western sage is more correctly called sagebrush, and certainly no other plant is so closely identified with the West. There seems to be sagebrush of some type or other just about everywhere. Big sagebrush, large and shrubby, inspired the title of Zane Grey's classic western *Riders of the Purple Sage*. Some 20 species inhabit the High Plains and Rocky Mountain region, all belonging to the genus *Artemisia* of the composite (sunflower) family. This fragrant group also claims as members the herb tarragon and Eurasian worm-wood, from which the liqueur absinthe is distilled. Many popular land-scaping plants—silver queen is one example—are artemisians.

What a lovely and poetic name, *Artemisia*. While their cousins the sunflowers and asters bear bright and showy flowers, the artemisians are dull, with tiny flowers barely visible. Yet they are namesakes of Artemis, Greek goddess of the hunt, a being of strength, power and confidence. Artemis rules the hunt not because she dominates and kills, but because she is mother of the animals, the animate spirit of nature. As such, she is a healer, a protector of the young and of wildlife, and she eases the pain of childbirth. Healers of body and spirit for many cultures, plants of the genus *Artemisia* draw their medicinal powers from their aromatic oils, particularly camphor.

Camphor gives sagebrush its olfactory kick and also makes it useful for treatment of colds and congestion. Boiled in a pot of water, sagebrush releases an aromatic steam that can be inhaled, or the warm, damp leaves can be applied to the chest and throat as a hot compress. Damp sage leaves can also be applied as a poultice on wounds and sore muscles, a sort of natural Ben-Gay ointment. Early pioneers brewed sagebrush into a tea to treat the effects of Rocky Mountain spotted fever. The leaves are chewed by some cultures to induce vomiting, a means of actual and symbolic purging. Native Americans use smoke from smoldering sage smudges in purification ceremonies.

Sage tea—it sounded wonderfully earthy and herbal to me. On one outing I picked a bundle of sagebrush on the prairie, dried it in the sun, then steeped it in boiling water. Straining the leaves, I poured the grayish-brown tea into a mug, cupped it in my two hands, and breathed in the steam. Hmm, smells like medicine. Then I took a sip. Ugh. No amount of sugar or honey made that bitter brew any better. It was like drinking cough medicine when you're expecting lemonade.

Now, while Joanne shows the house, I cut more sagebrush fronds to carry home to dry, wrapping and tying the bundles with blue grama grass. I will burn these as smudges to purify our new house, wherever we might end up.

Margo's energy is flagging; Cody's tongue hangs from his mouth like a long red tie. We're a pack of nomads who need to find shelter from the prairie sun. As the cool cease-fire period of early morning passes, the sun reminds me only too well who rules this land. From the northwest a dry wind sweeps in. "It'll suck the living juices right out of you," my father likes to say. I've progressively shed my layers—hat, jacket, sweatshirt—and now plod sweating into the sanctuary of a cottonwood grove. One sturdy old-timer extends an invitation. I lean against its dense trunk, slide to the damp ground to catch my breath. The dogs flop down next to me, their tongues hanging, mouths open in a vigorous pant.

Entered from the baked-biscuit scent of open prairie, this patch of woodland seems veiled in musk, its humid perfume clean and forthright. In contrast to the spicy, pungent scent of pine, cottonwoods have a damp and earthy smell. Their fragrance hints of secrets hidden below the dry prairie. The cottonwood might be insignificant in a hardwood forest dominated by maples with leaves the size of dinner plates, but on the shortgrass prairie, where each tree is revered, the cottonwood is a blessing. For a traveler, it becomes many things—a Samaritan, providing cool cover from the sun's intensity; a mother, offering wombs for cavity-nesting birds, bats, mice, packrats, raccoons and other creatures; a diviner, marking the treasure of water in an arid land. Cottonwoods must keep their feet damp. Visible at a distance on the open country, their obelisk shapes are a sure sign of a waterway or shallow groundwater.

The tree I sit beneath is a landmark I have often watched for in my ramblings, because it marks a crossing of the creek. Its roots reach into the sand of the dry creek bed where in wetter seasons they are gently stroked by the flow of the water. The tree's bark is deeply grooved with the years. I poke my fingers into the wooden channels and they are swallowed nearly to the third knuckle. Like us, a cottonwood is smooth and unlined in youth, the skin of its trunk soft and supple. As it ages, its bark adds lines and wrinkles, thickening with experience and wisdom.

This cottonwood is an old woman, a grandmother who has seen countless winters. She rises 80 feet high and her trunk is massive. We commonly praise trees when they are "straight as an oak." This tree is not. An oak, growing in a dense forest where the light is shaded and filtered, must climb up, up, toward the sky to reach the sun. The cottonwood has no such need, for on the prairie sunshine is abundant and the trees never grow so close as to block out the light. Settlers who tried to use cottonwoods for log cabins found the trunks to be less than cooperative as building materials; they were whimsical in design rather than straight and true, branching from the stout original into many trunks, each taking its own direction. True to form, the grandmother tree is bent and bowed on its way to the sky, branching into four main beams about 20 feet from the ground. I circle her trunk, embracing it with my outstretched arms, amazed at its girth. Marking my beginning point with a twig wedged in a deep groove, I inchworm around the tree with my arms, measuring its circumference. The old cottonwood's trunk is three and a half times the breadth of my outstretched arms. At home I measure my arm span at 62 inches fingertip to fingertip. That means the circumference of the old tree is an amazing 18 feet. Using my seventh-grade geometry, I calculate the tree's diameter. Its trunk measures five and three-quarters feet across. The trunk of the grandmother tree is broader than I am tall.

I fell into calling this tree a grandmother because she seemed so ancient and comforting, but she truly is a grandmother, many times over. Individual cottonwoods are either male or female, and it is the females that make the fluffy "cotton." In spring this grand old tree bears fuzzy, worm-like flowers which fruit into long strings of emerald beads. Tightly packed inside are bits of white silk fastened to tiny brown seeds, airborne troops rigged out in parachutes and awaiting the command to launch. When the beads ripen and give birth, the seeds spill out to loft away on the air in what looks like a summer snowstorm.

My neighbor sneers at cottonwoods as "trash" trees because they litter his yard with twigs and white silk and live fewer years than his favored maples and oaks. But settlers didn't have a choice of landscaping trees from a nursery. For them the native cottonwood, planted in windrows around homesteads and along fields, offered relief from the prairie sun and wind, and from the unrelenting openness. For settlers who drew their precious water from wells or hauled it from streams, nurturing a tree planted on the prairie was a challenge. Homesteaders cosseted their seedlings, bringing gifts of water and visiting them as if they were family members, to see how they got on. Cottonwoods standing in regimented lines remain as silent markers of prairie homesteads whose buildings long ago tumbled to the ground.

From where I lean against the tree's rough bark, I can see above me a messy tangle of sticks. This is no haphazard jumble of fallen twigs but a carefully constructed home. A domed roof covers opposing entrances that create a sort of breezeway. At the correct angle, you can see straight through a magpie nest.

From the outside, magpie nests seem haphazard, as if they are about to fall to the ground in a heap. But they don't. How can such messy constructions hold together, much less offer nursery for young magpies that must be a rackety, energetic brood? Magpies build these structures using impressive engineering skill. For hammer, saw and screwdriver, a magpie uses its beak. The architectural plans are age-old imprints within the bird's DNA. Inside the rough exterior is a bowl fashioned of clay and gently lined with fine root hairs and plant down. Magpies form what biologists call a long-term pair bond. I prefer to think of them like old married couples, looking so much alike you can't tell husband from wife. Having invested energy in building a nest, a bonded pair often repairs and reoccupies it the next year. If they don't like the old nest, they may still use it as the platform atop which to build a new nest.

As if dressed in sequins, the magpie's harlequin plumage shimmers to purple and emerald in the light. A black tail stiff as a crinoline petticoat trails behind. How came birds to garner so many gifts? God blessed them with the magical power of flight, and added grace and beauty in the bargain. But as if to offset these favors, magpies have the harsh voices and raucous behavior of all crow-family birds, and are almost recklessly bold. I've watched them hop past Cody, when he was fast asleep in the yard, to peck at a dog bone lying near him, nearly brushing him with their long tails. Lewis and Clark reported these striking black-and-white birds entering their tents and grabbing meat from the dishes. Magpies learned to exploit the food sources settlers brought to their habitat. Though protected now under federal law, through the mid-twentieth century magpies were despised as agricultural pests and killed by the thousands. Communities waged contests to exterminate them, their black-and-white bodies tallied and tossed in checkerboard heaps.

From somewhere above the magpie nest, a house wren sings, the music weaving through the tree with the bird as it moves busily branch to branch—a floating concert. A common yellowthroat makes itself known, a patch of yellow sun flickering in the tree, singing *wichity-wichity-wich*. From the coyote willows along the creek bed, a song sparrow tosses bright music. An ornament of orange and black alights in a higher branch and adds its voice—a northern oriole. The hanging-pouch nest of an oriole looks, as one acquaintance describes it, like a sweat sock left to dry on a branch. The intricate nest is woven of plant fibers, though I have seen some incorporating Christmas tree tinsel and monofilament fishing line. The female oriole weaves her nest fabric like the finest crafter, her bill the shuttle intertwining weft and warp. Her loom is the slender, springy branch tips from which she dangles. I find it a challenge to sew cloth using thread, needle and ten fingers, much less weaving a tight nest using just my mouth.

A large, gray shape looms above the tree canopy. From its size and wingspan, its reptilian beak and the slow, determined fashion in which it approaches, I think for a wild moment it must be a pterodactyl winging in from the Jurassic Period. But no, it is a creature of this millennium, a great blue heron.

The heron slowly circles the crown of the tree, settling finally in the topmost branches with a great maneuvering of legs and folding of wings. There it sits, long and slim, a bird made of sticks crowning the upthrust arms of the tree like a finger pointing to heaven.

The loud *chuk-chuk-chuk* of a flicker rings out. At times I've seen downy and hairy woodpeckers in this grove. Black-capped chickadees, lazuli buntings, American goldfinches, yellow warblers, long-eared and great horned owls, tree swallows, loggerhead shrikes...the birds fostered by this grandmother are many.

Drowsily I toy with a leaf, twirling it in my fingers. There's a family resemblance between this leaf of the plains cottonwood, *Populus deltoides*, and its high-country cousin, the quaking aspen, *Populus tremuloides*, both members of the willow family. Smooth and leathery, the cottonwood leaf is heart-shaped, with a finely serrated edge. Cottonwoods are chatty trees. Even a slight stir will set them to gossiping. As I daydream, this one talks to me, its triangular leaves like a thousand tongues all chattering in the breeze. It is a pleasing sort of discourse, gentle and droning, a perfect counterpoint to a lazy summer day, when a snooze beneath the cottonwoods is about all the activity I can manage. By winter the leafy chatter changes. A few of the paper-dry leaves remain on the tree, rattling and rustling in the chill wind, railing against the cycle of seasons which will force them, inevitably to lose their hold and drop to the ground.

Long ago an old man lounged in the shade of a cottonwood, absently playing with a cottonwood leaf, rolling it into a cone with his fingers. Lulled by the warm day, he fell asleep with the leaf still in his hand and dreamed of a cone-shaped shelter, one that would meet the demands of nomadic prairie life better than the small rounded lodges his people lived in at the time. So the cottonwood, according to this story from the Cheyenne, was the inspiration for the buffalo-hide tepee.

Every winter, when I sit snug inside my central-heated home as a prairie blizzard blows the snow sideways into big drifts, I wonder what it would have been like to endure that with only a skin tepee separating me from the elements. Historian Eliot West conjectures the Cheyenne could not have lived on the prairie in winter without cottonwoods. They moved into the relative shelter of cottonwoodlands along the river bottoms and hunkered down for most of winter, feeding cottonwood bark to their ponies and burning the deadfall as fuel. Before European settlement, there were three extensive cottonwoodlands on the Colorado prairie—along the Arkansas, Republican and Smoky Hill rivers—all of them called Big Timbers by the Cheyenne. The Big Timbers along the Arkansas stretched for 60 miles, from present-day La Junta nearly to the Kansas border.

I make a head count of the trees around me. Maybe a dozen gnarly-barked old-timers, not exactly a massive shelter. Maybe I will call my cottonwood grove Tiny Timbers.

A cottonwood is not always a pretty tree, its branches painting a tangle of lace against the sky. Its wood is soft and prone to injury, particularly when the prairie throws one of its rough-and-tumble weather parties. Wind, hail, snow, and lightning storms take their toll. In just such a storm writer and butterfly expert Bob Pyle found sanctuary in a grandmother tree of his own, remembered in the title of his book *The Thunder Tree*. Without that cottonwood, Pyle is sure he would have died at the age of seven.

He grew up in Aurora, an eastern suburb of Denver, in a neighborhood of strip malls, tract homes and sterile bluegrass parks where in later decades I played fast-pitch softball and flag football. In Pyle's youth during the 1950s the prairie was just falling beneath the bulldozer, about to be reborn as endless suburbia. Pyle and his big brother Tommy spent their days poking around the Highline Canal, an irrigation ditch that snakes circuitously more than 70 miles across the Denver metropolitan area.

One July day a sudden storm hammered the prairie. Rain quickly became hail. Caught in the open, the brothers ran for cover as the hailstones changed from pebbles to iceballs the size of grapefruits. Frantically, the two skinny boys squeezed inside the only shelter around, an ancient, hollow cottonwood. Tommy was struck on the forehead by a hailstone and knocked out, but the old tree protected them from the brunt of the storm and saved their lives. And so it became The Thunder Tree.

I notice my grandmother tree has been damaged since I last visited. One of her great limbs, ripped from the main body, lies naked and white on the sand of the dry creek bed. A rotted wound high up on the old tree, now sealed over and hardened like a woody scab, shows where the limb once grew. Such a wound on a human body would be devastating, but the grandmother tree endures.

The cottonwood leaves are chattering again. This ancient tree is a storyteller, foretelling a storm with fluttering leaves, announcing the arrival of fall, bowing finally to winter. In her pockets and crannies, in folds between her roots, she hides secrets. Cody knows this. He explores with his nose, seeking out her stories. Pausing at a heart-shaped track in the sand, the imprint of a deer's hoof, his rubbery nose searches for scent, gathering it up, turning it over, examining it. This is likely the step print of a white-tailed deer, a shy ghost that haunts the streamside woodlands of eastern Colorado.

Cody pokes his vacuum-cleaner muzzle among the fallen leaves, dead logs, and vegetation. To my surprise, and his, there is a response from the undergrowth, a loud rustling of dry leaves and trembling of stalks as some creature awakens at Cody's proddings. Is it a fawn? I wonder, delighted at the treasures we have found in this cottonwood village. Attracted by the commotion, Margo joins him, the two of them poking forward curiously, leaping suddenly back, pushing their noses again cautiously among the leaf litter, withdrawing with a start. I get up and start toward them, calling, "Cody, Margo, come here." Margo comes to me, but Cody is absorbed with curiosity. He still pokes and paws at the undergrowth. Then I see a flash of black and white among the vegetation. "Cody!" I shout, grabbing his tail and tugging, hooking his collar as he turns his head. But pulling a hundred-pound Chesapeake away from anything against his will isn't easy. We will be skunked for sure. Our only hope is to get as far from the oily spray as possible. Lit by adrenaline, dragging my unwary dogs away from certain stinkdom, I stumble frantically out from among the trees. But the skunk has shown its forbearance. By its blessing we all still smell as we should. Finally, at a distance from the cottonwoods, I sit down in the open, still holding the dogs by their collars, laughing through my gasping breath. Joanne the Realtor was right. A home shows a lot better without certain residents hovering around.

Chapter 3:
Wood Ducks

Joanne has done her job. The house showed well enough to sell. Now I sift through my accumulated belongings, sorting and disposing. Among an assortment of photos tossed in a shoe box I come across a picture of my ex-husband in hunting clothes, proudly holding a new shotgun. Another of me with my hand on the sleek head of a handsome black Labrador retriever who leans against my leg. In the last photo, a weathered farmhouse sags forlornly amid old fields glowing amber with the coming of fall. I look closely at the picture of the house. It looks so empty, its walls gray, its windows dark and blank despite the golden light illuminating its east wall. I peer in the windows as if I might see some spark of life there. I had forgotten that trip, forgotten completely about what must have been my first real outing on the prairie, made years ago in the company of hunters.

I occasionally went along with my husband, his father and uncle on their fall bird-hunting trips, not to carry a gun, but as a tourist of sorts, to enjoy the outdoors and to understand the process and events of the hunt. We hunted upland birds, pheasants and quail and mourning doves and sometimes ducks, the ones that migrate along prairie streams. The men in his family rarely sat in blinds on a frigid dawn to ambush geese. Instead we walked the fields and rangeland of eastern Colorado and western Nebraska, hunting the shortgrass prairie.

I remember those hunting trips well, the men dressed in their canvas hunting coats and wearing orange caps, their shotguns gently cradled in their arms. They carried the weapons somewhat lovingly, yes, but most certainly with respect. These were responsible hunters, men who had grown up hunting, learning from their fathers. They didn't get drunk the night before, didn't handle their weapons carelessly. They carefully made sure of permission before hunting on private land, got to know the farmers, and always brought a thank-you gift—a tin of fancy cookies made by my mother-in-law, or maybe a pouch of fragrant tobacco for one particular farmer who liked his pipe. These men enjoyed the entire experience, the time outdoors, the male camaraderie, the stalk, the kill. I liked those trips, too, being outdoors and close to the earth, walking the prairie, coming to understand the hunters and the hunt, though I didn't like the killing.

Strange how I enjoy some elements of the culture of hunting, especially working with hunting dogs, retrievers. I love to see the dogs work; I've owned retrievers myself for more than 20 years. I field-trained Cody, my Chesapeake, banging pots and pans when he was just a pup to get him used to loud noises, attaching an old pigeon wing with twine to a long stick to interest him in fluttering feathered things. I trained him to hand, voice, and whistle signals, though he only actually hunted a few times. But I loved to work him on retrieves, even though the quarry was only training bumpers; loved to feel his barely controlled excitement as he trembled at heel until I loosed him with a shout—*Cody!*; loved to watch him quarter a field, casting about with his nose to gather scent as if casting a net for fish; and I especially loved to see him hit the water with incredible, exuberant force, bounding in leaps till he couldn't touch bottom, then swimming with great, relentless strength, powerful shoulders hunched, hind legs churning as if pedaling a bicycle.

I recall the first time I witnessed a kill. We were on a farm in extreme southwestern Nebraska, though in our rambles that day we surely walked over the border into Colorado—birds don't respect such boundaries. We passed through farm fields and rangeland. Here and there a cock pheasant got up, the men fired but with no luck. We worked our way toward a prairie stream, its course marked by cottonwoods; it probably had a name though none of us knew it. The stream's meanderings, gnarled trees tucked into its bends, offered habitat for various ducks. When we heard birds coming in we looked down, hiding our faces so the sun wouldn't shine off them and alert the birds to danger. Fall hunting means overcast days in other parts of the country, but on the shortgrass it was always sunny, I remember, even though it was cold and there was often a skiff of snow on the ground.

I was walking the stream with my husband. He was carrying his new shotgun, a 12-gauge semi-automatic with a fancy gas recoil system that absorbed the kick. I was carrying a feather, a tuft of dried native grass or maybe a deer bone—prairie artifacts I had discovered. Rounding a curve of the stream, we stepped beyond the cover of a large cottonwood. Our sudden appearance surprised a pair of ducks. The ducks jumped suddenly from the water with a flurry of splashing, startling me. My heart raced, my husband raised his gun, fired two or three blasts, the ducks fell back to the earth, heavy now, no longer graceful. Uncle Rod's black Labrador retriever, a good hunter, knew her job, ran excitedly down the bank into the water, waded out. She didn't have to swim because these prairie streams are shallow. She brought the ducks back unbruised; she's a good dog, with a nice soft mouth.

The Lab laid the first duck in my husband's hand, turned back to the water after the second. I took the duck from him, its body still warm through the wet feathers, and laid it gently on the grass. It was a wood duck drake, one of the handsomest of ducks, its fine head emerald and chestnut, striped white like a warrior, with a fine trailing crest. I stroked the feathers of the folded wings backward, smoothing them, my hand sliding through blood seeping gently from numerous pellet wounds. The colorful feathers were dull now, lifeless. I knew the bird's iridescent color was due not to pigment but to the reflection of light through the branched barbules of its feathers, Lying in the shadows, the bird it would appear drab even if it was living. Still, the loss of color seemed a symbol of its death, the radiance gone from the bird.

The abstract of hunting is something I can accept, but seeing the drake, once handsome, now lying dull and dead, saddened me. My mind understands the hunt and the kill, but my heart never will. I have had some hunters profess to me, when the other men weren't around, a pang of sorrow for the death of the creatures they kill, though they still enjoy the hunt and are glad for the meat. It seems right that they should feel something at the death of the animal. We are not consummate carnivores, like mountain lions, who eat only fresh-killed meat. It is unlikely a lion empathizes with its prey or feels remorse at the kill. We evolved as omnivores, our ancestors as easily prey as predator themselves. It is not so far a leap between the two; empathy for the victim comes easily to us.

My husband cleaned the ducks; he has killed them, he says, and it's his responsibility. I will cook them a few days later, preparing them carefully because wild ducks are very greasy. I am rather good at cooking game meats. I bake wild ducks in a roasting bag, with wine and herbs. They are delicious and I enjoy eating them. And so I feel a bit of both sides of the hunting equation, the sadness and the satisfaction.

I doubt I could find that place now, that little prairie stream. I recall that it lay somewhere just over the state line from Holyoke, Colorado. I look closely again at the photo of the abandoned farmhouse. In our wanderings that day we came upon it, a sad place with hollow, dull-eyed windows. I remember its frame walls were silvered and weathered. Big old trees made a windbreak behind the house; cottonwoods, I think they were, planted by hopeful hands. I wondered if the planter had lived there long enough to see those trees grow to grandeur.

An ancient windmill stood guard over the place. It was still spinning in the wind, humming down all those years, but it wasn't spinning true, and the metal was grinding, grinding, with a metallic hum in the wind. There were some old sheds and outbuildings, inhabited now only by broken bits of machinery, and mice.

We walked about among the shadows without speaking, tourists from another time. It was a typical old farmhouse, certainly only one of hundreds, perhaps thousands, of such abandoned homes across the Midwest and West. The broken-out windows, adorned still with bits of tattered cloth, stared at us vacantly. The front door hung slack-jawed on one hinge. Peering through the windows, we saw broken furniture, trash, little drifts of dust. I could not enter the house; I didn't want its emptiness to get into me.

There is always an odd sense of human presence in such a place. The farm was long abandoned, yet the spirit of the people who labored there was deeply imprinted. They left a bit of themselves behind in little things. From whose dress did this tattered scrap of cloth come, its pattern now faded to gray? A fresh young woman worn down by life here? This worn-out boot, the toe dried and curling: Who had once walked in it over new-plowed fields, or stepped with vigor into a leather-covered stirrup? How many hands, small and large, carried this enameled basin, now made useless by a hole in the bottom?

I mine no artifacts here as I did on the prairie and along the creek. I won't adorn myself with bones and feathers from this place.

I wonder how long ago that old homestead was abandoned. Why did the people leave? Perhaps they gave up after decades of trying to make a living on the prairie. A family farm lost in recent decades to corporate agriculture? No, the emptiness here is of longer duration. Maybe the Dust Bowl drove them out. This land busted many people, many dreams, often because settlers came equipped with a body of farming knowledge dependent on rain. In an arid land, the rules are different. Those who tried to change the land rather than live with it failed. But then there are those who say you can't earn a living on the shortgrass no matter what, that with drought, hail, late freezes, and a dozen other difficulties farmers only get a crop two years out of five. But others survive here, multiple generations proudly calling themselves plainsmen. Perhaps they learned to live with the land, to wait out its moods, to blossom with it.

The prairie is a patient landlord. It endured through the occupation of this house and now, slowly, reclaims its land. One day this house will sigh and slide at last into dust, and grass will grow from the fibers of its wood framing.

We turned our backs on the house and its ghosts, headed again onto the prairie, pushing through the dry grass, the rough blades brushing and sighing against our pant legs. In the game bags the ducks bled from many pellet wounds, silently.

Chapter 4:
Buffalo Grass

T he movers packed the last of my furniture and boxes into the van, slammed shut the big doors, and pulled away to carry my possessions to my new home in Denver. Despite daydreams of skiing Steamboat all winter, I wasn't ready to leave the High Plains. Something held me here, a sense of treasures undiscovered.

The dogs and I followed the van in my 1976 GMC Suburban, driving away in the autumn sunshine from what was no longer my home. We traveled west through the rolling open country, my eyes scanning for the band of pronghorn, wanting to bid them a mental goodbye. They were busy about their own lives, I suppose, for I saw no sign of their sleek forms. At the highway we turned north, toward the city, leaving the open country behind. But I had brought some of it with me. After the moving van left me amid boxes and furniture scattered throughout my new home, I took out the bundle of dried sagebrush I had gathered on the prairie. Touching a match to the tightly wrapped smudge, I coaxed it to a glowing ember. Slowly, passing from room to room, I purified and blessed the house with the pungent smoke of sage, readying it for my occupancy.

My new house in Denver is really an old house. Built in 1907, this modest, one-story white frame home was once a farmhouse that sits now on an oversized lot out of place in this neighborhood. Most houses around here date from the 1950s—flat-roofed, car-ported ranch homes, sort of Frank Lloyd Wright-esque. They're handsome houses with a timeless contemporary feel but I prefer this stolid farmhouse that held its ground as city neighborhoods gradually grew up around it.

My house was built plainly by modest folk with a modest budget. It has no pretensions to split levels, great rooms, California kitchens or walk-in closets. Built as a simple rectangle, it has a living room, a dining room, two small bedrooms separated by a bathroom and a huge kitchen with floor-to-ceiling white cabinets. Within the last 10 years, a large room off the kitchen was divided to make another small bath and a tiny room that could be a study or another bedroom. On the back of the house is an enclosed porch with a shed roof, added sometime after the initial construction. The porch is where I have my office. The interior wall of this room used to be the back wall of the house, and it has a window through which I can peer into the kitchen. In the evening I like to sit in the porch swing on the covered front porch, ignoring cars and houses and city lights, and imagine that I look across open fields to the mountains.

Each of the house's tall windows—they rise six feet high beneath nine-foot ceilings—was handmade. The two in the living room vary from each other by a half inch in height and width. The glass is slightly bubbled and distorted, having flowed down with gravity over nine decades. To open the windows I "throw up the sash" like it 'twas the night before Christmas, and I can hear the sash weights banging inside the window casings. A pencil that falls to the floor in this house rolls off slowly, the corner it aims for varying from room to room. Doing a bit of remodeling, I pulled off some trim and found it attached with flat, square-headed nails, each different from the others—handmade, a carpenter friend tells me.

Farmers built this house, not well-to-do city folk, and it shows in the details. The built-in glass-fronted bookcases, the mirrored sideboard in the dining room, the door and window trim are plain and made of pine stained mahogany-dark. I find none of the intricately turned oak trim the wealthy put in their Victorian mansions on Capitol Hill. Even the wood floors are of pine, which is soft and prone to scratching, chosen instead of sturdier oak because it was cheaper.

The house was an aging diamond-gone-back-to-the-rough when I first toured it. The kitchen dated from the 1940s, ceiling water-damage needed repair, and in places wood lath peeked out beneath broken plaster like ribs through a wound. But I suppose I have a weakness for wounded birds, and the quaint little farmhouse enduring amidst the city captured my interest. Once I saw the big kitchen with floor-to-ceiling cabinets, so like the kitchen in my grandmother's big home in Kansas, I knew I would buy this house.

What I know of the house's history I've learned from Morris Pierce, my next-door neighbor. Now in his late seventies, Morris brought his bride Evelyn home in 1946, after the war. His house was built on one of the first lots carved from the farm. My house, in turn, was not the original homestead.

That farmhouse still stands east of here on the corner, though you'd never know it beneath its remodeled exterior. Covered with siding, peeking out through modern, double-hung windows, it is not recognizable as an old house. My house was built for the oldest daughter of the family when she got married, I guess to keep her near home. At one time the entire front yard held raised vegetable gardens—"hot beds"— growing truck crops for the Denver grocery market.

Morris recalls how our busy residential street was a dirt country road when he moved here in the forties. "In those days, Mary," he says with his wry smile, "if you saw one car a day, it was a big event." I imagine corn and wheat fields where houses now lie and envy the view that once greeted the house's occupants. My six-foot picture window overlooks my neighbor's house, but if I'd lived here in farming days I would have had a panoramic view of the Front Range, from Pikes Peak in the south to Longs Peak looming up out of Rocky Mountain National Park to the north. Oh, the sunsets the farm family must have seen from that window, when their place was just a gash on the newly plowed prairie and this white house a lonely outpost. Considering the expense of such a large window, I realize the view of the mountains must have been important to them.

Exploring the backyard, I discover a strange artifact. Resembling a straight-sided pagoda, with an arched opening at the base, it is of masonry, about three feet tall and topped by a domed iron plate with a spiral-shaped handle. If I were to come upon this item in some intriguing spot, I might think it an altar, but in the backyard of this old house in Denver I know it is something a good deal more banal. It is an old trash incinerator.

A trash incinerator may seem hardly worthy of notice, but I am an archaeologist discovering the secrets this old house holds and to me it is a clue. Outside burning has been banned in Denver for decades but this funny old device, obviously home-designed and poured in place, served the family at a time when nobody worried about the brown cloud of pollution hanging over the friendly cowtown. A narrow sidewalk leads from the back door across the yard to the trash incinerator. On the way it stops at the clothesline, two sturdy T-shaped poles set above a concrete pad. The walk was poured by papa, I suppose, so mama could get to the trash incinerator and hang her wash easily without wading through mud or snow. I imagine her hanging her husband's shirts in the sunshine as the prairie wind whips the wash, wrapping her skirts around her legs. The old Siberian elms planted in a row along the northwest would have been just seedlings then, offering no shade on the open land that only recently had been broken from prairie to cropland.

When this house was built, the coyotes must have paid visits to the chicken house, tumbleweeds blown down the road, and yucca scratched the children's legs as they played in the yard. The yard has not been tended for years and I find clumps of buffalo grass growing among the weeds. Lying low and defiant, jaw thrust out like a street tough, this hardy native has persisted here somehow. I wonder sometimes, if I dug deep enough in the backyard, whether I would unearth the long-buried bones of prairie dogs, relics of an ancient community. And with those perhaps I might find the skull of a black-footed ferret, a truly rare artifact of a prairie Atlantis lost beneath the city.

The buffalo grass sets a seed of an idea in my brain. My yard covers four city lots. I'm not eager to water and cut bluegrass so I decide to try establishing a bit of native prairie behind the house. First step is to kill off the weeds. "Cover the weeds with black plastic until fall," says Betsy Baldwin who raises native plants professionally for commercial greenhouses through her business, Sunchaser Natives. "Then sow your native grass seeds, mulch, and you'll have the beginnings of a prairie in late spring." So I borrow Morris' rototiller and set to work. Instead of busting sod, my mini-plow will return this bit of ground back to prairie.

Grand schemes require sweat equity. After a few days of sore muscles and head-to-toe dirt, I have the ground nicely turned over and raked smooth. "Amend the soil," says Betsy. "Even native plants need help getting started in our sandy soil." So I drag in bags of sheep-peat—sounds like the name of a Scottish highlander—and rake that in too. Now I roll out yards of heavy-mil black plastic and peg it down. Then I wait.

In the fall I pull up the plastic and dig out the surviving weeds. After living for months on stored food in the roots, they are too weak to put up much of a fight. A local seed company mixes me a 50/50 batch of buffalo grass and blue grama, 80 pounds worth, and I spread it with Morris' seed spreader—he is a marvelous neighbor, his garage filled with eager-to-be-loaned tools.

"Water it well," Betsy advises, "then mulch to hold the moisture." The grass seeds need a season of dormancy in the soil so they will germinate when the soil warms. I follow her advice and mulch with straw. It's not until early spring, when tendrils of green grass emerge much too early for my two shortgrass species that I suspect a problem. "You didn't use certified weed-free straw," Betsy says matter-of-factly. I didn't even know there was such a thing. Instead of a native shortgrass prairie, it seems I have sown a healthy crop of cheatgrass. This truly noxious Eurasian weed, which piggy-backed a ride to North America in shipments of Russian wheat in the late 1800s, has taken over millions of acres of rangeland; neither cattle nor wildlife will eat it. Now it threatens my backyard prairie. Cheatgrass is a cool season grass that will shade out my natives, which need hot prairie sun to thrive.

"Mow it when the heads emerge but before the seeds set," Betsy advises, undaunted by my setbacks. Cheatgrass is a pretty grass, its fringed, reddish seedhead tipping over like a courtesan's hankie. But I don't let a pretty face stop me. I am ruthless with the lawn mower and cut down the cheatgrass wherever I find it. By midsummer, the cheatgrass is exhausted, nothing but standing straw.

But as I triumph over the cheatgrass, I discover another invader. Frill-edged leaves of deep jade sprout on hardy taproots throughout my prairie. As they grow and thrive I thumb through plant guides, struggling to identify them. Then I have it—common mallow. They are everywhere, thousands of plants, growing larger and stronger by the day. The cheatgrass was an easy foe compared to this. I can mow and chop, but the mallow only sends out new leaves from its hardy taproot. I won't consider poisons. There is only one solution. I must hand-pull them. Like a peasant gleaner I bend to the task of weeding. Obsessed, I hand-pull weeds like a madwoman, till my fingers crack and bleed from the fibrous stalks. My fingers callous over, and I weed on.

I am gaining on the weeds! Swaths of bare earth emerge like sand traps on a fairway. Beneath the weed cover I discover tiny tufts of newborn buffalo grass, sprouted on the bare earth like soft hairs on a bald man's pate. I bring them precious water, using a watering can to carefully nurture each tuft while denying moisture to the adjacent weeds. And I visit my tender native grass, just to see how it gets on.

It takes several seasons of vigilance, ruthlessness and nurturing to defeat the weeds and foster the natives. Now I watch as my buffalo grass and blue grama rise for the summer sun, unaware of the struggles I have gone through to assist their birth. The two are like siblings with different personalities. The blue grama sprouts in small clumps, sending up delicate flags, seedheads that brush my knees. The low-growing buffalo grass is the rowdy kid, aggressive, sending runners across the ground like recon patrols to dig in at new outposts. The buffalo grass will eventually take over, Betsy tells me, will even form a ground-covering mat of vegetation. Until then I should enjoy my pretty grama.

I've finally found success with my reborn prairie. Eventually I will add rabbitbrush for autumn gold, and maybe yucca. But my favorite plant lies quietly in two or three places among the grass—delicate fringed sagebrush planted from seeds I harvested on the prairie last summer and scattered with the grass seed in the fall.

Not far from my Little House No Longer on the Prairie, I discover a much older home. If I get on my bike and ride north, zipping down a steep hill to Cherry Creek a mile and a half away, I come to the oldest home in Denver. Four Mile House lies four miles from the confluence of Cherry Creek and the South Platte River, where Denver was founded. By Colorado standards, this log and frame home dating from 1859 is ancient. Once a stage stop along the Smoky Hill Trail, a major route between Denver and the Colorado gold camps, its history is cloaked in the romance of the Western frontier. Fortunately the historic old house, despite its prime location, has been rescued from the developer's bulldozer and is now a museum operated as a living history site by the City and County of Denver. Just blocks from the raging torrent of Colorado Boulevard traffic, chickens peck in the dust while heavy-bodied draft horses graze in a pasture. A few years ago a pesky red fox, sneaking up at night from its lair along the creek, decimated the population of the chicken house. After working its way through the chickens, it moved on to the ducks. The entire city followed the events in the morning Rocky Mountain News as the fox, or foxes, picked off the birds, one a night, despite frantic efforts by the museum staff to save the poultry. It's been a long time since Denver has had foxes in its henhouse, except maybe at the City and County Building.

Not far downstream, the creek's overgrown banks transform to a neat, concrete-lined channel, like a wild child sent to the barber. But along this stretch a dense forest of cottonwoods, braided with numerous mountain bike trails, offers a bubble of nature amid the city. A great blue heron stands motionless on stilt legs where a bend in the creek creates a quiet pool. A kingfisher flies upstream with a rattling cry. I find the chiseled stumps of cottonwoods, like gnawed pencil stubs, where beavers have been at work. They den in the bank of the creek, cutting the trees to build their dams, sometimes venturing beyond the unkempt cottonwoods to fell the neatly planted ornamentals lining the parks along the creek. Beavers drive the Department of Parks and Outdoor Recreation crazy. DPOR doesn't like wildlife—they upset the neat order of parks management. The parks department thinks of open space as nicely clipped expanses of bluegrass, bordered by ranks of evenly spaced lollipop trees. They like parks with plenty of lawn for picnicking and volleyball. Wildlife and native plants have no place in the picture; too messy, too disorderly, too hard to control. I think the city defines any creature that's not a robin or a fox squirrel as a varmint, and any plant that doesn't need watering a weed.

My move into the city has definite advantages. I'm close to grocery stores and cappuccino bars. The marvelous Tattered Cover Book Store, an independent bookseller with a national reputation, is only 10 minutes away. Here I can order any book that's still in print or sit in an overstuffed chair and read my way through the inventory, if so inclined. The art museum and, more importantly, the central branch of the Denver Public Library are both just a few more miles, if I follow the urbanized course of Cherry Creek downtown. Since I'm not living close to nature anymore, I can go see it on display at the natural history museum and the botanic gardens. But city living is a mixed bag. My sky is a good deal reduced here, squeezed between roofs and the tall trees of the urban forest. I miss watching the advance of storms across the sky, sweeping from mountain to open country like Patton rolling toward the Rhine. Instead, the clouds surprise me, showing up suddenly overhead. My dawns no longer rise on the eastern horizon in a silent symphony. I settle for a mirror of their colors, a wash of vermilion painting my white house a glowing rose.

*   *   *   *   *

It's early on a crisp October morning. A snap in the air confirms the radio's report of a cool 34 degrees. I'm headed for the Plains Conservation Center, a prairie preserve at the edge of Aurora, to help build a classic plains dwelling—a soddie, a house of earth.

At the turn of the century, my farmhouse family lived close enough to the commercial center of Denver to build with wood. For earlier prairie settlers, however, timber was not an option, so homesteaders turned to the materials at hand. They cut into the prairie sod and pulled up bricks of earth held together by the deep roots of the grasses. Now I will build a soddie as they did.

In recent years Aurora, sprawling to Denver's east, has worn the dubious crown of being one of the fastest growing suburbs in the country. Like bindweed, suburban sprawl creeps further and further out on the eastern plains, entwining everything in its path. But at the PCC, 1,900 acres of prairie are protected from development, at least for now.

I drive past endless tract homes and strip malls, striking in their mediocrity, devoid of spirit and character. On every corner is a shoppette of small service businesses. At larger intersections are chain groceries and big-box stores—Safeway, WalMart, Home Depot—American culture nicely homogenized like a bottle of milk. In between are lines and lines of nearly identical homes that house the consumers who support the retail glut. The houses and developments look so much alike that without street signs I might become completely lost. This cookie-cutter development serves the desire for single-family home ownership—the modern spin on the primal need for shelter, I guess. Meeting that desire has mutated in the hundred years since a farm family built my little house for their eldest daughter. Sprawl in those days was a handful of farmhouses on the prairie. Modern suburbanites are no different than farm families in seeking to make a home here. But their need is met now by an industry, mass homebuilding that produces a zillion widgets. While meeting a need, the homebuilding industry also creates the need—"They come and so we build, then we build so they will come." Can't we satisfy the American dream of owning a home in a way less lacking in identity, and without so completely destroying the native character of a place? We even give these developments silly names like Hunters Glen and Acres Green that have no relationship to the communities of plants and animals that have typified this landscape for 10,000 years.

Suddenly I reach a frontier, the edge of development. Emerging from the sterile forest of tract homes and discount stores, I see the open prairie spread out before me, a sweep of grassland so abrupt and so bright it makes me blink. The sky is still vast and blue here, the wind sometimes gentle and sometimes brutal. Living in the city, I forget how stunning the open country is. I forget its power. Now the effect is almost physical as it seizes my heart and flings it wide, and I am spinning across the openness. I gulp it all in with the air—the clean feel of grass and sky, the intangible wonder of space and horizon.

Housing developments lie in ranked formation on three sides of this prairie preserve, each house like a soldier in a vast and growing army moving inexorably eastward. Poised all around the PCC, the houses await the order to advance, held at bay by a tenuous truce. If the boundary is ever erased, if the decision is ever made to develop this preserve, the tract homes will rush over the hills and roll over the prairie grass like hounds let off the leash, till this place, too, is lost beneath the waters of suburbia.[1]

The remnant of prairie at the PCC is like a wounded battle survivor, born of devastation and locked within a tiny demilitarized zone. How did this patch of prairie survive the development juggernaut of recent decades? The PCC is owned by the West Arapahoe Soil Conservation District, itself a product of the Dust Bowl. When the droughts of the 1930s ravaged the Great Plains, busted farmers abandoned their land to the federal government. The government formed soil conservation districts, special units similar to school districts, with the mandate to teach farming methods that conserve topsoil and prevent erosion. So the feds handed this surplus 1,900 acres to the WASCD to be used for education. These days the PCC educates urban kids instead of farmers, teaching them about the prairie and how Native Americans and early settlers lived on the land.

Getting out of my car at the PCC headquarters, I have a sense of stepping into a gentle river. The landscape flows around me, the grasses a rolling swell, the wind passing across the grass like a hand stroking velvet. To the east, the sky curves down to meet the earth.

In a canvas tent behind the main building, a group of people bundled in coats mills about large urns of coffee and trays mounded with muffins. I join them, shivering in the morning chill as I fill a paper cup with coffee, warming my hands around it. In about 10 minutes the sun moves above the horizon, and the change is almost immediate, altering the light and warming my back through my wool coat. The sun is everything on the prairie: creator, preserver, destroyer. It turns a winter day to spring, sends the snow away, draws plant life from the earth, bakes the land to hard brown and, when it withdraws, banishes the world to dark and cold. In mountain forests the trees are allies to the snow, sheltering it, prolonging

---

1. Since my first visits in the early 1990s, the Plains Conservation Center has sold a portion of its land and purchased a 5,700-acre parcel of prairie farther east along West Bijou Creek.

its life. In canyons, the incised landscape fosters micro-worlds safe within folds of the earth. But the open country offers few intermediaries between sun and land. The sun's decrees are immediately carried out. On the prairie, the sun rules unchallenged, benevolent queen, and despot.

Still sipping coffee, munching muffins and chatting, our work crew, a straggling army, marches down to the patch of open ground where we will erect our sod house. Dividing into teams, we begin to build. Our building materials are fresh-cut bricks of prairie sod, marbled with the live roots of grasses and squirming with worms and grubs. I'm surprised how quickly we evolve into a crew of specialized laborers. The mudders mix soil with water for mortar, learning the right consistency by trial and error. They paste a layer of mortar atop the growing wall, smoothing and leveling to make a sound base for the next course. Two sod carriers slide a sod brick onto a board and carry it to the work site. The drying sod is fragile. The carriers must handle it gingerly. They lift the brick carefully into place. Now two other workers, the cutters and shapers, set and trim the brick. Since our bricks are not uniform and sometimes crumble, we need to shim the edges. The shapers cut slices of sod and wedge them into gaps. The chinkers add mud, filling gaps and holes between the bricks. There are even jobbers who glean the loose dirt fallen from the sod, because only prairie soil, not just any dirt, can be used for our mud mortar. I apprentice at all these tasks, finally settling in as a journeyman cutter-and-shaper.

It took an acre of virgin prairie to provide the sod for a 16-by-20-foot, one-room sod house. As I help these earthen walls rise—bristling with roots and grass, dirt constantly sifting down, insects clambering out of the sod—I realize that sodbusters who came to "tame" the plains lived physically within the prairie, within the womb of the earth. They cut the soil, built a shelter of it, then crawled within.

Slowly the walls rise, like a stack of flapjacks from the stovetop. We add the door and window frames, of precious lumber, and continue raising our sod walls around them. The work is slow; it must have taken a single family weeks to do this. Helpful neighbors hastened the task. I think of the Bohemian family in *My Ántonia,* Willa Cather's classic story of life on the Nebraska prairie, who lived through the winter in a house dug out of an earthen bank because they had started their soddie too late in the season and couldn't cut sod from the frozen ground. "As we approached the Shimerdas' dwelling, I could still see nothing but rough red hillocks...and then I saw a door and window sunk deep in the draw-bank...The oldest son came out of the cave...(then) the father came out of the hole in the bank." What was it like to live in a pit house, virtually in an earthen womb? In past centuries, Europeans considered aboriginal peoples living in dugout homes savage and uncivilized. Yet, with no other options, Europeans who came to this land went back to live in the earth.

People have long lived in earthen shelters. The mesas of the Four Corners region, where Colorado, Utah, Arizona, and New Mexico come together, are dotted with remnant pit houses. Ancestral Puebloans, commonly known as the Anasazi, built these partially subterranean dwellings atop Southwestern mesas, later moving to greater safety in cliff dwellings within the canyons.

Earthen houses reached a zenith with adobe building, using bricks formed of mud and straw. The Spanish brought the Moorish craft of adobe building to Mexico, then to the American Southwest, where it became synonymous with the identity of the region. In a marvelous irony of our techno-world, hand-crafted adobe bricks of dried mud and straw are now among the most expensive building materials.

At midday my crew breaks for lunch. We sit on the ground in little groups, eating, chatting, relaxing. A breeze carries the scent of sagebrush and the songs of crickets, mimicking the quiet hum of conversation. We feel satisfied by our physical labors, our work of the hand. I look around at the assembled company, only their shoulders and heads visible above the dry grass. The sun glints off their hair, the breeze stirs their clothes, heads bob back and forth as the talk is broken by the sound of laughter. How much like a scene from the nineteenth century this must be, when folks lay about chatting during a break from a day's good labor.

By the end of the day we feel tired but accomplished. We take our plates and mugs and are served a "mess" of elk stew cooked over an open fire in a big iron pot, chased down by chunky homemade applesauce and crispy air-filled fry bread hot from the skillet and slathered with honey. We sit around on the ground, dry grass prickling our behinds, swapping the day's war stories. We relish our elk stew and with it the physical work, the building of a structure with our own hands, the making of a shelter, the handling of materials from the earth. All these are the making of our satisfaction.

I am so intrigued by the PCC that I return to write some magazine articles on the place. "We could use extra hands putting up our tepees," says the Center's director. I put down my notebook and pitch in on a balmy spring afternoon to help erect a Plains Indian tepee for use in the Center's education programs. I've built a soddie, now a tepee. I'm going to end up an expert on prairie dwellings.

The sky looks as if a horse has kicked over buckets of paint, sending a swirling mix of blues and grays across it, with trailing wisps of white. The rise of the land obscures the suburban development to the west, hiding it within the seam where sky meets prairie. Our group of workers is the tallest landmark in sight. I turn slowly in a complete circle, surveying the land of grass and sky that flows from me to the horizon. How often have any of us stood where we had a 360-degree view around us, unobstructed by house or skyscraper or vehicle or tree, as if we were the central hub of the great wheel that is the earth?

On the ground before us lie our materials—fifteen 25-foot-tall poles, made of peeled lodgepole pine; ropes; stakes; and a white canvas lodge cover (buffalo hides being in short supply). The poles are five inches across at the base, tapering to perhaps two and a half inches at the tip. Our first step is to take three sturdy poles, lay them side by side, and lash them tightly together with rope about 18 inches from their tips. Once upright, these poles will form a tripod, the base upon which the rest of the framework is laid. If we don't do this step right, the whole structure could come tumbling over or blow away in the prairie wind. Some Plains Indian tribes used a four-pole base for their tepees, but the Cheyenne used a tripod and the Cheyenne are the focus of the PCC's Native American program. They are also the indigenous people most associated in recent history with the Colorado prairie.

The wood creaks with the pains of compression as the hemp rope (the Cheyenne would have used leather thongs) is drawn tighter and tighter around the lodgepoles. Two of our crew sit on the ground across from each other with the poles between them, bracing their feet on the poles and leaning back against the pull of the rope like two kids holding hands and playing a game of see-saw. The rope is drawn over and under, over and through the pole tips several times. Then we knot it tight. We must cinch this first joining as tight as possible for the stability of our tepee.

With the pole ends tied together, we are ready to set up the tripod. We set two poles in position, then winch up the peak of the frame by pulling on the long end of the rope that lashes the pole tips together. Like a giant rising reluctantly to its feet, the 25-foot-tall tripod of lodgepoles looms up and into position. We swing the third pole out into place, and our tripod stands alone, the beginnings of a tepee frame.

A tepee seems like a simple structure, but there is a great deal of consideration of physics in its design. Our tepee is not a perfect cone, because the legs of the tripod are not set equidistant. Instead, they form a rough isosceles triangle with sides measuring 14 feet, 18 feet and 18 feet 9 inches (Cheyenne women would have eyeballed this but we use a tape measure). The two poles that are closest together stand most upright, and we place this side to face the wind. Once the tepee is covered by its skin, the force of the wind blowing against the upright face will drive the leeward poles, which sit at a steeper angle, more firmly into the ground, bracing the structure. After the tripod is standing, we add the additional poles to the structure vertically, but we don't just lay them on haphazardly like sticks on a fire. We stack them from the tip of the cone down in a twisted spiral, as if we are going 'round the Maypole, each lain on the one before to lock it in structurally and keep it from shifting.

Our tepee cover is made of heavy white canvas, with buffalo hide reinforcing the stress points and the edges. Traditional Cheyenne tepees were made entirely from buffalo hides, but not just any skin would do. When it was time to make a new tepee cover, the hunters had instructions from their wives and mothers to kill several old buffalo cows. These hides were easiest to tan because the old cows were thin and scrawny so the flesh came off easily. The best time of year for this was April or May when the animals were shedding their winter coats.

When the Cheyenne lived on the Colorado prairie, the number of horses a Cheyenne man owned, and therefore his wealth, was reflected in the size of his lodge. It required two horses just to haul the poles of a large lodge, and another to carry the cover, plus more animals to carry all the family's belongings. If a man had only a few horses, his family could move only a modest lodge.

Tanning fresh hides into skins, then piecing and sewing the skins together into a tepee cover, was a social event among women, like the quilting bees of white settlers. Helping make a lodge cover was a service returnable in kind—help your neighbor today and she helps you tomorrow. Thus a task that would have been difficult and drudging to do alone was accomplished by a community of women working together.

It takes our community of six laborers two hours just to erect the tepee frame, with many pauses for measuring, poring over the instruction booklet and discussing how best to do our task. We laugh at our inefficiency as tepee-raisers; a group of Cheyenne women would have had this tepee up and covered in 45 minutes.

By the time we are finished with the tepee frame, our lodgepoles spiraling against the sky, the clouds of late afternoon have gathered and darkened ominously. The wind, benign when we started, has become brusque and threatening. Though our task isn't done, we'll have to come back another day to place the tepee cover over the frame. The prairie wind is a power to respect. If we tried to hoist the canvas cover, clumsy and inexperienced as we are, the wind would take it like a sail and probably carry us all stumbling across the prairie. So instead of a white cone against a blue prairie sky, our tepee frame stands skeletal and forlorn, exposed like bare bones to the elements.

A few days later we hoist the cover over the frame, stretch it and stake it around the perimeter. A light breeze is blowing and within minutes I am covered with a fine layer of dust—a fact of life on the open prairie. A flap controlled by another lodgepole allows us to open and close the smokehole at the top of the tepee. We add an interior liner—which rises from the floor some four feet up the insides of the tepee—lashing it to the poles. This liner creates an insulating air space and keeps the wind from blowing under the edge of the tepee. So the tepee is a durable structure—portable, quick to put up and take down (if you know what you're doing), ventilated, cool in summer and warm in winter. What a marvelous technology, composed of rope, poles, animal skins... and human ingenuity.

I'd slept in a tepee numerous times when I was a camp counselor during college. What remains in my mind is the curious experience of sleeping in a circle with other people. I felt like we were a pack of wolves curled up together, each one of us continuing into the other. Or maybe I felt like a she-wolf with a litter of pups, since I was in charge of about 10 ten-year-old campers. But when my ten little Indians were done telling ghost stories around the campfire, and drifted off to dreams of living wild and free, I lay on my back looking up to where the smokehole made a dark portal to the sky, with vague visions of rising to heaven on the smoke from our fire.

Twenty years passed before I stepped inside a tepee again. A skin tepee seems poor shelter from the cold, but one brutal December day, when the Fahrenheit hovered around 15, I found out how warm a tepee can be. I was visiting Bent's Old Fort National Historic Site in southeastern Colorado, a living history site re-creating an important trading post along the Santa Fe Trail. Volunteers dressed in period costume re-enact the era of mountain men and Indians in early Colorado.

The day was bone-numbingly cold, a frigid wind blowing off the Arkansas River dropping the wind chill below zero. But prairie life continued in winter as well as summer. Smoke was seeping through the smokehole of a tepee in front of the fort, as if a Cheyenne family was sheltered in their winter camp in the Big Timbers along the Arkansas. The ends of the tepee's interior liner overlapped at the entryway as a seal against the cold. Bending over, I stepped through the oval doorway into a space about 15 feet across, heated air warming my face.

A fire of cottonwood sticks crackled in a pit in the center of the tepee. "Come in, come in," said a woman seated at the edge of the tepee floor. A buffalo robe, hair side in, wrapped her body, and her black hair hung in two braids. A smile lit her face and her friendly eyes sparkled in the dim light. She was enjoying herself. She spoke with a slight lilt, and judging by her round face, I was pretty sure she was of Indian heritage. "Come in, sit down. All the smoke's up there where you're standing," she said with a grin, pointing up towards my head. She moved over to make room for me, so I sat down on a padded seat covered with buffalo hide.

We sat for a while just watching things. It was really quite toasty, a small space that heated nicely with the fire in the center, and I wasn't eager to go back out in the cold. The liner was a good insulator. I began to understand how Plains people made a warm and comfortable shelter for themselves against the prairie winter.

A man and a boy wearing a Boy Scout hat sat across the fire from us, part of a Scout troop visiting the fort. "Are you the one they call Red?" the

Boy Scout asked the woman next to me. "Yes," she said, smiling. "And that's Buffalo Woman," she added, pointing at the other woman across the tepee. Unlike Red, Buffalo Woman, though dressed in a buckskin dress and beautiful knee-high moccasins with intricate panels of beadwork across the feet and up the sides, was of European background. "Why are you called Red?" asked the Boy Scout's father. Red laughed and pointed to her hair, which had a reddish tint to it, and to her dress, made of red cotton trade cloth. "Red," she said.

We all sat awhile in silence. "I can't believe how warm it is in here," I said in a hushed voice to Red. "We gather wood from around the trees along the river," she said, speaking in the first person, present tense, as re-enactors do at a living history site. "But," she whispered to me, girl-to-girl, "we slept in here last night and it was co-old. You gotta keep the fire going all the time, and even then it was really cold. I didn't want to go out to go to the bathroom, you know," and she gave me a huge grin and began laughing again.

"What did the Indians do all day when it was so cold out?" asked the Boy Scout. "We just stay in our tepees all the time," said Red, back in character, "and tell lots of stories and sometimes play games. That's how we pass along our history, with stories."

We started talking about the artifacts in the tepee—a backrest made of slender willow sticks, a bone hide-scraper, an elk-hide drum. Red explained their uses, always keeping to the present tense as if she had been scraping and curing buffalo hides that morning. The Southern Cheyenne were moved out of Colorado and onto a reservation in Oklahoma in the 1870s. But many had married white ranchers and traders like the Bents, who had operated this trading post. I'd heard that their mixed-blood descendants still lived in Bent and Prowers counties. "Are you Cheyenne?" I asked Red. She leaned towards me like a conspirator and whispered, "No, I'm Cherokee, but don't tell anybody." Then she began laughing again.

I thanked Red and Buffalo Woman and stepped out into the bitter afternoon. I was convinced now that a tepee could be kept relatively warm, but of the prairie dwellings I've experienced, I'll stick with my snug frame farmhouse.

Chapter 5:
Turkeyfoot

I 'm 600 miles from home and driving south along Kansas Highway 7 through humidity that smothers me like a wet blanket. My prairie journey has brought me to this green land along the Missouri River, where the scent of damp hangs heavy as incense. On this September day the leaden clouds move slowly, like a mare soon to foal. My dry Colorado prairie seems a world away, and yet it is to prairie of a different sort that I have come. I'm in search of beginnings—my own and the prairie's.

"Our family has roots on the Great Plains, you know," my mother commented one day as I told her of my growing interest in the prairie. "Your grandmother was born on a farm in Kansas, near a place called Wilder."

My aristocratic grandmother a Kansas farm girl like Dorothy of Oz? My grandparents had a grand Victorian home in Leavenworth, in eastern Kansas, and I remembered that my grandmother had grown up not far from there. (My sisters and I have always gotten a lot of mileage out of saying we were going to Leavenworth to visit family.) But that riverside town is built over rolling hills and steep hollows, trees still growing thick wherever they haven't been cut for farms or houses. I looked at my mother skeptically, "That's not really prairie around there."

"It was the beginning place," Mom said, "where the wagon trains started out across the plains." A faint image from early childhood tickled my memory. We'd been stationed at Fort Leavenworth, the historic Army post on the hill above town, when I was a little girl. Hadn't my sisters and I played in the century-old ruts of the Oregon Trail where it passed through our backyard? The deep trench gouged into what is now a grassy hill had been our hideout, deep enough that our mother couldn't see us unless she stood at the edge and looked down. Though the Missouri has shifted its course a mile or more east in the intervening 150 years, that cut still marks where the wagons, heavily laden with household goods and dreams, once pulled up out of the river and headed off across the prairie.

"Where is Wilder?" I asked my mother, sitting down next to her and unfolding the Kansas map across our laps. "I don't know exactly," Mom said. "When I was a girl, we visited my grandmother's home after church one Sunday a month, and it was somewhere between Leavenworth and Olathe." She drew her finger along the 40-mile route, now Highway 7. We scanned the names of small towns along the route that lie in the growing shadow of Kansas City to the east. Wilder was not on the map.

A call to the Kansas State Historical Society led me to the Johnson County Archives. "I'm trying to locate a town site called Wilder," I told the clerk. "I don't think it exists any longer." She agreed to send me what information she could find.

Mom continued telling me what she knew. "My grandmother, Katie Marilla Hoard, came west to Kansas from upstate New York about 1875, when she was ten years old," Mom said. The death of his wife had left Katie Marilla's father, Levi, with two motherless children—she and her little brother Lewis—and in need of a new start in a new place.

"Come west to us," Levi's cousin wrote to him. Auntie Frame ("that's the only name I ever heard her called," said Mom) and her Scottish husband were prosperous farmers in eastern Kansas and had room for a single man and two children. Katie Marilla grew up on the Frame farm. At 19 she married Robert Goddard, a neighbor's son, and moved to her husband's farm near the town of Wilder.

Wilder was the only clue I had to my family's roots on the eastern prairie of Kansas. But the West is a land that changes quickly, where the vestiges of a family's history are quickly blown away, built over, forgotten. Did Wilder still exist? I wondered if I might find it, might actually locate the family farm, if anything was left of it.

The manila envelope from the Johnson County Archives and Records arrived, containing photocopied pages from an 1874 atlas and a modern 1989 map of the county. On the modern map I immediately found a handful of intersecting streets about a quarter-mile square tucked in a bend of the Kansas River along Highway 7—Wilder—20 miles from

Leavenworth and about 15 miles from Kansas City. What had been there 100 years earlier?

The 1874 map of Monticello Township was a treasure, a Rosetta stone for my research. It showed landscape features, improvements...and the name of each landowner. Wilder didn't exist yet but near its future site was a large farm bearing my grandmother's family name—Goddard. Carefully matching the section lines and the roads, I outlined the farm's boundaries on the modern map. The Goddards had a sizable place, nearly a section, though it was oddly shaped, undoubtedly bought up from various landowners. A little black square on the old map indicated a farmhouse, almost certainly the house where my grandmother had been born in 1889.

On the old map, a belt of native timber ran between the river and the farm, and the house sat at the edge of a bluff where a small stream passed. From the river west was farmland and open country. "I remember Mother talking about those river bluffs," Mom recalled, "how they lived where the land rose up from the river and the farmers hadn't cut the trees there because the land was too steep."

What had this place, where river woodlands gave way to prairie, looked like before settlement? I found a description in *The Oregon Trail* by Francis Parkman, the journal of a wealthy Bostonian who traveled west in the 1840s. Parkman crossed the Missouri at Westport, now engulfed by Kansas City but at that time a major river crossing 15 miles east of Wilder: "Emerging from the mud-holes of Westport, we pursued our way for some time along the narrow track, in the checkered sunshine and shadow of the woods, till at length, issuing into the broad light, we left behind us the farthest outskirts of the great forest that once spread from the western plains to the shore of the Atlantic. Looking over an intervening belt of bushes, we saw the green, ocean-like expanse of prairie, stretching swell beyond swell to the horizon."

My thoughts flew on an imaginary journey, from my home at the foot of the Rockies, over the Eastern Plains of Colorado, across the flatlands of Kansas, eastward toward where the sun rises. Far across the open country, on the bank of the Kansas River, the family farm had lain at the doorway of the Great Plains.

What was left of the Goddard farm site? I wondered. Could I find it? What would the landscape be like? I knew I had to go there, stand at the site where the farm had been; if I could, find the place where my grandmother was born, see where my prairie roots began.

I spread out my state maps, tracing the Kansas River with my finger. The Kansas is a river born of the shortgrass, from a marriage of two smaller rivers, the Republican and the Smoky Hill, that emerge from Colorado's Eastern Plains. The tributaries of these two rivers drain millions of acres of prairie. Dry washes and seasonal streams with names like Hell Creek and

Wildcat Canyon live a dual life. Slumbering much of the year they awaken in brief but glorious bouts to dance furiously across the open country, swollen with rain, hail and snow. Moving along myriad undulations of rangeland and field, arroyo and canyon, they migrate unerringly along courses they have ordained for themselves season after season.

The Republican River, following a haphazard path out of the northeastern Colorado prairie, like a first-year bird on an uncertain migration, heads up through Nebraska before turning south into Kansas. The Smoky Hill River begins its journey in the eastern suburbs of Denver not far from my home and moves more certainly, draining across Colorado's central plains, then across the flat, open country of western Kansas, to join waters with its Republican cousin. At Junction City the two merge, giving birth to the Kansas River.

The prairie rivers travel eastward toward the Missouri. I would too.

*   *   *   *   *

My journey takes me from Colorado's shortgrass to the tallgrass prairie of eastern Kansas. Across this expanse from the Rockies to the Missouri River, from Denver to Wilder, the North American prairie changes, takes on different faces.

The prairie is not a land to tell its story easily. It shows no age, no cataclysms, no passage of time. Researchers have learned the prairie's story by looking beneath its skin, at details gleaned from pollen images in core samples, from tales told by ancient animals abiding in the earth, from tablets of shale that once lay upon a sea's bed. But I see the tale as more of an epic. The prairie is like a mythic beast, born of the Cretaceous Sea, transforming over countless time to damp forests and marshes and then to a parkland of woods and meadows. Wildlife of all manner and form walked the land then, many creatures of which today we can only dream—giant dire wolves, mammoths, saber-toothed tigers—and other beasts that now live only in faraway places—rhinos and camels, cheetahs and lions. Millennia passed until again the great forces of climate, like the wrath of a creator god, changed the landscape. The trees receded and the grasses surged forth, forming an immense valley of grass down the center of the continent. The cornucopia of mammals that had roamed the parklands disappeared; they fell into the earth and turned to stone. Only those who loved the grasses were spared, the bison and pronghorn and prairie dog, and they multiplied a thousand-fold and spread across the land following the grass. For 10,000 years the Great Plains of North America lay within its own rhythms, each season giving birth to the next, mother to child, transforming again to mother and again to child. Hemmed on the east by vast forests and banked to the west by the upsweep of the Rocky Mountains, the land lay gently breathing in an endless cycle.

Within this valley of grass were three regions, each with an individual face and called by the name of the grasses that grew there—the lands of the tallgrass, midgrass and shortgrass. More powerful than great armies, the forces of fire, wind, water, topography, and climate sculpted the three, and the immutable laws of terrain, moisture, temperature, soil, and climate governed what plants would grow where. Perhaps the three grasslands might best be thought of as sovereign nations, similar but disparate, delineated not only by geography but by race. The community of life inhabiting each was definable and different from its neighbor. Like any set of neighboring countries, the ethnic makeup of each prairie nation was blurred at the edges. As climatic conditions varied from year to year, the boundaries of each prairie ebbed and flowed and plants associated with one prairie grew into the margins of the next. Plants typical of one prairie also showed up like squatters within their neighbors' borders wherever conditions welcomed them.

Though different from one another, the prairies shared certain features—flat or rolling terrain, wind, fire, periodic drought, scarcity of trees, and grass as the dominant vegetation. A grassland is in many ways an upside-down world. Absence of trees does not mean absence of organic life. Life thrives in an underworld of roots, which are the living heart of grasses and perennial plants. Snug in the earth, they are protected from sun, wind, weather, and physical injury, unless plowed. A grass' large root network may grow down as far as the height of a man, then branch sideways even further, spreading its skirts like a gypsy dancer catching coins, netting and holding water. In turn the roots anchor and stabilize the soil and keep invaders, such as trees, from establishing.

Prairies are born of air, earth and light, but also of fire. Before settlement, prairie fires—caused by lightning or intentionally set by native people— raged where they would like a cadre of light cavalry, moving quickly with the help of the wind. Fire was a giant broom that whisked through and tidied things up, burned off dead plants, enriched the soil by releasing nutrients, and kept the trees at bay, which allowed sunlight to reach the ground so new plants could germinate.

Of the prairie nations, the richest one, the one with greatest rainfall and the darkest, most humic soils, was the tallgrass prairie. Encompassing the eastern edges of Kansas, Nebraska and the Dakotas, most of Iowa and Illinois, and at times swelling like a prairie peninsula into parts of Indiana, it ranged north into the prairie provinces of Canada and extended south into Oklahoma. Its boundaries, like those of all prairies, were amorphous, constantly expanding and retracting. To the east, forests constantly laid siege to its ramparts, sending seedlings like pioneer homesteaders surging past the frontier to root on open ground. In the battle on this forested eastern front, the prairie's greatest ally was fire, which killed trees without harming the roots of the grasses and thus protected the integrity of the Great Plains. Though it burned off the blades of the grasses it did not kill them, because their essence was safe below ground in their roots. In a wet year, the tallgrass plants in their turn might creep west into the domain of the midgrass prairie, and the midgrass push its frontier westward into the shortgrass.

Among the prairie nations, the tallgrass was the most handsome, seemed the most gifted—tall, rich and robust. Its dominant grasses such as big bluestem and prairie cordgrass could reach a midsummer height of 12 feet. I once walked amid tall grasses along a river channel, finding myself in a surreal forest of slender-stemmed trees nearly twice my height. I pushed through the yielding stalks, which parted without protest only to close behind me with a sigh. I became disoriented, perhaps even a bit frightened, hemmed in by a prairie with no horizon. I recalled reading how cowboys tending their grazing herds amid the tallgrass stood on their saddles and scanned the sea of grass for movement to find their cattle. Now I was a cow lost in a forest that should have been a prairie. Only by reaching the river and following its course did I find my way, like Hansel and Gretel, out of the eerie wood.

The tallgrass prairie was a wondrous ecosystem but because of its rich, fertile soil, it drew the lustful gaze of settlers and was the first prairie nation to fall victim to an indomitable foe—the plow. It took barely half a century to defeat the tallgrass, replacing its diverse, interdependent community of native plants with monocultures of crops. The wildflowers and plants of the tallgrass, many with wonderfully poetic names—blazing star, rattlesnake master, compass plant, queen-of-the-prairie—were paved over with wide, uninterrupted swaths of corn, wheat, and oats. These grain crops support human life but little wildlife. Today the tallgrass nation is in tatters; less than one percent of the original tallgrass prairie remains, protected in a handful of fragmented public and private preserves scattered through Kansas, Iowa, Oklahoma, and other areas of the Midwest.

The fate that befell the tallgrass nation was not long in coming to its closest western neighbor, the midgrass, also called mixed grass prairie. The midgrass prairie of the central Great Plains was the lyrical land of Willa Cather. The largest in size of the three nations, it extended in a broad swath from central Texas up through the Dakotas into Canada. It was drier than the tallgrass prairie, so its grasses—little bluestem, Junegrass, western wheatgrass among others—grew not quite so high as their stately neighbors, only reaching two to four feet.

As the juggernaut of settlement advanced across the Great Plains, the wild bullock of the midgrass prairie was broken to the yoke, its sod plowed under and converted to wheat, hay, barley, sugar beets, and, with the advent of pivot irrigation, corn. Cather grew up on a farm on the Nebraska frontier in the 1880s. As an adult, a celebrated New York writer far removed from her midgrass prairie homestead, she remained in her heart a

Nebraska farm girl who never forgot the achingly beautiful land of her girlhood. Cather's love for her prairie home is captured in *My Ántonia:*

> *I felt motion in the landscape; in the fresh, easy-blowing morning wind, and in the earth itself, as if the shaggy grass were a sort of loose hide, and underneath it herds of wild buffalo were galloping, galloping....I wanted to walk straight on through the red grass and over the edge of the world, which could not be very far away. The light air about me told me that the world ended here: only the ground and sun and sky were left, and if one went a little farther there would be only sun and sky, and one would float off into them, like the tawny hawks that sailed over our heads making slow shadows on the grass.*

The third of the prairie nations, the shortgrass, dwelt beyond the pale like blue-painted Scots ranging ragged and fierce beyond Hadrian's Wall. The shortgrass was the last to be harnessed and even today seems at best only halter-broke. While the tallgrass has largely disappeared beneath benign farms, and the midgrass has been tamed into endless Nebraska corn fields, the shortgrass, because it made poor farmland and was often only good for grazing cattle, was spared the most brutal consequences of the plowshare knife.

Lacking the elegance and refinement of the tallgrass and the stolid utility of the midgrass, the shortgrass prairie lies like a shaggy mustang between the western edge of the midgrass prairie and the Rocky Mountains—high, lonesome, and windswept. Stretching from Canada to Texas, it spreads eastward from the skirts of the Rockies into the Dakotas, across eastern Colorado, the western regions of Nebraska and Kansas, the Oklahoma panhandle, and a large portion of northern and central Texas. The shortgrass prairie is dry and stern, the driest prairie nation of all, in some locales receiving only 10 inches of moisture a year. It is a puritan land whose rules, once broken, extract their own hard price.

Yet the shortgrass bears a rough and feral beauty evident to those willing to see with different eyes. "Nowhere has Nature presented more beautiful scenes than those of the vast prairies of the West," wrote artist George Catlin, who visited in the 1830s. "Soul-melting scenery was about me. I mean the prairie, whose enamelled plains lay beneath me, softening into sweetness in the distance like an essence." Catlin described the handsome plains antelope as "one of the most pleasing living ornaments of the western world."

If the shortgrass is a nation, it is ruled by a tyrant—water. Moisture is the great limiter of this land; its decree governs what plants will grow and demands that all animal life survive within its terms. The shortgrass suffers for its proximity to the mountains, for it lies within a rain shadow created by the Rockies. Moisture-laden clouds rise and cool as they move eastward across the mountains, becoming less able to hold moisture. As they pass over the peaks, much of the moisture they carry is lost in the form of rain and snow. By the time the clouds reach the prairie, little is left, creating the dry environment that fosters the shortgrass community.

When I lie and watch the play of clouds above the mountains, I see wild ponies—blue roans with manes of thunder—striking lightning with their hooves upon the rocky peaks. They bear rain in clay-lined baskets slung across their arching backs. But as they gallop eastward across the mountains—I hear the rolling cadence of their hooves—the mountains toss up horsehair lariats and rope them fast. The roans rear and buck, but the mountains snub the ropes tight to their rocky ridges till the ponies spill all their precious cargo and shed more moisture with their weeping. Only then, with the ponies spent, their sides heaving, their baskets dry, do the mountains loose the lassoes and send them on.

Unlike the ponies, the native plants of the shortgrass waste no moisture in weeping. They long ago adapted to the harsh, dry climate, knowing the value of a drop of rain. Shortgrasses conserve precious resources by staying close to the earth—they are typically only six to 12 inches tall. The two generals of the shortgrass nation, the keystone plants, are buffalo grass and blue grama. Though buffalo grass looks a bit scruffy, a clumpy grass sprouting unkempt runners, it is so nutritious it was a favorite forage grass of bison. These shortgrasses lead a fleeting life. They are warm-season grasses, waiting to green up till summer is well on its way and the soil has warmed. Then their stay at the ball is brief, from May through midsummer, when the clock strikes midnight and they enter the pumpkin carriage, drying to gold and surrendering the prairie to the cool-season grasses of autumn.

I have come to know the shortgrass well. Now I will travel east to the tallgrass of eastern Kansas, to discover the land and my ties to it.

*   *   *   *   *

The maps lay open on the car seat beside me, the 1874 atlas like a treasure map with secret clues. In 1874, the atlas tells me, the bridge over the Kansas River which I am approaching was a ferry crossing, and the Goddard farm lay just on the other side of the river. Wilder didn't exist yet, nor did the rail line, but the contours of the land, the bend in the river, the section lines, the country roads all correlate to landmarks on the modern map.

The farm country on either side of Highway 7 is trim and handsome, with neatly tended farmsteads and broad hay meadows. I come to the Kansas River at Bonner Springs, an unimpressive little town built into hollows along the river. High bluffs border the water, the banks steep and covered with timber except where the bedrock limestone lies exposed like pale bones. An immature red-tailed hawk wheels and banks, using the updraft off the face of the bluff for lift. The trees rise tall and slender like the lodgepole pine forests of the Rockies, overgrown with vines where the sun hits the edges of the woodlots. Osage orange with hard, globular fruit; wild persimmon;

oaks and cottonwoods with a tangled understory of poison ivy and other plants—these remnants of the native woods that once covered the riverside hills were the last frontier of the eastern forests. I've come to the doorstep of the Great Plains, the edge of what once was tallgrass prairie. From here the plains spread west to the Rocky Mountains, to my home. The prairie begins here, I realize, and so do I.

Crossing the river, I see far below me its muscular waters moving slowly eastward. The river fascinates me. Where I live we have no robust bodies of water writhing like green snakes, deep between banks grown thick with vegetation. Back home, the South Platte River is lazy and shallow most of the year, spread across its sandy bed a mile wide and an inch deep. But the water I stare at now below the bridge is not really unknown to me. It has come as far as I have. It fell on me as rain or hail this summer before flowing into the Smoky Hill, traveling all these miles to meet up with me here.

The site of the Goddard farm is just beyond the bridge, on my right. The highway, in fact, is its eastern border. I cross the bridge and within a quarter mile a road turns off the highway and passes among green farm fields tinged with autumn gold. I swing the car in a right turn, slow down to negotiate a few curves, then pull off to the side of the road along rows of low, wide-leafed soybeans. I step out into the humidity and walk around the car to the edge of the field. I can see the tree-lined bluffs of the river just beyond. One hundred twenty years ago, my family lived here in this place, farmed these fields, mined the riches of the prairie. I'm standing on the Goddard farm.

A nappy border of weeds and grasses edges the neat soybean field. Knee-deep at the roadside, lacy sprays of switchgrass, a keystone grass of the tallgrass prairie, brush my bare legs and I recognize the compact seed-heads of timothy, a prime hay grass. Wild clumps of big bluestem, bowing slightly, with unkempt golden seedheads and broad green blades, rise shoulder-high. Back home on the shortgrass, big bluestem only grows in low, moist spots or in the floodplains of rivers. I'm not used to grass that brushes my cheek as I walk through it. The bluestem is too unmanageable to collect. Kneeling, I grasp a handful of switchgrass, pulling a bunch to dry and take home as a memento.

I continue slowly along the road. All around me are the flat fields that had been the Goddard farm, full now with corn and soybeans, the corn tall and golden-brown, the soybeans low, bushy and yellowing. Windbreaks of cottonwoods border each field, limiting my view. Wilder, if it exists, is just past the screen of trees. Then suddenly I'm there, at a collection of maybe ten ramshackle houses among tall trees, each sitting on two or three acres along a handful of intersecting streets laid out in a square grid. No shops or businesses, just houses. Though the town site is wide and flat, Wilder sits shaded among tall trees in the shadow of the river's limestone bluffs. The humid air hangs hazy around me, and I feel like I'm in a hollow.

My grandmother was right. Wilder isn't much of a place. It's no El Dorado, just the remnant of a little railroad village. I turn up Railroad Street, then onto Parish and back down Prairie, driving around Wilder in about five minutes. Each street is perhaps two blocks long, and I drive slowly past frame houses in need of paint, the yards housing collections of vehicles old and new, metal Tuff Sheds and old barns. Gnarled oaks and ash trees stand in neat rows along the edges of pastures behind the homes. Back at the main road, I stop at a lemonade stand operated out of the back of a Honda Civic hatchback by four smiling kids. Excited at the prospect of a customer, they hurry to pour a lukewarm serving of pink lemonade in a paper cup. One of the girls, with a sly look in her eye, accepts my dollar bill for the fifty-cent lemonade and conveniently forgets to bring my change.

"My grandmother was born here a hundred years ago," I tell them. They're excited at meeting a stranger, all trying to talk to me at once, though I doubt if they can imagine life in their tiny town a century ago, or a grandmother who would be 100 years old.

"There's gonna be houses here soon," they tell me, breathless to out-talk each other. "And a recreation center down by the river."

"You mean you will all have to move?" I ask them.

"Well, yeah, but we got paid enough money so we don't care what happens here," they answer breezily, echoing their parents.

I realize I have found Wilder just in time, seen it just before it vanishes beneath a subdivision. This area is undergoing gentrification, part of Kansas City's exurban sprawl. In time I suppose it will bear some silly name like River Oaks Estates or Carriage House Acres. How surprised Nana would be to think of her rural birthplace that "wasn't much of a place" transformed to overpriced mini-estates for expatriates from Kansas City.

Finding the actual site of the Goddard farmhouse seems even more imperative now. Might the old home still exist? It would be of frame, I imagine, as near as it is to this wooded strip along the river. My 1874 map indicates the house quite clearly, at a rise where the road makes a sharp bend to the south. The existing road still follows that exact path, curving south just past the tracks of the Atchison, Topeka & Santa Fe Railroad. I drive across the tracks and the road begins to rise. Just back from the road sit two small, one-story gray houses. Nothing about the homes stands out. I can't judge their ages, cloaked as they are in neatly painted siding, but they're both well-kept, the windows trimmed in white and appearing newly painted. A little stream runs past the place; I cross it on a small wood bridge and pull into the yard. A white birdbath sits beneath a tree, ringed by fall-blooming tulips. These people take pride in their home.

A young man is clearing brush with a Bobcat tractor. I park the car and walk around to where the man can see me. He's in his thirties, wearing a seed cap and a Harley Davidson T-shirt. Noticing me, he shuts off the machine and looks at me questioningly. "Sorry to bother you," I say, "but I'm looking up some family history and I think my grandmother was born here in 1889." The young man extends his hand and introduces himself as Tim. He grew up here, he tells me. His parents live in the closest house and he lives in the further one. Tim is very friendly and interested in chatting and looks at my maps with great interest. Might he know when these houses were built? "My granddad built both these houses," he says, though he's not sure when. I feel a bit of disappointment, though I hadn't really expected the original farmhouse to have survived more than 100 years.

Tim's father, who is 66, was born in the nearest house, and Tim thinks his family has probably lived here since the 1930s. "You know, my granddad said he tore down a much older farmhouse when he built this one." Tim points to an open patch of green lawn just beyond his father's house. "Over there."

I walk "over there." The spot is flat and open, now the yard of the present house. I am as close as I'm going to get to my family's home, I realize. It's a nice enough spot, shielded from the road by the inevitable row of trees and a tangle of shrubs, the little stream passing by just beyond, a corn field visible on the other side of the railroad tracks. For a moment I imagine my grandmother as a little girl, with braided hair and long skirt flying, running down this dusty road to play with friends in Wilder, a girl with all her life ahead of her, with children and family as yet unknown that will make her life, and bring me mine.

The information from the county archives included a one-paragraph mention of Wilder from a 1915 county history. In those days this area had been potato fields. My mother's cousin, Dr. June Miller, had told me that when she was a girl the farmers around Olathe, 10 miles south of here, raised garden vegetables to serve the Kansas City grocery trade. This prairie, with a grand river at its back, suffers no shortage of water. How different from the dryland wheat farms of the shortgrass.

The Goddard farm site holds one more surprise for me. When I later re-read Parkman's description of the area in *The Oregon Trail*, I find something astonishing. After crossing the Missouri, Parkman arrived at the "Methodist Shawanoe Mission," a log church and schoolhouse, around which the Kansas City suburb of Shawnee Mission will eventually blossom. The Shawnee Methodist Mission was founded in 1830 by Rev. Thomas Johnson—Johnson County is named for him—and is now a state historic site. On the wall of the girls' classroom is a portrait of George Washington, who must have seemed strange and foreign to Indian children forced to sit at the hard wooden desks and learn the history of the culture that had disenfranchised them. Originally from Ohio and Kentucky, the Shawnees had been forcibly moved west by whites in successive stages. Finally pushed west of the Missouri, they displaced the native tribe of this area, the Kansa (or Konza or Kaw), called the People of the South Wind because the wind blew always from that compass point. The Kansa were few in number but handsome of person and gracious in manner.

From the Shawnee Mission, Parkman continued on until "a few hours' ride brought us to the banks of the river Kanzas." The rich green prairies with their mosaic of wildflowers were broken by stands of trees flushed red with the buds of maples. Parkman's party camped in a meadow near the river's edge, at the Lower Delaware Crossing. The Delawares, originally from Pennsylvania, were another eastern tribe pushed west, eventually to a reservation established for them in 1835 west of the Shawnees.

The meadow where Parkman's westbound party camped sang with the plaintive whistling of quails and, after dusk, the calls of whippoorwills. Though Parkman grabbed his shotgun to try his luck with the quails, he saw no game, only some turkey vultures roosting in a dead sycamore. The next day the party made a difficult river crossing, rafting their horses and supplies across and struggling up the steep bluffs on the other side. "A military road led from this point to Fort Leavenworth," Parkman wrote.

An established crossing of the Kansas River west of Shawnee Mission, with steep bluffs on the north side and, beyond, a road leading directly to Leavenworth. Is Parkman describing the site of the Goddard farm? Wilder lies about 13 miles due west of the Shawnee Methodist Mission. The Highway 7 bridge across the Kansas River is a major crossing, replacing what had been a ferry 125 years ago. I had already seen how modern crossings and roads follow older established routes, and no other roads lead directly north in a beeline to Leavenworth. My evidence is circumstantial, but if Parkman camped on or near my family farm, he left me a fine description of the land as it had once been.

Fifteen miles south of the Goddard farm, at the far edge of Olathe, I find a tiny remnant of the ancestral landscape. The Prairie Center is a tallgrass prairie preserve, a 300-acre sanctuary with 45 acres of virgin tallgrass, land that has never been plowed. The day is warm and the air hums with insect song as I walk a trail mowed through the grass. The stalks rise above my head, reedy and golden, the wind stirring the stems with gentle music, like a wispy clarinet. The seedheads of big bluestem flop like the bird's foot from which they draw their nickname— turkeyfoot grass. I grasp one gently and bend it down like the springy limb of a tree, splay the seedhead on my palm. Nearby I see the handsome heads of Indian grass. Below these towering grasses grows an understory of other plants, clustering thick as the shrubs and vines of a moist forest, dense enough to leave no patch of earth exposed. A beetle lumbers over a stem; a small native bee buzzes past; an eastern meadowlark sings from somewhere beyond, its song foreign to my ears, different from the tumbling notes of its western cousin. For just a while I let myself be enveloped by this odd tall prairie, pretending I am seeing it as it once was, vital and unbordered, no roads or houses, only the native plants and the mighty grasses growing higher than it can be possible for grass to grow.

I've finally found the tallgrass. I've found Wilder. I've found the Goddard farm. Now only one landmark of my family in this county remains for me to find. Mom remembered as a girl visiting family graves at an old church cemetery at Monticello. Down the road I come upon the small country church flanked by a tidy cemetery. Surrounded by a black iron fence, the graveyard is quiet and unimposing. I walk through the open gate and directly on my right find a red granite headstone with the surname in bold relief—GODDARD. Below that: Robert 1856-1924 and Katie 1865-1940. My great-grandparents. Just to the right, a smaller single headstone with the simple inscription, Deleo 1887-1912. Deleo was my grandmother's beloved eldest sister who fell ill and died at the age of 25. The pictures I've seen of Deleo reveal a lovely young woman with large dark eyes, fair hair swept up softly and pinned in a roll atop her head in the style of the day. In my jewelry box I have a quaint school medal awarded for "elocution." On the back is engraved the name Deleo Goddard. My mother found this antique trinket among Nana's things after she died. For more than 60 years my grandmother had kept that small memory of her sister.

I search now for more family markers. Twenty feet beyond the Goddards I come upon a gray granite stone set flat in the ground, a few dry maple leaves fallen artfully upon it. Levi Lewis Hoard, it reads, 1869-1941, with the symbol of the Masons. This is Uncle Lew, Katie Marilla's little brother who became the bachelor great-uncle my mother remembers seeing only once a year, at Christmas. But what of Levi Hoard, the patriarch, who brought the family west to the edge of the Great Plains in the 1870s? I search the area with no success till I finally look closely at a worn, four-sided column of white marble. The chiseled letters are partly obscured with moss, and the lines from Emily Dickinson come to my mind: "until the moss has reached our lips and covered up our names." But I am here to read the name and recognize it—Levi C. Hoard, d Sep 25 1881 age 55y 10m 24d "Sacred to the memory of our father." I have found my great-great-grandfather.

It is strange to come to a place where you have never been before and find family. I don't know this place, but I have ties to it. I go back five generations here, brief by some standards, but a wondrous concept for an Army brat like me, a rolling stone raised all over the world.

Great-great-granddad Levi brought the family to the edge of the plains, but they didn't stay here. Like the restless Ingalls family, the Goddards moved further west, to Hutchinson, Kansas, where Great-grandfather farmed and bartered real estate. Forty years later some of the family moved west again when my Uncle Bob moved his family to Loveland, Colorado, along the Front Range north of Denver. When my father retired from the Army, we followed them and made our home in Loveland too.

Over three or four generations we had gone as far west on the prairie as we could, rolled from the Missouri River to the Rocky Mountains. Growing up I never felt I was from anywhere, never felt I had a home until I came to Colorado. Now I know I am from two places, from where the prairie ends and from where it begins.

Chapter 6:
Black-tailed Prairie Dogs

I'm walking through a ghost, a weedy patch of throwaway land surrounded by the Denver metro area, where native prairie lingers in echoes, a pagan Avalon hovering in the mists of a Christian world. Now that we've moved into the city, finding prairie is not as easy as walking out the door. I had remembered coming upon this place by accident several years ago. Now I come back in search of open ground where I can exercise Cody.

These hundred-some acres of open space avoided development for many years because they lie in the flood spillway of Cherry Creek Reservoir. Now they are for sale, optioned by a commercial development company. One day an office building will rise to convert this shameful, useless ground to revenue-producing real estate. Until then, it is my little patch of neighborhood prairie.

Most Denverites whiz past on busy Hampden Avenue completely unaware of this place; if they should happen to glance over they see nothing but a worthless, weed-filled field. What I've found in this raggedy spot is a remnant of prairie, a reflection in a cracked mirror of the native landscape that once defined the High Plains. In a bow to the irony of its location next to fastidiously groomed links, I call this the golf-course prairie.

To many eyes this is an ugly place, the vegetation on this November day gone crackly brown. Few trees relieve the horizontal lines of the land. But it was the very ugliness that first drew me here. No one else would come to this unkempt plot, I reasoned, I could let Cody run off the leash. We would bother no one and in turn remain unbothered. I never expected to become so enamored of its rough attractions. But I'm learning to take my prairie where I find it, delighting in the discovery, here and there, of a native plant surviving among the weeds—buffalo currant bearing tart-sweet berries; bunches of blue grama with seedheads like curving sickles; defiant yucca bristling with attitude.

This is an odd little patch of ground, this urban wilderness. North across Hampden Avenue lies a seemingly endless expanse of homes, offices and strip malls; to the west, townhomes and more city. To the east, beyond the fence, is Kennedy Golf Course, with emerald lawns and stately shade trees maintained by the City and County of Denver. Next to the golf course lies a pair of soccer fields, busy on weekends spring through fall but abandoned the rest of the time. The manicured fields look out of place here amid this remnant grassland, like two kids with polished shoes and combed hair surrounded by a ragtag band of seedy urchins.

To the south is an interstate highway, but not one that connects cities or states, more of an intra-state, really. These six lanes of racing urban whitewater known as I-225 are just a connector, running up the east side of the Denver metro area to link I-25, which flows north to south between Wyoming and New Mexico like a major river, and I-70, which passes east to west out of the Eastern Plains eventually defying gravity to flow up and over the Continental Divide.

Just beyond I-225 rises a great earthen dam, a monument to the U.S. Army Corps of Engineers. The dam holds back the waters of Cherry Creek, a little prairie tributary which, restrained, swells up to form an impressive reservoir. Around this man-made lake is a state park. The creek, the dam, the lake, and the park all bear the same name. I wonder if they would have christened all these developments in honor of this prairie stream if it had been called Rattlesnake Creek?

When I first discovered the golf-course prairie several years ago, a good-sized prairie dog colony bustled with vitality here. Several months passed between my visits. The next time I reached the top of the rise overlooking the village, I expected to see the usual galloping brown ground squirrels and hear their high-pitched barking. But the place was silent. Nothing moved, no sentry sounded a warning. The 'dog holes lay ominously empty, like so many eyes staring blindly at the sky. Weeds grew over the burrow mounds, the tunnels had collapsed and were filling with debris that no self-respecting prairie dog homeowner would have tolerated. The skulls of prairie dogs gleamed white in the dust around the burrows. The colony had been wiped out by plague.

Called sylvatic plague when it sickens rodents, the disease is caused by the same organism that ravaged Europe during the fourteenth-century epidemic of bubonic plague known as the Black Death. Like humans, the communal prairie dogs are highly vulnerable to plague. Once it struck, this village was devastated, as black-tailed prairie dog populations have been throughout Colorado's Eastern Plains. Plague is not a native disease, so our North American rodents have no evolved immunity to it. Like so many non-native life forms brought to the New World by European settlement (including many of the noxious weeds that surround this prairie dog town) plague was a stowaway, harbored within other unwelcome émigrés which have themselves become major nuisances—Norway rats.

"What's the incidence of transmission of plague from prairie dogs to humans?" I ask John Pape, epidemiologist with the Colorado Department of Public Health and Environment. Prairie dogs as dangerous transmitters of death is frequently used as justification for exterminating them, when what people really want is the land the 'dogs inhabit. Between 1957 and mid-1998, Pape tells me, there were 43 cases of plague afflicting humans in Colorado, but only nine of those were associated with prairie dogs. Of those nine cases, only one resulted in a death. So, one human death in more than 40 years from prairie dog-borne plague. By contrast, in 1996, four people died from being struck by lightning, which kills on average three people a year. Lightning is obviously a much greater threat to public health and safety than prairie dogs. I can't resist asking about the statistics for motor vehicle-related death. In 1996, 538 people died in auto-related accidents on Colorado roads. I guess the way to really live dangerously is to drive your car through a prairie dog town during a thunderstorm.

In the years since the plague die-off, the 'dogs have re-homesteaded this bit of turf and are back in force. The change is dramatic. The burrow mounds are tidy and free of weeds, the town itself a flurry of activity and noise. The extended village covers perhaps 30 acres now, right up to the edge and onto the neighboring golf course. I'm sure they drive the groundskeepers crazy. I can't resist smiling at the idea of prairie dogs with such prime real estate—*Townhome community on 7th fairway, view of mountains, custom floorplans, alarm system.*

I imagine them pitching in to spruce up the old burrows, the industrious males diving in with both paws to excavate and rebuild the tunnels, sending dirt flying out the entrance. With T-squares, plumb lines and surveyor's tape they reconfigure the placement of the burrow's various chambers. Even the female 'dogs perched upright on their mounds play a role in the drama, standing with paws on hips, tut-tutting at all the clutter and mess.

I challenge anyone who contends a prairie is empty and silent to venture through a prairie dog town. With my appearance, the residents disappear from view, but their squeaky alarm barks blossom all around me. I walk through a garden of sound. *Chirk, chirk, chirk* erupts in front of me, behind me, to the right and to the left. I recall Tennyson's *Charge Of The Light Brigade*, though here it is rodents to right of me, rodents to left of me, that volley and thunder.

For sheer entertainment, there's no place quite like a prairie dog town. The village is a noisy carnival. Sentries bark out their alarms. Neighbors pay calls on neighbors, visiting between burrows. Moving in a slow, rolling gallop, the 'dogs scurry along familiar paths pounded into the earth by many rodent feet. In winter, when the surrounding cover is especially sparse, these prairie dog paths stand out, radiating among and between burrows like the lines on a Chinese checkerboard. Those who say there are no straight lines in nature have never seen the burrow-to-burrow paths within a prairie dog town, as straight as if drawn with a ruler. Prairie dogs don't need to study geometry to know the shortest route from burrow A to burrow B is a straight line; a meandering prairie dog is soon hawk food.

Prairie dogs are heliotropes; they rise and set with the sun. You never see or hear them from evening until morning and they stay underground on overcast days when the light is flat. Again it is the constant fear of death that rules their lives. Their only defense is seeing predators and diving to safety. On overcast days a hawk dropping from the sky casts no shadow.

I once puzzled over the many indentations I saw on some burrow mounds, like the pattern of dimples on a golf ball. Then I watched prairie dogs at work on burrow construction. Using their flat-nosed heads like battering rams they pack the soil around the entrance—*bonk, bonk, bonk.* Those dimples were the 'dogs' noseprints in the packed dirt.

From a distance I watch two prairie dogs greet each other face-to-face and embrace with a kiss, or so it appears. Touching their paws to each other's shoulders they nuzzle noses, a way of identifying the other by sniffing its breath. Biologist call this naso-nasal contact, an ungracious term for a charming behavior. They remind me of two Frenchmen kissing each other on both cheeks, "Bonjour, Jean-Paul. Ow goes zee burrowing zis morning?"

In spring, I see the pups, just emerged from their underground nurseries, clustered in groups on the mounds above the family burrow; a class picture of fourth-graders, everyone facing the same direction, everyone's right shoulder pointed to the camera. Dotted about the village are residents sitting upright atop their burrow entrances like retired farmers rocking on the front porch. Some of the adults jump for joy, throwing their heads back and jumping up with a yip. Many of them are actually sentries, keeping watch for all manner of dangers, as prairie dogs are the food of choice for hawks, owls, coyotes, and other predators. Prairie dogs have come to know one of their most dangerous predators is two-legged and armed with a shotgun loaded with varmint shot.

I have watched prairie dogs a thousand times over the years, but it wasn't until I focused on them with my binoculars that we became intimate. I watch one sentinel barking out his warning, the pink lining of his mouth flashing like a semaphore with each bark, bark, bark. Dr. Con Slobodchikoff, a biology professor at Northern Arizona State University, says prairie dogs have the most advanced form of natural language known to science. In other words, they can talk. He should know. He's studied prairie dog communication, particularly their alarm calls, for 10 years, observing from a blind atop a tower set at the edge of a prairie dog town. They have hundreds of words, he claims. Walk into their town and they can describe you to each other not just as a human, but also what color shirt you're wearing and whether or not you're carrying a gun.

Of course, the 'dogs didn't talk directly to the professor. He had to interpret their language by eavesdropping on their conversations. When he sent a graduate student through the town armed with a stick "gun" and wearing a white shirt, he recorded the prairie dogs' calls. Later, when the same student came through, the 'dogs remembered him and made the same unique set of calls, distinct from sounds they made when a non-threatening student, unarmed and wearing a dark shirt, appeared.

Slobodchikoff identified four distinct alarm calls for four different predators—coyote, hawk, dog, and human. Now when I venture through this prairie dog town, tripping the invisible alarm wire, I wonder how the sentries describe me. I hope it's complimentary, not as some two-legged god-awful-ugly varmint with no business in their town.

One day I noticed two little boys, probably about eight years old, poking around the 'dog town. They were half crouched, skulking along amid the burrows. What are they doing? I wondered. The 'dogs were sounding off grandly, the entire village a cacophony of high-pitched yips. Abruptly one of the boys rushed a prairie dog sitting up on its mound. Predictably the animal disappeared down the burrow with a flutter of its black tail. The boys, I realized, were stalking prairie dogs.

They reminded me of coyote pups, repeatedly trying to sneak up on the wary rodents, rushing in just as their quarry dove for cover. Foiled on his first attempt, the boy whirled to race after another prairie dog barking behind him. I wondered how many animals the boys had chased underground this afternoon. The boys would learn their lessons, just like young coyotes; learn patience, how to save their energy and invest themselves only when chances are good for a payoff.

I understand their fascination with these communal rodents. My oldest sister claims it was prairie dogs that first won me over to the prairie. Buffalo, coyotes, and pronghorn get all the glamour press but like workers who keep the factory operating, the prairie dog is the key to much of the shortgrass prairie ecosystem. The eagles and hawks and badgers need someone to eat and the prairie dog obliges, involuntarily, of course. Ecologists claim up to 140 species or more depend on prairie dogs. I've personally seen, either in or over a prairie dog town, ferruginous, Swainson's, red-tailed, and rough-legged hawks; bald and golden eagles; prairie falcons; kestrels; meadowlarks; mountain plovers; great horned owls; coyotes; badgers; burrowing owls; bullsnakes; prairie rattlers; cottontails; jackrabbits, and many invertebrates.

My favorite 'dog-town squatter is a creature many people are surprised to learn about. Familiar with the Rocky Mountain Arsenal National Wildlife Refuge after years of writing about it, I volunteered to help out for a Migratory Bird Day celebration by leading a public tour. As the bus passed a prairie dog town, an older couple reported that one of the 'dogs had suddenly jumped from atop a burrow and flown off. Their flying prairie dog was one of the little ground owls of the prairie, a burrowing owl, which nests in abandoned prairie dog holes. Burrowing owls are much too small to prey upon adult prairie dogs—the owls are all air and feathers, weighing about five-and-a-half ounces compared to the hefty two- to three-pound rodents. But the shape of the two is similar—both have rounded heads, are about the same height, and both perch atop the burrows. Nesting in prairie dog towns offers the owls more than ready-made homes. The prairie dog alarm system protects the owls as well. When they hear all those squeaking alarm barks, the owls know to watch out for danger.

The idea of ground-dwelling owls is bizarre to many people. As I talked with Refuge biologist Jane Griese, two workers in hard hats approached us, a tall young man and a stocky older man. The younger man jerked his thumb towards his friend as he spoke to Jane. "Tell him about those owls," he said, then added earnestly, "those owls live in the ground, right?"

"Yes, they're called burrowing owls," Jane affirmed, proceeding to explain about the birds to the skeptical older man.

"See, I told you," said the younger hardhat when Jane had finished.

"Well, I just never would have believed such a thing," said the older. "I was ready to bet my paycheck!"

"Oh, don't do that, don't ever bet your paycheck," Jane said with a grin. The two men went off still wrangling amiably between themselves. "I told you those were owls," said the young man. "Well, I wasn't going to believe just you," said the other.

Burrowing owls don't tolerate human activity well. In fact they have abandoned all the nesting sites around the Denver area where I used to see them because of the offensive encroachment of houses, traffic, and dogs. Prairie dog towns hemmed in by human development no longer attract burrowing owls as seasonal tenants. I once saw seven burrowing owls perched on fence posts along a road on the west side of Cherry Creek State Park, one owl every other pole, but I haven't seen owls at the park now for several years. I feel as if I've lost family members when I revisit 'dog towns where I'd watched burrowing owl young develop each summer, only to find a parking lot instead. In 1998 the state of Colorado listed the burrowing owl as a threatened species.

Livestock growers have no love for prairie dogs, considering them an enemy and major pest. The grass-eating ground squirrels compete with cattle for range and it's hard to argue that a prairie dog town looks pretty, overgrazed and bare of grass.

Aided by the federal agency formerly known as Animal Damage Control, now gone undercover as Wildlife Services, private landowners across the West have waged a campaign of extermination against prairie dogs for 100 years. Plowed under and poisoned out, the once-prolific prairie dog remains in remnant populations, inhabiting scattered fragmentary colonies, its numbers reduced by as much as 99 percent from pre-settlement levels. In 2000, the U.S. Fish and Wildlife Service ruled that listing of the black-tailed prairie dog as a threatened species was "warranted but precluded," supposedly because the Service lacked the manpower to work on them and felt other species were more important. But the more likely truth is that prairie dogs are far too hot politically, with too many enemies who would rather see them exterminated than protected.

Estimates of how many prairie dogs there might have been before Europeans arrived in North America are only guesses. But in 1901 Vernon Bailey, a researcher with the Bureau of Biological Survey, the precursor of the U.S. Fish and Wildlife Service, rode for most of a day through one continuous prairie dog complex in Texas. He guessed this 'dog metroplex covered 25,000 square miles. The number of individual 'dogs estimated to inhabit such a vast community? Four hundred million. Based on these kinds of anecdotal reports, the pre-settlement population of prairie dogs is thought to have been something around five billion. By way of comparison, in 1990, the world's human population was 5.3 billion.

Prairie dogs may have gotten a bad rap as ravagers of the range. There's evidence, says Dave Seery, prairie dog biologist at the Rocky Mountain Arsenal refuge, that on a healthy prairie, with native plants that evolved with the 'dogs' munching, the rodents don't overgraze. Studies at Wind Cave National Monument in South Dakota have shown that "managed" grasses and forbs atop a prairie dog town are higher in protein and nitrogen. Bison, pronghorn, and even cattle prefer grazing in prairie dog towns—more bang for the bite, nutrient-wise.

The 'dog town at the golf-course prairie has managed to hang on at least for now, a strange bedfellow to the golf course next door. I occasionally find golf balls gleaming incongruously white among the brown landscape of this 'dog town—a Top Flite XL or a Titleist 4. These refugees from the golf course escape the 7th fairway, flying over the fence to freedom on the loft of some duffer's hook shot. The little white balls lying vulnerable and exposed on the open ground immediately catch Cody's interest. At last, something that doesn't squeak then disappear down a hole! He brings the balls to me eagerly and sometimes I toss one for him to chase, playing a crazy version of golf among the prairie dog holes, though my goal is to not sink the golf ball. Once, in the process of retrieving a golf ball, Cody took a sudden detour to investigate a barking prairie dog. Peering curiously down into the hole, his floppy ears hanging down the sides of his face, Cody simply opened his mouth and watched the ball disappear down the burrow.

Prairie dogs don't seem upset by such detritus. Lots of stuff ends up in and around prairie dog holes. I've seen their burrow entrances carved around chunks of concrete, plastic anti-freeze containers, even old car radiators. If you can't dig it out, go around, seems to be their motto. Sometimes, like archaeologists, prairie dogs unearth precious relics. The skulls and bones of endangered black-footed ferrets occasionally materialize atop prairie dog burrows. Alas, these bones are not the hoped-for proof that free-living ferrets miraculously survive but the remains of ferrets long-dead, unearthed by a 'dog re-excavating an old hole.

Beyond the 'dog town, Cody snuffles busily at a low-lying patch of mud that holds the impressions of slender, four-toed paws. He sniffs with gusto, milling about excitedly. His bulbous nose is more sensitive to trace chemicals than the finest gas chromatograph; he would not, I think, show such excessive interest in the scent of another domestic dog. He is on to the scent of his wild cousin, a coyote. I see coyotes often out here, haunting this remnant grassland, as if no interstate or golf course or city defines the boundaries of their turf. I see coyotes here almost every day, usually just one alone, but sometimes two together, as well as raptors of all kinds. The predator interest in this bit of real estate is a dividend of the burgeoning prairie dog community. Wildlife are like the ballplayers in the movie *Field of Dreams*—give them habitat, and they will come.

While coyotes are frequent voyagers here, I see red foxes only across the fence on the carefully groomed fairways. Coyotes, the larger of the two, will keep foxes out of their turf. The sleek red fox, urbane and cosmopolitan, is most at home amid the manicured green grass of the golf course. The coyote, much more the Western ruffian outfitted in grizzled gray and moving with a cowboy's saunter, haunts the rough and weedy world of this remnant prairie.

On a wide, low railing edging the highway I find splashes of dried blood lying in circles like red nickels. Here too I see the whitewash of bird droppings and a bit of the entrails of a rodent, dark red and leathery like a dried-up worm. A raptor sat here, eating its catch from the surrounding grasslands, holding its prey in sharp talons and tearing the animal to digestible bites. Who it might have been, what hawk, I cannot know, though the rail is rather low to be the preferred perch of a large raptor. I have seen several kestrels in the last 20 minutes, perched on power lines. Perhaps the diner was one of them, though kestrels, small falcons not much larger than a robin, hunt mainly grasshoppers and other insects. There are no hawk pellets on the ground below the railing, so this is not a favorite perch where a bird might sit and rest after eating, coughing up neat packages of bones and hair, the indigestible parts of its dinner. No, this was an expedient place to gulp down a meal, sort of like sitting in the car to eat a fast-food hamburger instead of carrying it home.

As if on cue, a large bird passes me silently, its shadow raking the ground, sending the prairie dogs tumbling down their burrows with a frenzy of squeaky barks. A handsome ferruginous hawk lands atop a nearby power pole. Its head bows to work at something clenched in its talon. I follow the path that leads past its pole. The hawk, of course, knows of my approach; it probably eyeballed me from the moment I topped the rise that overlooks this patch of open land. Tiring of calling the hawk "it" I decide to presume her to be a female. This, then, is a woman hawk, a fierce huntress, an Artemis of the air.

As the she-hawk turns her head at a certain angle, I am reminded of an Egyptian hieroglyph of Horus, the sky god, a hawk whose eyes are the sun and the moon. I look at her and wonder at the marvels she sees with her moon eye and her sun eye. Horus was the son of Isis and Osiris, but myth often blurs the distinction between male and female and I allow that this mythic hawk will be a daughter. Horus of the Horizon, the image of the rising sun.

She seems otherworldly, with the moon in her eye, carrying the wisdom of her species. Yet she is very much of this world, this prairie world, what's left of it. This ferruginous hawk may not be a god, nor a hieroglyph, but she is certainly a master crafter at her task, and that task is hunting prairie dogs. The ferruginous hawk, dubbed "ferrug" by birders, is a consummate prairie dog hunter. It will wait on the ground at a prairie dog hole, just below the rodent's line of vision, then grab the 'dog when it pokes its head up to look for danger. Researchers once puzzled over why some ferruginous hawks, which have creamy-white heads and breasts, sometimes appeared to have "ring around the collar." Then they observed a ferrug land near a prairie dog burrow and poke its head into the hole, looking for dinner. Sadly, with the development and loss of so much prairie, these greatest of grassland hawks, found only on the Great Plains of North America, are rapidly disappearing.

I see the she-hawk many times through the fall and winter, at least I assume the hawk I see is the one I call Horus. It pleases me to think so, that she and I have a nodding acquaintance, both drawn to this place by the remnant grassland and its prairie-dog town. She, of course, seeks immediate fulfillment in the meals she takes among the resident small mammals. I settle for more abstract rewards.

In what must be the hawk's own little joke, she never appears on the days I remember to bring my binoculars. As if protecting her privacy from my peering eyes, or perhaps afraid that if I look at her too keenly, too close, I will see she is just a hawk after all and not a god. What she can't know is that to me she could never be anything less than magical and her appearance here, within the city, is a special gift.

The remains of a narrow asphalt road hide beneath the weeds here, as well as the foundation of a building or two. The old road, dissolved into a dirt path in many places, leads to an abandoned overpass that crosses I-225. Curiously, the overpass wasn't built for cars, but for people and farm equipment. This land is owned by the Cherry Creek School District. Cherry Creek High School lies across the interstate to the south, next to the state park. In the days when the high school operated an agricultural program, this patch of ground was known as "The Farm." It was a school farm where the kids learned the art and science of raising crops. When I see the students around the high school today, for the most part children of great privilege, I can't imagine any of them in overalls and seed caps operating a manure spreader or milking cows. These kids are destined for law school, Wall Street, and Junior League, not a prairie farm.

At the base of the overpass a sprouting of cattails along a little runoff stream marks a tiny wetland that hosts red-winged blackbirds in the spring and summer. A few years ago the school district had managed to sell this area, despite the looming presence of the dam and its millions of acre-feet of water, pent-up and restive behind the earthen barrier, to a prominent local developer. Under cover of darkness, an army of earthmovers rolled in, their mission to fill the wetland before anyone was the wiser to avoid any potentially costly government-mandated mitigation that could have interfered with development plans. But somebody already was the wiser and had tipped off the Environmental Protection Agency. Perhaps the neighbors looked out and saw the equipment or maybe a traveler passing on the highway thought something suspicious was underway. The developer was caught red-handed about to destroy the wetland and was charged with violating environmental laws. The school district regained control of The Farm and the golf-course prairie earned a reprieve for a few more years.

I hike up from my grassland patch to stand atop the overpass. Gazing mesmerized at the passing traffic, hypnotized by the motion and the noise, I feel myself peering from another time and place into the present. From this land of grass and big sky where I am an occasional visitor, I look into the world that I really inhabit. I travel this particular piece of interstate myself quite often. Funny how I never noticed this overpass from my car, though I'd driven beneath it a hundred times.

It's a bizarre catwalk, traveling from one patch of bitty prairie to another, a bridge across the modern world. After a winter snow, I often find the fresh tracks of a single coyote traversing this bridge. No boot prints, no bicycle tires, just the fine, teardrop-shaped tracks of a coyote. It seems right that they should be the first to turn out after a snow, to make first tracks here, since it is their home. Coyotes, after all, are supreme opportunists. I imagine them trotting blithely across the highway bridge, the traffic zooming by below, for all the world as if this overpass were built just so coyotes could get from one prairie-dog town to another.

A few years ago a rogue band of pronghorn roamed briefly in the city park across the old overpass. Only about half of the park is developed, given over to well-tended athletic fields. The rest is more battered prairie, weed-choked waste ground where city workers by day, and the neighbors by night, dump building materials, unwanted sod, old furniture. But here, as in the land next to the golf course, I had discovered prairie survivors—red-tailed hawks, prairie falcons, western kingbirds, coyotes. And now pronghorn. Only the appearance of buffalo here could have surprised me more. I imagine the pronghorn trotting across the softball diamond, perhaps stepping on second base for good luck on their way to the outfield.

Pronghorn are wonderfully adapted for life in this landscape. They can thrive on sagebrush, a rare talent. Cattle will starve to death if sagebrush is all there is to eat. A pronghorn's telescopic eyes seem to know no limits; they mock the endless distances of open ground, noticing anything on their prairie. Clocked at up to 60 miles per hour, pronghorn are among the fastest land mammals in the world, ranking somewhere behind cheetahs and whippets. Like fine-tuned race cars they are turbo-charged with oversized windpipes to take in more air and fuel their speed. These startling speedsters so impressed explorer Meriwether Lewis that he described their movements in his journal as "reather the rapid flight of birds than the motion of quadrupeds. (sic)" Hoping to shoot one, he stealthily approached to within 200 paces of a buck and six does, but the animals "smelt me and fled." Hustling up to the spot where the pronghorn had been, he saw them racing across a far ridge, now an estimated three miles distant. Lewis at first doubted they could possibly be the same group of animals, but soon acknowledged their amazing speed. Ever the sportsman, he noted, "the speed of this anamal (sic) is equal if not superior to that of the finest blooded courser."

A pronghorn can easily outrun all North American predators—wolves, coyotes, bears, mountain lions. I recall how they kept pace with my speeding sports car out near Parker. How did they evolve to be so much faster than the competition? The answer lies in a world quite different from today. During the Pleistocene Epoch, more than 10,000 years ago, cheetahs lived in the American West. Slow pronghorn became cheetah food; fast ones survived.

Pronghorn are often called antelope—as in "where the deer and the antelope play"—but they are not antelope. Antelope are Old World grazing mammals, animals of the African and Asian plains. Pronghorn are creatures unto themselves, the sole living representative of their family, the *Antilocapridae*. Paleontologists have found many of the pronghorn's relations written in the fossil record of North America, but their last cousin died out tens of thousands of years ago. The pronghorn lives on, the lone survivor of its taxon, a survivor from the great Age of Mammals, a survivor of the more recent shortgrass prairie community; in brief, a survivor.

Now I find this desperate band of pronghorn numbering only about ten animals. Might these be my pronghorn, I wonder, come from the open country several miles south of the city? They could have followed the course of Cherry Creek, migrated through the state park to this side of the dam. Or, being open-country animals rather than stream-course dwellers like white-tailed deer, perhaps they trekked cross-country to get here, hopscotching from pasture to open space between the office parks and housing developments, dodging detection. Are they seeking me?

The first time I noticed these pronghorn they were running along the base of the dam next to the interstate. The outer flank of the dam is a fairly steep, grassy slope where each year seniors from neighboring high schools burn their school's initials into the grass—CC for Cherry Creek, SH for Smoky Hill. The lower reaches of the slope are broad and open, offering sufficient running space for suddenly urban pronghorn.

As I zoomed by in my sports car at 60 miles per hour, listening to rock tunes on the radio, I once again found myself racing a band of pronghorn just beyond the fence. I looked, then looked again. Pronghorn have not roamed this patch of ground in many decades. In this place they are not sleek princes but wild things lost in the city. They run in fright, seeking an outlet. They are like skittish colts, large-eyed and fluttery, bewildered by the madness of a city that has grown over their prairie. I cry out to them, "There's no way out for you this way!"

I see the pronghorn almost daily for a week or two, in the undeveloped land around the park across the unused highway overpass from my golf-course prairie. They are elegant animals, these *Antilocaprids*. They lie at rest, their long slender legs folded beneath them, prairie remnants among the weeds as surely as the blue grama and rabbitbrush. They are fish caught in a weir—having swum in the narrow neck, they find themselves in a basket, hemmed in by interstate, reservoir, and city. They cannot find a way out. It is only a matter of time; they don't belong here. They must go.

Irrationally, I consider the pronghorn my own little secret, like refugees I've hidden in my basement. I want to help them, but what can I do?

My refugees are not well hidden. Others have seen them and eventually the Colorado Division of Wildlife descends with traps, nets, and manpower. I open my morning paper to find my pronghorn caught in the arms of the law. Chased into catch nets, their eyes rolling wild, their dancers' legs kicking and thrashing, they are bundled up in the tangling nets and deported. Several animals must be destroyed, their legs broken in the capture. Another dies from stress, the biologists report. But it is fright they die of, these prey animals who have known only wide open country. They are devoured by fear from being chased and grabbed and held.

I can't help but cry for them, as I sit in my kitchen reading their fate in the newspaper.

I know it is really the only solution, and a humane one, to trap and move them. I work often with the wildlife division; I know the biologist who runs this operation. She is a competent, no-nonsense professional, good at her job, good at dealing with these sorts of freakish culture clashes—wildlife in the city. This may have been prairie for millennia, but it is no longer. Red-tailed hawks, coyotes, and prairie dogs may sneak in at the fringes and get away with it. Not so these timid, leggy pronghorn, who need lots of room and suffer from an excess of sensibility. I've never seen pronghorn again in the city. They have no place here; they are the echo of a fading symphony. Their sojourn in my neighborhood was really a time of entrapment. But I still miss them, these elegant animals that seem to me like wild prairie in animal form. Their visit touched my heart. Will they ever call again?

Chapter 7:
Prairie Pony

Pulling the borrowed horse trailer behind my weary-but-working old Suburban as if I were a ranch girl hauling my barrel pony to the rodeo, I tried to look like I did this every day. Inside, though, I shivered with excitement and secret pleasure. Loaded in the battered blue trailer on the way to his new home near the prairie was a sure-footed, 14-year-old Arabian gelding named Thunder. At 33 I was finally fulfilling the dream of every American girl. I had just bought my own horse.

"When did you ever learn to ride a horse?" my father asked when I told him about Thunder. As a young girl, taking riding lessons was my heart's desire, but my father, judging horses to be too dangerous, refused to grant it. He suggested ballet instead. I was aghast. I knew that inside I was a cowgirl. Somehow I learned to ride in spite of Dad. I rode whenever I had the opportunity, hanging around with friends who had horses, taking lessons here and there, riding by the hour at rent-a-horse stables. I managed to become a competent rider in a Western saddle, but I still hadn't much knowledge of true equitation.

Once in college at Colorado State University, which has an excellent equine science department and a large riding stable, I signed up for courses in English and Western equitation. In between coursework on developmental biology, animal behavior, and organic chemistry I learned to ride properly, to communicate with my mount, and to groom and care for a horse.

Working part-time at the CSU Veterinary Hospital, mainly in small animal surgery, I occasionally helped out on the large animal side, going out on house calls (horse calls?) with the mobile vet. I learned to give inoculations, worm horses with a tube through the nose into the stomach, doctor wounds, and grind down or "float" teeth. I helped out at foalings and geldings. After college, I was primed and ready to own a horse, but again I had to wait.

It had become a fun habit over the last several years to scan the Horses and Tack column of the Sunday classifieds. Finally I asked myself, "What are you waiting for? You've got your own money. You've got the time. And you don't have anyone telling you that a horse is a foolish waste of time and money." Damn straight!

"Grey Arab gelding, 14 yrs, easy keeper, good feet, gentle," the ad read, listing a reasonable price. I picked up the phone with determination and dialed the number. A day later I was on my way to see a woman about a horse. I drove into the yard of the place where the horse was boarded. As I got out, a young woman rode up on a compact Arab, all rigged out in Western gear including a striped Mexican blanket over the saddlepad. The gelding was short but sturdy and moved nicely. "Hop on," the woman said as she dismounted. I mounted him as she climbed on a sorrel quarterhorse and led us up a hill. She broke into a canter but I held in the Arab, only letting him run once I asked him to. He was eager and responsive, moved out with just a squeeze of my legs, a sliding of the reins up his neck. Before long I had bought myself a horse.

Thunder is a good, steady horse, blessed with speed and stamina, a sweet temper, steady nerves and sound feet. True to his Arabian breeding, he is not large, standing 14.3 hands high. Back in the mists of history, horse traders measured how high a horse stood at its withers, or shoulders, by a hand held with fingers parallel to the ground. So a 14-hand horse was equivalent to the width of a man's hand stacked 14 high. Today the hand is standardized at four inches, with one-inch increments expressed as .1, .2 and .3; thus at 14.3 hands, Thunder stands 59 inches. By definition, an equine is called a pony up to a height of 14.2; above that it is defined as a horse. So Thunder makes it in just under, or over, the wire.

Thunder has a registered name that is nonsensical to me, one of those elaborate references to his lineage. Even his common name, Thunder, sometimes sounds a bit dramatic for this compact horse, so I often just call him Pony. The nickname suits him, not in the sense of a child's Shetland, but more in the way of a prairie pony. Thunder is a Western horse. He's never been confined to a stall, had his mane braided or his hooves painted. A corral is his habitat, with weathered fence rails and an old shed of silvered pine. He's the kind of backyard horse you see all over the West, the ones grazing in the long grass behind someone's house, the horses that come to the fence to see the kids when they pass by after school.

With his fine head, intelligent eyes, delicate nostrils, "dish" face, and miles of heart and stamina, he is a classic Arabian. Most people would describe him as a white horse, but in horse parlance, a whitish horse with hairs of any other color mixed in its coat is called a "grey." Horse folks would call Thunder a flea-bitten grey for the reddish freckles flecking his pale back. While the American quarterhorse might seem the ideal plains horse to many people, this trim little Arab has been my prairie pony, carrying me many miles across open ground.

Thunder is a mirror reflecting the prairie's moods. On a frosty morning, he prances with eagerness, ears alert, eyes bright, spirit tingling. He is a different horse on a sultry afternoon when, like me, he plods sullenly in the heat. And when the wind is strong or gusting, the kinetic energy sets him on edge; he becomes skittish and jumpy, the brush of the wind charging him with electricity.

Sometimes he moves with a lulling rhythm, walking oh-so-slow, with a hip-swinging stride, placing each heavy-hoofed foot with a thud. With a little urging he might speed it up to a jog, broad butt shifting left-right, left-right in an equine samba. Or he may trot out officiously, clip-clop, clip-clop, his unshod hooves striking the ground in a muffled tattoo. Leaning forward slightly, sliding the reins up his neck a bit, I urge him into a canter, what Western riders call a lope. The shifting forward of my weight, the encouraging slackness in the rein, the growing energy of anticipation, all convey a building urgency for speed. He reads my cues and, gathering his legs up under him, springs into a three-beat lope. The rhythm of the canter is mesmerizing, a rolling gait, easy to sit—1, 2, 3; 1, 2, 3; 1, 2, 3—flowing across the ground in a horse's waltz. The rhythm of the lope rings over and over, pleasing to the human ear, to the body, to the spirit. I center my weight, settling in the saddle, rocking with the motion of the lope. Feeling the rhythm, balance, and motion is important, or my weight becomes a burden to the horse. We are partners in the waltz, pressing close, picking up each other's cues for the dance, whirling across our prairie ballroom.

The canter is a pleasant gait, but to truly fly we move into a ground-gobbling gallop. We race across the earth, so smooth I am floating. Each of Thunder's hooves strikes the ground separately, sounding its own blow, but in quick succession like a battery of rapid-fire cannons—*ta-ta-ta-ta; ta-ta-ta-ta.* Over and over, the four beats flow effortlessly into each other, with a momentary pause between the sets, no more than a heartbeat, when all four hooves are in-air and horse and rider are flying. The gallop is the smoothest gait of all, easiest for a rider to sit because of its even rhythm and the steadying influence of motion and speed.

The boarding stable is a short drive from my home, between the city and the open spaces to the east. When I arrive at the corral, Thunder ambles over, whuffling with his soft nose, lowering his head to be stroked, liking the attention and the grain in my hand. I put my arm across his withers, lean my weight against his shoulder, place my face against his neck. He is a wall, warm and vital. I feel his drumming heartbeat, the reassuring lift and fall of his breathing. I stroke his neck, warm silk the color of ivory. Beneath my touch he trembles with vitality. His coat is sleek in summer, woolly and thick in winter. He smells like horse, the scent mingled with the wonderful aromas of fresh hay, oiled leather, and steaming, organic manure.

My saddlebags hold a thermos of coffee, a few bagels, and my journal. I buckle them to the saddle, mount up and head out into the fresh day with Cody and Margo following. We are a caravan—horse and rider, big dog, little dog. We ride for a while, not heading anywhere in particular, just ambling, wrapped in the warm arms of the sun and serenaded by a fragrant breeze. The dogs trail in our wake like porpoises flanking a vessel on the high seas. High-stepping through the grass, Cody discovers an entire universe with his nose. A dog on scent is both fascinating and comical. Cody's body moves almost mechanically, kept from disastrous misstep by the automatic pilot of his eyes. But the real field commander is his nose, gathering in scent like a vacuum cleaner. When something intriguing registers, the whole ship lurches suddenly to starboard, like a fish snagged by a baited hook.

We find an inviting spot to stop for breakfast. I dismount, unbuckle the saddlebags from the saddle. Thunder is good at staying ground-tied, doesn't stray or spook easily, so I simply drop his reins to the grass, trailing one rein along the ground near me, just in case. I settle down, the midsummer grasses rising above my head, enclosing me in a secret world like a flea amid the hairs of a dog.

We've ridden not only onto the prairie but also through a time warp into another place. The modern world has shimmered and vanished, a mirage. The sound of traffic fades; planes no longer pass like compass needles in the sky. Above us a red-tailed hawk soars, cruciform against a cloudless sky. It pauses, tail dropped to maintain position, motionless on trembling wings, and for a moment I fly with the hawk, godlike, seeing myself below in the grass. Then the hawk drops for a kill, not quickly but slowly, gliding down as if to deliver me softly, wings outstretched, talons ready, settling upon its prey like a net rather than an arrow. And I am back on the ground, human again.

Cody comes to lie by me, my silent guardian. I peer close at the soft forest of grass around us. Come autumn these stalks, dried and brittle, will make a harp for the wind, but now they bend with only a soft *whish*. A ground beetle lumbers over ripples of earth that to him are mountains. I hear the yip of prairie dogs, and overhead the hawk once again soars with grace. Nearby my horse grazes companionably, his soft nose pushing through the tender grass, snorting as the blades tickle his nostrils. His lips are thick, fleshy and mobile; they wrap around the grass stalks like a monkey's tail. He grabs the grass in strong, square teeth, then breaks the stems with a jerk of his wrecking-ball head. Deer, sheep, and cattle—cloven-hoofed members of the bovine family—have no upper front teeth, but instead a bony plate which the lower incisors press against to crop grass. Horses, like people, have incisors top and bottom, and they nip the grass as we bite into a sandwich.

Thunder's jaws grind with a circular motion, his back teeth sturdy millstones. He breathes gently as he feeds, his soft nose blowing warm air through large, round nostrils. A horse's nose is a wonderful thing, soft and nuzzling and sensitive. You must treat a horse's nose gently, with respect. Expressive of its emotions, a horse's nostrils flare with fear or lust or hormonal challenge, or blow softly with a contented *whuff*. Friendly horses greeting each other will tuck their heads nostril to nostril and blow gently, a means of identification and greeting, I suppose, gathering information about the other animal, much like one dog sniffing another.

I pluck a new stalk of blue grama, nibble off the sweet, tender base, then tickle Margo's ear with the seedhead. She shakes her head, floppy ears flying, then looks at me reproachfully. Of the three species enjoying this prairie morning—*Homo sapiens, Canis familiaris, Equus caballus*—Thunder seems most to belong here. If this were a different time, if I weren't here, if there were no city near, no contemporary world, he would still be doing the same thing he is now, slowly, determinedly cropping grass. Thunder and the grass are kinsmen, they belong on this prairie. He and the grass are direct trading partners in the energy chain of the ecosystem. Thunder can feed directly on the grass and gain sustenance. All 900 pounds of him is made, for the most part, from grass, cropped and chewed then tumbled through his long intestine. Horses aren't ruminants like cattle; they lack the bovine's pouched stomach, substituting instead a very long intestine. On the journey through this digestive factory, the cellulose of the plant material ingested by the horse is gradually broken down, with the help of cellulose-busting intestinal flora. The grass' energy is extracted then processed into horseflesh. Perhaps the horse's scientific name should be *Equus gramineae,* because he is as much grass, *graminoid,* as he is horse, *equid.* Neither the dogs nor I can break down the grass' cellulose to mine its value. We need an intermediary, a processor like Thunder, to convert the grass' energy to a form we can use. Not that I plan to render Thunder up to the dinner plate. The French may smack their *bon appetit* lips at the thought, but our culture is aghast at the idea of eating horsemeat. Horses are our workmates, our companions, and our friends.

The breeze brings Thunder the scent of another horse. This coded message on the wind, hidden from me as if written with invisible ink, summons forth a strange excitement in my horse. He ceases his grazing, raises his prick-eared head, his entire body suddenly taut. I watch my gentle horse fade and another creature step forward from him, wild prairie in his eyes. He trumpets a call of greeting, a mighty neigh that starts at his hooves and gathers power up through him till it blasts forth, rippling his entire body with the effort. He awaits a reply from his far-off kinsman, who thunders back despite the bit in his mouth and the rider on his back. I watch Thunder's fine-boned head and sparking eyes. He does my bidding willingly enough, but he has memories of wildness in his heart. Does he dream at night of an open plain, of jostling bodies in a wild-eyed herd, pressed close, smelling one another's fears and desires? Does he call to mares in his sleep, trumpeting like a warrior, battling other stallions? Does he dream of running and running without boundaries, beyond this tame existence, running wild with others of his kind, his spirit charged with fire? I think of him, this creature of open ground who awakens each morning in a quiet pasture, to hay tossed twice a day, and I wonder: Does he dream?

The other horse and rider pass at a distance and Thunder's excitement fades. He becomes again my saddle horse with the bridle about his head, contentedly grazing.

I open my journal and flutter the pages, past an account of harrier hawks dancing in the spring sky, past a sketch of sand lilies just appeared in April, to a blank page. My drawings would pass no critical muster; they're for my eyes only. I am no artist and my illustrations are for my own pleasure, and as an aid to memory. From my vantage point seated cross-legged on the ground, I appraise my placidly grazing horse, working to capture his shape on paper, suggesting rather than illustrating the basic lines of his form. In clean strokes he takes shape on the page, long-legged, long-necked, amid slender grasses that echo his lines. I found permission to draw this way, rather than attempting realism, in a ledger book of illustrations containing a remarkable series of drawings made by Cheyenne warrior-artists. This treasure, part of the collection of the Colorado History Museum, records the battle exploits of Cheyenne Dog Soldiers during the Platte River raids of 1864 to 1867. At first glance the drawings seem primitive in style, but they are actually detailed records made by men for whom war, horses, and deeds of valor were paramount. The drawings, made in colored pencil (both pencils and ledger book were taken in raids on white settlements), show in precise detail the weapons, battle dress, horse accouterments, lines of attack, numbers of shots fired, wounds inflicted, and other important particulars of battle.

But it is the portrayal of horses that I find most magical. The horses fly across the pages, suspended above the ground. Forelegs reach out, hind legs trail in full extension as if just launched in a mighty, sailing stride. No earthbound beasts these, but airy, elegant creatures, their gracefully arching necks tapering to tiny heads. Dramatically elongated, the animals' bodies bear muscular shoulders and hindquarters. Their legs, long and sleek, are the limbs of dancers, tipped with dainty hooves. Rendered in an almost mythic style the drawings sing with an image of the horse as a magical being, at once both a necessary tool and an extension of one's spirit.

My sketch shows Thunder as I see him, all curving lines, no saddle on his back or bridle about his head, an animal born of the grass and sky and far horizon.

Horses seem such a part of the Great Plains and the American West it's hard to believe that they were a European introduction to this continent, at least within the era of recorded human history. The fossil record, that enigmatic storybook buried in the earth, tells us that horses evolved in North America some 57 million years ago. Best known among the modern horse's ancestors is eohippus, a small agile mammal with four toes on the front feet and three on the back, whose fossilized bones paleontologists have found in Colorado, Wyoming, New Mexico, and Utah. Though these Western states conjure images of mountains and canyons, prairies and deserts, they were very different when eohippus roamed the land. Then a great moist forest covered much of the West and this unassuming "dawn horse" bounded about browsing on shrubs and green growth like a deer. Eohippus was a little guy, standing between nine and 20 inches tall— imagine a horse the size of a small dog—but he cast a tall shadow. Over millennia he gradually lost his toes, till only one remained on each foot. The bones of his feet elongated, the foot's angle becoming more upright, till he stood like a ballerina on pointe. His weight was now borne on the grossly modified nail of that single toe, the nail now a hoof. In pursuit of greater and greater adaptation for running, he had stretched the extension of his leg to the absolute limit. He was superbly adapted to a runner's life in open country. The dog-sized eohippus had become *Equus caballus*, the modern horse.

Able to cover long distances on a marathoner's legs, horses drifted gradually into Asia from North America over the Bering land bridge, the same route humans traveled, in reverse, to come to North America from the Old World. Toward the end of what is known as the Age of Mammals, some time about 10,000 years ago, horses died out in North America along with many other large mammals—rhinos and cheetahs, mammoths and tigers—that now exist in other forms in other places. No one is really sure what did them in, though there are several theories. One blames the American horse's extinction on overhunting by Stone Age hunters, who also preyed upon giant bison and other now-extinct species. Other scientists pooh-pooh this theory, citing the low numbers and thin distribution of humans across North America at the time. These scholars attribute the horse's disappearance to climate and habitat changes that transformed the central part of the continent from a savanna of mixed woodlands and meadows into a broad swath of grassland best suited to true prairie specialists like modern bison. Whatever the cause, horses disappeared from their continent of origin, not to return for 10,000 years. In 1519, Spanish conquistador Hernán Cortés brought horses back to the New World on his expedition to conquer Mexico. Like a prodigal child, the horse returned, this time in servitude.

The story of the horse's evolution in North America, its disappearance and return with Spanish conquistadors is often told these days, but I remember when I first heard it. I must have been in about the sixth grade, a child who loved to read and loved the West. I'd spent my childhood summers playing cowboy on a rugged mountainside literally at the gate of Rocky Mountain National Park—the western fence line of my grandparents' property was the eastern boundary of the park. When I discovered that the mounted Plains Indian warrior and the wild mustang of the West were products of European settlement, I was stunned. My first reaction was disillusionment. But that soon evolved into fascination and I read everything I could about Dawn Horse, its descendants, and the North American plains.

In 1541 an unusual party of travelers visited a village on the southern plains in what is now western Texas. The villagers, probably Plains Apache, were farmers who seasonally hunted buffalo on the prairie to supplement their diet. Having no draft animal larger than a dog, the villagers followed the herds on foot, laboriously dragging the meat back to the village using their dogs and their backs. Plains life proceeded year after year in a cycle of seasons. But the visit by the travelers presaged great change to come.

The villagers had never seen such strange creatures. They were men from the waist up, but they had four legs and the bodies of elk. Then the creatures separated from their elk bodies and stood as men. They were Spanish explorers under the command of Francisco Vásquez de Coronado, the first party of Europeans to reach the Great Plains of North America. Coronado and his party retreated back to Mexico, their visit having little immediate effect on plains dwellers. But within less than 200 years, horses would became a part of life for native people. Descendants of horses brought by Spanish colonists to their haciendas in the Southwest percolated north across the Great Plains through tribal trading, theft, and natural migration. Ideally suited for life on the prairie—they had in essence come home—horses provided a giant leap in technology for prairie people, transforming life on the plains of North America just as they had thousands of years before on the Eurasian steppes where horses were first domesticated.

Over successive centuries nomadic horsemen of Eurasia, under leaders like Attila the Hun and Genghis Khan, rode and raided their way across China and Asia, across Europe and down into the Indian subcontinent where they ruled as the Moghul Empire. Carried on swift animals, they rode with the same arrogance and sense of freedom and power as did the mounted warriors of North America hundreds of years later. Though half a globe apart, these tribes, Asian and American, were kindred people joined by a similar landscape and empowered by the same animal. Whether prairie, plain, or steppe, these nomads lived in open country—horse country—and the fabric of their lives was interwoven with horses. Their horses made them masters of the land, not minions. In 450 B.C., Greek historian Herodotus described the Scythians, a nomadic, horse-based Asian tribe who sound curiously familiar: "A people without fortified towns, living in wagons which they take with them wherever they go, accustomed, one and all, to fight on horseback with bows and arrows, and dependent for their food not upon agriculture but upon their cattle." Substitute tepee for wagon and bison for cattle and you have the Plains Indians of North America 2,300 years later.

The bond between horses and humans dates back at least 5,000 years. It's likely horses were first domesticated as food animals, but their value as transport soon outweighed their appeal as edibles. Experts debate when and where horses first entered our service, but they were being used in what is now Turkey before 3050 B.C. Who, we might wonder, was the first bold dreamer to throw himself upon the back of a horse? Surely humans had watched these sleek animals thunder across the plains and thought, "I, too, could fly if you carried me on your back." It is likely the first mounts were horses already in use as draft animals. But even a partially domesticated horse would not have taken kindly to a rider suddenly on its back. Imagine summoning the courage to climb upon that powerful animal, particularly since it was probably rearing and bucking and sidling. Once astride, what a wild ride that first equestrian must have taken! Truly it began a journey into a brave new world, a world of partnership with a creature who gave *Homo sapiens* the key to world domination. As draft animals, horses allowed nomadic people to carry a wealth of material possessions. Their great strength eased grueling tasks like plowing and milling. As transport, horses carried us swiftly across Asia and Europe, and eventually much of the rest of the world. As animals of war, they bestowed enormous advantages; a mounted man, or one riding in a chariot, was faster and stronger than an earth-bound enemy, with height and leverage advantages, and a pronounced psychological edge, in battle. Many a great warrior, I am sure, must have quailed in the face of horse cavalry, as the great beasts charged down upon him, all muscle and weight, heavy hooves and armed rider.

One summer I witnessed the power of mounted men over those on foot. I wasn't on a battlefield but at a street fair where things got a little out of hand. The beer was flowing freely, the rock music blaring, and a group of drunks got rowdy and began throwing fists. In a flash, the mounted police officers patrolling the fair were on the scene, pushing their way into the midst of the brawl, the crowd parting like rows of wheat before each sturdy horse. The rowdies' bravado evaporated as they found themselves butting chests with 1,000 pounds of horseflesh, the men astride the horses looming over them with sturdy nightsticks. Though the street fair brawl did not require it, I saw how one mounted man with a club could overpower a group of opponents on foot.

It's not the ability to vanquish ruffians that I value in my horse, rather the dialogue with the land he offers me. To know the horse is to know the prairie, for like the pronghorn, the horse is an animal embodiment of prairie, his limbs, his form, his eyesight, his reflexes molded by this landscape. The prairie speaks in a different voice when I am on horseback. I am not just a visitor but a part of the land. I glide above the grass, skimming the top like the shadow of a hawk. Thunder's unshod hooves help me feel the contours of the earth; through him I discover its wrinkles and ridges, as if moving my fingertips across corduroy.

When we ride over open ground, pushing through belly-high grass, leaving a wake marking our passage, or gallop freely across high prairie beneath mountains standing watch like a gallery of titans, I know an immense feeling of personal power. The horse brought much to prairie people—improved hunting success, the ability to transport greater material wealth, power in warfare. But the horse's most precious gift is to make us greater than we are. Astride a horse I am tall above my world. My horse magnifies my size and strength, my speed and spirit. My vision stretches to a farther horizon, my legs are longer and stronger, my strength that of ten, my speed that of the wind.

As a human I am earthbound, but mounted on horseback I am capable of flight.

Chapter 8:
Chokecherry

lunk! I drop the first ruby-hued chokecherry into my bucket, then peer in at it, raising my eyebrows at the single fruit lying in the cavernous pail. It looks so lonely in a bucket holding nothing else but anticipation. I have many cherries to pick, many, before I've gathered enough to work with.

The chokecherry thicket outside my bay window is laden with fruit—glowing, plump, ruby cherries. I sit at my computer trying to work, trying not to turn my head and gaze out at these fruits hanging like jewels on the emerald-leafed bushes, but they call to me like Sirens. I can't resist, I am drawn to them. I must harvest this bounty.

Chokecherry pickin' is one long strip of highway. Each cherry is about the size of a fat pea, most of the space within taken up by a big pit. It takes lots of these Lilliputian cherries to make any kind of food. Fortunately, chokecherries grow in a cluster like grapes and I can gently grasp the bunch and strip them from the stem with one motion. I toil, gathering the cherries within reach from the ground, reaching in again and again to gather the crop. My fingers stain deep red, the skin growing sticky from the juice of the cherries, and still I work.

A ripe chokecherry is a sensual fruit, plump and swollen, with a lustrous red skin, dimpled like a navel where the stem attaches. A member of the rose family and closely related to sour pie cherries, Bing cherries and wild plums, *Prunus virginiana melanocarpa* is often called black chokecherry for the rich, dark color of its berries. (Some modern plant taxonomists reclassify them in the genus *Padus*, but I prefer the old association.) The chokecherry is well-named. Eaten straight, the plump fruits could choke a bear. They're bitter, astringent, and unpalatable, with a large pit that leaves little room for fruity flesh. But crushed, covered with water and simmered, they render the most pure, the most wonderful, the most truly wild-cherry flavor imaginable. Once I have several buckets of cherries, I will do just that, preparing an infusion to extract the flavor.

Gathering wild prairie plants and making them into food has become a favorite pastime of mine. When I eat the products of my efforts, the feeling of fullness, of satiation, is marvelous. The food I make from the prairie nurtures me, as the prairie nurtures my spirit. I enjoy gardening, but by preparing and consuming wild foods I've gathered myself, I somehow make the prairie part of me. In my way I am reestablishing a dialogue with the land where I live, rediscovering in this small way how it nurtures and sustains life, physical and spiritual.

The chokecherry is a handsome shrub, growing perhaps 20 feet tall. Its lustrous green leaves resemble those of cultivated cherries. Chokecherries are found along waterways and in rich soil throughout much of North America. They often grow in large thickets, offering not only food for wildlife but cover as well. My earliest cherry gathering was done on the prairie, wherever I could find a wild thicket. I could rely on one particular patch of cherries, tucked in an oxbow of Cherry Creek where it meandered south of the state park, for a decent crop most years. But when I bought my old farmhouse, I discovered an abundance of chokecherries growing in the backyard.

In spring I watch with anticipation as my chokecherry bushes flower with drooping white clusters. I cheer the honeybees and bumblebees as they visit the flowers and carry out their pollination chores. I check daily as the bunches of unripe cherries, like strands of emerald beads, grow and ripen slowly into plump, apple-cheeked fruit, lustrous and full of promise. The birds are watching too, so I must be quick to beat the robins and occasional troops of cedar waxwings that arrive to divest me of my fruit crop. Birds have a different concept of property ownership than I do. They consider my fruit theirs, of all the nerve. We've arrived at a compromise. I gather the cherries I can reach from the ground and they get all the rest.

The birds, the chokecherries, and I cooperate within a synergy. The birds will benefit the plants in a way I can't, by distributing their seeds, which pass through a bird's system undigested. I help the chokecherry thicket when I water my lawn, and with occasional pruning, though I much prefer to let it tumble wild and unkempt like an unruly child, building a dense thicket for the birds and a place for the dogs to seek shelter from the summer sun. The shrubs in turn provide us avian and mammalian life forms with sustenance.

Most people these days, even if they might be able to identify a chokecherry, pass right by without a glance, but to Plains Indians, chokecherries were like gold, both a staple food and an important trade item. When the Cheyenne lived on the Colorado prairie, they used chokecherries in all kinds of ways. They pounded them with rocks, pits and all, into a mash which, mixed with buffalo meat and fat and dried, became highly nutritious pemmican. Sometimes they shaped the mash into cakes that were dried in the sun and stored for later use, or they dried the cherries whole. I've got my own uses for these sour little fruits.

Chokecherry wine. What better way to invest my chokecherries? I recalled once tasting strawberry wine—sweet, with the truest strawberry bouquet and a lingering sensuality. So too would be my cherry wine. I'd tried making chokecherry wine once before with cherries I'd picked on the prairie, following a recipe given to me by a friend. But that wine hadn't worked out—too sour. I found a new recipe in Euell Gibbons' paean to wild foods, *Stalking The Wild Asparagus*.

In July the fruits were ready, plump, and ripe. No anemic cherries for my wine. I chose only the best, at the height of ripeness, full-blown Rubenesque maidens with skins lustrous and red. Carting my first bucketful of cherries into the house, I washed them and picked out the duds and any leaves or stems. Pitting chokecherries is out of the question, since the pit occupies about 80 percent of the fruit's volume. Instead, I must extract the cherry flavor from the whole fruit, later discarding the skins, pits, and pulp.

My first step is to crush the pert, firm cherries. To corral them for crushing, I poured the cherries into a large ceramic crock. Ripe chokecherries are interesting to handle. A few always make a break for freedom, bouncing out of the crock and pinging around the kitchen like mini-tennis balls. Cherries are not a fruit you crush by stomping on them, so any image of myself dancing in a vat of cherries like a Tuscan wine-maid was fleeting. Instead I turned to my meat tenderizing mallet. Cherry-crushing requires diligence as the cherries easily roll out from under the crusher and the firm skins are quite stubborn. After much work I had a crock full of fragrant red mash.

I had started with three quarts of cherries. Now I boiled two quarts of water, dissolved eight cups of sugar in the water, then poured this over the mash. Sufficient sugar to feed the yeast during the fermentation process is essential, otherwise the wine will come out too sour. I was determined to produce wine, not cherry vinegar.

When the brew cooled, I stirred in a packet of bread yeast. Wine-making yeast purchased from a home-brewing shop is best, but I used what I had at hand.

I covered the crock with cheesecloth and stored it in a quiet corner of the basement where the mash would ferment for eight days. On the first day of the second week, like an impatient child waiting for homemade ice cream to freeze, I went to the basement to check on my creation. Taking the crock from its dark resting spot, I peeled the cheesecloth carefully back from one edge and peered in. Are you wine yet? I wondered. My brew was deep red, bubbly and frothy, with an intriguing aroma of cherry brandy. On to the next step.

Lining a funnel with cheesecloth, I strained the wine into a large glass jug, stuffing the neck with cotton. Oxygen is important to the ripening process and the wine needed to breathe. Unfortunately I still had to hold my breath for another 30 days as the wine aged and mellowed in the basement.

After a month aging in the jug, my wine was ready for bottling. Preparing for this grand event I had saved several empty wine bottles, washing them and soaking off the labels. My prairie wine would carry no reference to the Rhone River or Napa Valley. Carefully I decanted the liquid into the bottles and corked them, leaving behind a dark, silty residue in the jug. My wine was ready to drink!

I poured the wine into a balloon wineglass, one designed to capture the hearty bouquet of red wines, and held it to the light. The liquid gleamed a deep cherry red. Now the true test, the first sip...Wonderful! The wine had come out just right, sweet but not syrupy, fragrant with the taste of brandied cherries.

After my initial success with cherry wine, I ventured into other cherry products. Pouring several quarts of cherries into a deep stock pot, I crushed, boiled, and infused, strained the juice, added cups and cups of sugar, then boiled some more until the juice thickened into syrup. The test came on Sunday morning. Dragging out my grandmother's cast-iron griddle, burned black with years of cooking, I poured whole wheat pancake batter in neat circles onto the hot, butter-coated metal. When the bubbles rose and broke, I flipped the cakes then shoveled them onto my plate. Lifting the flask of syrup almost reverently, I poured the newly minted chokecherry syrup over the cakes in a gleaming, red cascade. Oozing slowly like red molasses, taking its time, the cherry syrup pioneered a thick path across the smooth ground of my pancakes, dripping over the edges to gather on the plate in ruby pools. I swished a piece of pancake in the syrup to coat it well, then savored the purest, most intense cherry flavor imaginable. The syrup has since flavored cakes and icings, and, cooked to the hardball-crack stage and poured into molds, made cherry hard candies.

As I became more interested in the prairie, more under her spell, I wanted to harvest the fruits I saw ripening each season. I wanted to touch them, feel them on the tongue, taste them. It didn't matter that I wasn't going to prepare complete meals. I selected my bounty arbitrarily, picking whatever I found and making it into something that pleased me. I didn't need to camp like a hermit in a cottonwood grove and live off the land. I was content with my token bits of food, like symbolic offerings to my spirit. I knew of a thick cluster of currant bushes growing atop a steep cutbank at a bend of Cherry Creek. The shrubs, with pale green leaves looking like a gloved hand with fingers spread, grew near a crossing marked by two ancient cottonwoods where I often rode across the creek bed. Several species of currant, of the genus *Ribes*, grow on the prairie, their ranges extending into the foothills. Golden currant, *Ribes aureum*, is the most palatable, forming large, plump berries ranging in color from pale gold to ruby. The golden currant blooms in April and May, offering up clusters of fragrant, trumpet-shaped yellow flowers that are quite sweet when plucked and nibbled, and a favorite of bumblebees and butterflies. I'd planted several golden currants beneath my bedroom window and on spring nights the evening breeze carried the delicate fragrance of the blossoms to me as I lay in bed. But the thicket of buffalo currants along the creek was a different species, a little rougher around the edges, the flowers less fragrant, the berries pithier and not quite so sweet but still fine enough to make into jelly.

By midsummer buffalo currants color up from yellow-pink to red. Allowed to stay on the shrub until their peak ripeness, they mature to a deep red, almost black, with a sweet, pleasing flavor. As I watched them over spring and into summer, the currants turned from tart little berries to fruits sweet enough to eat. Currants are a firm fruit with a waxy skin that makes them durable, easy to pick, and able to withstand transport, unlike fragile strawberries and raspberries. As the flower's ovary ripens into a currant, the flower seems loathe to part company, and the currant bears the dried remnant of the flower as a papery bill poking up from the fruit.

Finally in August I tucked several Tupperware containers in my saddlebags and rode out to gather currants. Like chokecherry picking, gathering wild currants, which are about the size of a small juniper berry, is a time-consuming process. Steady picking under a hot sun finally garnered enough currants to make jelly. To help the currants jell up, I added a few pectin-rich apples I'd found growing on the site of an old farmstead upstream. The gnarled apple trees, their limbs twisted and knotty like the hair of an unkempt child, grew in a small cluster where they'd been planted decades ago. The trees and a rusty clothesline pole leaning at a forlorn angle were the only reminders of the human life that once inhabited that spot. Though small and misshapen—as fruit left to their own devices and not showered with pesticides are—the apples were tart and tasty and did the trick to jell my wild currant concoction.

The prairie might seem the last place to look for fruits, but by learning the right season to forage, I kept finding more choices. West of the old farmstead with the gnarled apple trees, where the creek splits into a series of meandering braids, I recalled a dense thicket of wild plums. Each winter the thicket sheltered black-capped chickadees who moved down from their summer nesting grounds in the mountains to the milder habitat of the prairie. Wild plums, *Prunus americana*, are close relatives of chokecherries, blooming before the leaves appear. They can begin as early as March, depending on the warmth and wetness of the spring. Draped in clusters of white blossoms, wonderfully perfumed, a wild plum stands out like an angel against the still-drab prairie.

Plums take longer to develop and come to ripeness than the smaller cherries and currants, so I waited till after Labor Day to finally gather them. I rode up to the thicket and dismounted, absently leading the horse with the reins in my right hand. As I approached, a frantic thrashing sounded from within the thicket. I stumbled backward, holding tight to Thunder's reins as he pranced and tossed his head. Then a mule deer doe scrambled from among the shrubs and bounded away across the prairie in the boing-boing flight peculiar to muleys.

Since I'd unintentionally chased off the locals, I turned my attention back to the inch-long plums. I picked one, polished its whitish blush on the sleeve of my jacket, and bit into the golden yellow flesh. It wasn't as juicy as a domestic plum, but it was plenty sweet. Anthropologist George Bird Grinnell, who spent a great deal of time with the Cheyenne between the 1880s and 1930s, reported that Cheyenne children were so eager to pick and eat wild plums that they stripped the bushes near their camps, leaving none for the women to gather. The Cheyenne name for wild plums translates to something like big berry.

I knew the wild plums would make a fine jelly, but somehow I never quite got around to making any. Instead, tired of looking at them in the refrigerator and afraid I would let them rot and go to waste, I finally spread the plums out on my brick patio to dry in the sun. My winter larder that year included many tiny, rubbery, but still tasty, wild prunes.

Natural food guides claim that rose hips provide the most concentrated natural source of vitamin C. Wild roses bloom wonderfully through summer, their branches untamed and tumbling, armed with small thorns a good deal less fierce than those of their domestic cousins. My image of garden roses is of closed buds just opening; by the time the center is laid bare to the sun, we consider the flower blown and we clip it off. But the tiny bud of the wild rose soon spreads its dainty petals wide, painting spots of pale pink on the earth-tone prairie. The petals fall and the ovary ripens by autumn into a fruit—the hard, red "hip." On horseback I rarely notice wild roses snagged among the grass but on an autumn hike I found the knobs of rose hips persisting stubbornly on thorny twigs, the leaves dried, the flowers long faded. I filled my jeans pockets with this vaunted source of vitamin C, popping one in my mouth to chew on as I walked. In a moment my face screwed up in a grimace and I spat out the fibrous mess.

The hip was dry and pithy, filled with tiny seeds—not exactly candy. But I had a pocketful of hips and I couldn't just throw them out. The rose hips sat on my kitchen counter in a dish for a month or more, reminding me they needed my attention. Finally I ground them with a mortar and pestle and steeped the grindings in hot water to make a tea. Helped out by several spoons of sugar, the tea was quite pleasant, pinkish in color and tart, with a vague flavor of rose.

I'd known that the bulbs of mariposa lilies—mariposa means butterfly in Spanish—were an important food for the Cheyenne. Grinnell described how Cheyenne women dug the roots with pointed wooden sticks and cooked them fresh till they were tender and falling apart, or dried the bulbs and pounded them into a powder that was cooked into a sweet porridge. I've found mariposa lilies blooming on sunny, open hillsides in the mountains, at the edge of ponderosa pine forests, but never on my prairie haunts. Hiking with friends in southern Colorado one Fourth of July, I discovered mariposa lilies blooming in a dry meadow bordered by piñon pines, their demure heads nodding on tall thin stems.

I knelt by the lilies, trowel in hand, ready to dig them from the ground. Picking fruits and berries from a tree didn't bother me but as I looked close at one of the delicate flowers, its creamy, three-petalled head forming a dainty cup around a yellow and purple-tinged center, it didn't seem right to dig up and kill a whole plant. I wasn't dependent upon these flowers for food. I do my hunting and gathering at the grocery store. My prairie food preparation is a lark, a hobby, an experiment. I decided to take George Bird Grinnell's word on the sweetness of mariposa porridge and settled for admiring the flowers.

I was determined to try my hand at the most important prairie food of all, bison. Not that I would ride out to bring down a buffalo bull myself. I settled for buying my bison meat at the natural foods grocery. I was eager to try preparing buffalo meat not for its health considerations—it is lower in fat than beef—but because bison were what drew humans to the prairies. The buffalo steak on my cutting board comes from a ranch not the wild prairie, but it still pleases me to prepare and eat bison, re-creating in the only way left to me this age-old connection between prairie people and the land.

Between 30 and 70 million buffalo are estimated to have wandered the Great Plains prior to 1870. By 1900, the great herds were reduced to fewer than 1,000 animals, destroyed by a determined effort by the U.S. government to eliminate the economic base of Plains Indians. The destruction of North America's buffalo herds is perhaps the most shameful chapter in our not-too-honorable history with wildlife. With their passing, the prairie is forever changed, forever less than it was. Grass alone does not a prairie make. The grazing and trampling of these large mammals was an integral part of the ecology of the grasslands. I have been overwhelmed at the sight of half a million sandhill cranes along the Platte River in Nebraska, or tens of thousands of snow geese wintering at the Bosque del Apache National Wildlife Refuge in New Mexico. But what of seeing millions of bison drifting across the plains in a milling brown mass? Migrating bison herds halted wagon trains for days. That the Great Plains supported these enormous mammals in such astounding numbers —a mature bull buffalo can weigh nearly a ton and a half—testifies to the vibrancy of the prairies. The grasslands in the center of the continent weren't deserts or wastelands, as the first Europeans thought, but gardens.

The last wild bison in Colorado was killed sometime between 1897 and 1904. Bison have been legally defined as livestock in Colorado since 1974, a degrading fate for animals once sacred to the people who depended on them. I've had a tense moment or two encountering buffalo face-to-face while hiking in Yellowstone National Park, held my breath as I skied very near them on trails there in the winter, and at those moments they seemed godlike. If you are a wrathful god, I thought as I skied past one huge bull—taller than me at the shoulder, his massive body mantled by a cape of woolly hair—you can choose to destroy me, but I pray you show mercy to one so puny. I breathed a sigh of thanksgiving that the grass he had uncovered below the snow was of more interest than I was, and he allowed me to pass.

Though bison in Yellowstone and other parks appear wild, all bison are managed to some degree and no true, free-roaming herds exist. Bison ranchers have told me they have no wish to genetically alter and domesticate bison, but the animals must be fenced, inoculated, and handled by humans, and there is no intermingling of genetic material from free-roaming animals. Bison growers inevitably select breeding animals for specific characteristics. Buffalo are evolving inevitably into domestic animals.

I plunk a buffalo sirloin on my cutting board. Sharpening my knife till it would slice a piece of paper held in the air, I set to carving the meat into slices as thin as possible. Buffalo is a very lean, coarse-grained meat and is consequently a deep, dense red. I laid my strips out in a pan and rubbed them with cut cloves of garlic, doused them with soy sauce and red-wine vinegar, then sprinkled them liberally with red chile powder I had ground from dried pods purchased at a Hispanic market. I grind my chile pods in the blender, which can be hazardous as the potent powder, bearing that marvelous and terrible element capsaicin, gets into the air and soon has me coughing.

I pounded the chile into the meat with my tenderizing mallet, then spread the strips one row thick in the trays of my food dehydrator, careful not to overlap the meat. The traditional way to make buffalo jerky is to hang the strips to dry in the sun on racks made of branches lashed together. I had already made concessions on not hunting my own buffalo, so, no longer able to call myself a purist, I didn't feel too bad using the electric dehydrator.

Finally my buffalo jerky was ready. I peeled it from the drying trays, still warm, and bit into it. Or tried to. I clamped down with my jaws and tugged on the strip to tear off a bite. The meat held firm. Finally it gave way and I rolled a hunk of buffalo jerky around on my tongue—salty, chewy, with a real kick from the red chile. Stored in Ziploc bags in the refrigerator, the jerky can last a couple of months. I usually carry some now on rides and hikes, discovering what all earlier dwellers on the Colorado prairie knew, that buffalo jerky is a high-quality, lightweight, easy-handling protein source.

I doubt if native prairie people ever made some of the things I have from wild foods. What is a hobby for me was survival to them. Food is the most basic human connection to the land, an umbilical cord that links us to all other life, and to the earth itself. Gathering wild foods reminds me what every human culture since the dawn of our awareness has held sacred, that the land is our mother. We gather and eat the food that grows from the earth and it nurtures us and gives us life. The image of the earth as a living, sentient being is not an obscure or New Age idea. It is in fact quite old age. Many human societies have known that the earth lives. As I learn her rhythms more intimately, watch how the calendar follows her lead as she breathes with life, falls to sleep, then is again reborn year after year, I know this too.

Now, as snow falls outside my bay window I sit sipping my chokecherry wine, gazing through the bare branches of the cherry thicket to my neighbor's yard. The summer's dense jungle has transformed with autumn to a barren collection of spindly branches. A mountain chickadee hops twig to twig, flying in to my feeders for a single sunflower seed, then flying off to secrecy to crack the seed and eat its meat. Handsome juncos, their eyes smeared with the kohl of courtesans, scuffle their feet amid the fallen leaves in a curious dance, seeking the seed I have tossed there. The chickadees and juncos are winter visitors to this cherry thicket, though it offers them no food or cover. It is me they come to see or more accurately, the seed I put out for them. We share a secret, all of us, that this is not the season of death but of sleep. My cherries know this and wait through the dormant time until they come forth again, as they always have. I am waiting too.

Chapter 9:
Tumbleweeds

I walk through brittle grass in late summer along open fields northeast of Denver, grasshoppers leaping ahead of me, spring-loaded. They ricochet at odd angles, colliding with my bare legs, scratching me with whiskery feet. Fallen to the ground, the 'hoppers laboriously gather their backward-bending legs beneath them and leap off again. Grasshoppers seem born of drought, speckling the grassland like surrogates for the drops of rain that haven't fallen. Today, like yesterday and the day before, the land and air are hot and dry. Scant rain has fallen this summer. I pass wide farm fields of bare dirt plowed into furrows, other expanses broken by earthmovers preparing an invasion of tract homes. The wire fences bordering these acreages are heaped with breastworks of dirt and tumbleweeds piled up like pennies pitched against an alley wall. There's a strange symmetry to these slopes, which rise always on the west side of the fences. Wind following the work of the plow and the bulldozer has carved these mounds. The scene seems strangely familiar, though I know it only from old photographs dating from the 1930s and from my mother's stories.

"It was Dust Bowl days then." That's how Mom always begins her stories about her journeys as a young girl in the 1930s across the eroded deserts that had been the wheat fields of western Kansas and eastern Colorado. She was little Patty then, about 12 years old, with two big brothers—Bert and Bob—and a baby sister, Emma Jean. Mom grew up in eastern Kansas, not on the dry prairie, but along the wooded, hilly banks of the Missouri River where flood is a more fearsome foe than drought. That part of Kansas at the edge of the prairie, with its hills and stands of native trees, feels more like the East than the West. To escape the hot, humid weather, my grandparents began the family tradition of spending a few weeks each summer in the cool air high in the Rocky Mountains. In 1934, Granddad left his Chevrolet dealership in the hands of a manager and drove the family on the first of many road trips to Estes Park, a cross-prairie migration that survived into my childhood. But between the Missouri River and the Rocky Mountains lay 600 miles of the hot and dry, then the heart of the Dust Bowl. The images from those trips are burned so vividly on my mother's memory that even after more than 60 years, she relates her stories in great detail.

I've heard the stories before, but I have a new interest in this time when the prairie, like an angry, wounded bear, turned on the people who had been such poor stewards of the land. "Tell me what it was like during the Dust Bowl," I ask her.

"It all started with the long drouth," Mom explains. She always pronounces the word drought with a "th" in the Midwestern fashion. The newspapers of the time, of course, were full of the devastating dry-up of western Kansas, the failure of crops, the blowing clouds of topsoil. My grandparents planned the trips west carefully, figuring on a two-day hard pull to get to the mountains, with one overnight stop midway. The family road trips when I was a kid were long and dull, but we were always sure of finding places to buy gas and food. Not so in the 1930s, when travelling across the Dust Bowl was a serious undertaking. In those days, there were no McDonalds where families could stop for a quick hamburger. Knowing provisions might be hard to find along the way, my grandmother packed big jugs of water and baskets of food to carry with them. They held the sandwiches, fruit, and cookies that make a road trip more bearable. As usual, Patty was squeezed in the backseat between her two big brothers, while Emma Jean, the baby, sat between my grandparents in the front seat. No one was comfortable, of course, since August on the prairie is mercilessly hot, drought or otherwise. Car packed, people and vehicle fed and watered, the family pulled out of Leavenworth and away from the Missouri River.

Rolling along through the shadeless open country, their car became a convection oven, baking the family inside like a batch of powder biscuits. There was no air conditioning in those days, so they had the windows rolled down, since a dry breeze was better than being closed up in the stifling car. The sun burned bare arms leaning on the window sills. Dust blew in the windows, coating sweaty bodies with grit. My grandmother wet towels and draped them across the open windows trying to cool the air by evaporation, but it didn't work very well.

Granddad was a formal man. Even on vacation in the mountains he wore a starched shirt, creased trousers, and wingtip shoes. But that prairie heat forced him to relent. Gone were his usual coat and tie. The sleeves of his white shirt were rolled up above the elbows. It was the only time Mom remembers seeing her father dressed so casually.

The family headed west along two-lane highways that today still bear the same number designations as they did 60 years ago, US Highways 24 and 40. Their Chevrolet sedan, a big boxy car with sturdy fenders and a big engine, motored along like some great, dark beetle crawling over the dun-colored plains. In those days most cars were painted in dark colors—black or navy blue—which only made them hotter inside. The interstate highway system didn't exist yet but in that wide open country, speed limits didn't mean much anyway. "My dad drove way over the speed limit out there most of the time," Mom says with a conspiratorial smile as if tattling on her father.

The road was lonely. Theirs was usually the only car on the highway and meeting another vehicle was an event. They'd watch its approach from a long way off, appearing as a speck trailing a plume of dust, then growing larger and larger. The boys, both enthralled with cars, tried to be the first to guess what model of car it was. With not much to do to pass the time on the long trip, they played cards and word games—I am Annie from Atlanta and I'm carrying an apple, I'm Bert from Baltimore and I've got a baseball. "My mother was a real bee on those word games," Mom remembers with a laugh. Singing songs was good for burning up the miles. They sang lots of folk songs like *Rolling On The River,* and silly pop tunes of the day like *The Flat Foot Floogie.* "The Ding-Dong Daddy song?" I ask hopefully. "I don't remember that one till a lot later," Mom says with a smile.

Despite their diversions, the emptiness of the land was oppressive. It wasn't just the sameness of the open landscape, which would bore my sisters and me in later decades, but the deadness of the miles and miles of abandoned farmland without a hint of life that wore down their spirits. Humans need the affirmation of life around them, but in that desolate country there was no wheat or corn growing in the fields, no grasses or wildflowers, not even a coyote or jackrabbit or meadowlark.

"The worst part was the ghost towns," Mom remembers. Many towns along the highway were empty, the inhabitants gone, fled perhaps to California, like the Joads in Steinbeck's *Grapes of Wrath,* but just as likely to somewhere else in the Midwest. Entire towns, which a few years earlier had been bustling farm communities, were completely abandoned. These collections of empty buildings were eerie and disheartening to the young family driving into them, reinforcing their sense of being the only living things in a land of the dead. The feeling that someone had been in these towns before her, leaving behind traces of their lives and a bit of their spirits, was very strong to Mom, a feeling she has never forgotten.

As they approached a town, Granddad would slow the car, never knowing if this place was still inhabited or had been left to the wind. The whole family, their anxious faces peering out the open windows, searched hopefully for signs of life. They would have welcomed the sight of a weary farmer, or even a scrawny dog. But town after town held nothing except empty frame houses, worn out and peeling, their shutters banging in a ceaseless, dry wind. The wind was everywhere, whispering a constant shhh. Mounds of dirt sloped against the houses in drifts like the fallen snow of a brown blizzard. The hurly-burly rolling of tumbleweeds replaced the motion of living things, blowing up against buildings and catching in fence lines, their round, skeletal bodies piling up like the ghastly remains of a holocaust. There were no crops in the fields, just drifting rows of dirt. Curtains of dust blew incessantly, carried by a wind that never stopped. Here and there amid the fields of dust stood forlorn farmhouses and barns, all abandoned. Only ghosts walked among those fields and homes.

The family motored through this devastated landscape like odd tourists in a surreal world. The emotional impact aside, there were some real concerns over making it through. Like twentieth-century pioneers, they headed off across the plains never knowing where they might find an outpost offering supplies. Finding gas was a concern and when they came to a town with an open filling station, Granddad would pull in and fill up, even if the tank was only down five gallons. The towns that still had occupants and offered a few services posted warning signs that underscored the desolation of the country—"No Gas for 100 miles." The men at those gas stations looked gaunt, dried-up, and dusty. Granddad always chatted with them for a while, asking what was up ahead, inquiring about how things were going, whether many people had given up and left, commiserating over the lack of rain. Sometimes the station owners seemed exhausted by it all, but often they had a survivor's wry outlook: "The land already blew five states over so if we hang on long enough it'll blow back around to us." In one town some jokester had put up a hand-lettered sign—"Land For Sale, Cheap" with an arrow pointing up to the sky.

The kids used the gas stops for a chance to go to the bathroom and stretch their legs. Nana refilled the water jugs and bought cold Coca-Colas for everyone, and sometimes candy, though never candy bars, which would melt to a chocolate mess in the heat. Patty liked the chance to step inside out of the sun, which beat down mercilessly without a cloud to offer relief. Entering a small filling station in one town whose name she has long forgotten, its once-white walls battered to weathered gray, she stood blinded for a moment after the glare outside. As her vision adjusted to the dark interior, she saw a boy about her own age sitting on a stool by the cash register, watching her. The boy wore tattered overalls and scuffed shoes, and his dark, straight hair was blunt cut at the level of his chin. With a start Patty realized the boy was really a girl, and she looked grimy all over, covered with a coat of dust. While Patty's own clothes were soiled from the trip, her white blouse and plaid skirt still looked new, her brown leather shoes had the sheen of a polish, and her dark hair was clean, brushed and clasped on the side by a barrette. Patty felt embarrassed at her own good grooming and for the other girl, who looked like a ragged, dirty boy. But the girl didn't seem conscious of her scruffy appearance. Her face brightened at sight of another her own age. "Where you heading?" she asked in a friendly voice, and Patty felt ashamed of her judgment of the girl.

"To Colorado," Patty said, "to the mountains."

The girl grinned. "I'd sure like to go there. We never been but I've seen pictures and it's cool and blue and clean there."

Patty didn't know what to say. She felt suddenly sad for this bright-eyed girl trapped in this dreary brown place who dreamed of a land that was cool and blue and clean.

The big Chevy was a workhorse of a car, holding up admirably under the extreme conditions. Since Granddad was a cautious man, they never ran out of gas in all of their trips, but occasionally the heat got the better of the car. When it overheated, Granddad would pull over to the side of the road and carefully raise the hood to avoid being scalded by steam. When the radiator had cooled, he'd carefully refill it with some of their precious water.

One year the family had made it across Kansas and over the state line into Colorado. As they approached the town of Burlington from the east, my grandfather glanced to the southwest and saw something dark and ominous heading toward them. The swirling, boiling ghost of a dust storm was on a collision course with the car. Everyone living in the Midwest had heard the horror stories about the dust clouds. Cattle out on the range with no cover when the dust storms blew in were found drifted over, suffocated by dust. People caught outdoors by one of these dust clouds were in real danger of being engulfed and smothered. Even indoors the fine dust found its way through tiny cracks and crevices, under doors, down chimneys and around windows. Dust-caused asthma and pneumonia sickened people and many children would die of respiratory problems before the "Dirty Thirties" were over.

"We've got to beat this storm to Burlington," Granddad told my grandmother in a low voice. Her face grew taut and pale. She glanced over her shoulder at her children in the backseat. The whole family, even little Emma Jean, fell silent, knowing the gravity of the situation. The only sound was the rhythmic drone of the tires and the increasing roar of the wind.

As if trapped in a Jungian nightmare, chased by a dark cloud of doom, Granddad floored the gas pedal, whipping the Chevy like a team of horses in a neck-and-neck race with the storm. Face grim, head bent over the wheel, shirtsleeves rolled up, sweat making his shirt stick to his back and shoulders, Granddad piloted his Chevy in a sprint for safety. The car barreled along, the storm loomed closer.

Finally the grain elevators of Burlington came into view. "When we get there, you kids don't stop for anything, you just run inside as fast as you can," my grandfather said sternly. They pulled up at the little hotel. The day had gone dark, the cloud was almost on them. Without pausing to grab their luggage the family jumped from the car and dashed for the hotel just as the dust descended. The hotel owner and her daughter had seen them pull up and were waiting at the front door like guards at the castle gate. As the family reached the door the two women threw it open just long enough to let the frantic arrivals dart through, then slammed it shut behind them as the dust storm hit. Driven by the wind, the pitiless dirt pelted the building, rattling against its frame sides like hail. The hotel owner passed out damp towels for the family to hold over their faces to keep from choking as the air in the room filled with powdery dust, sifting in through the cracks despite wet rags stuffed around windows and under doors. Holding the moist cloth to her face, Patty walked with her mother into the living room that also functioned as a lobby. A handful of people sitting and standing around the small room with their faces obscured by towels looked like a strange tribe of desert people. They regarded each other silently with eyes that were tired and fearful. Some covered their faces completely with the towels. Nobody spoke. The room was eerily silent of voices but loud with the pattering racket of the dust storm. It was only about 5 p.m. on an August afternoon, but the day had turned as dark as dusk as the dust filled the air and blotted out the sun. The dim glow of candles offered the only light; the electricity had been knocked out by the wind.

The hotel proprietor managed to make sandwiches to serve everyone for dinner, buttering the bread, adding the meat and cheese, then slicing the sandwiches all by feel because she had covered the food with dish towels to keep out the dirt. The dining table where the small group of guests ate together family style was covered with a thick film of fine dust. There wasn't much dinner conversation, just coughs and sneezes. Sitting at the table eating her sandwich beneath a cloth tied around her face like a stagecoach bandit, Patty idly began writing her name in the dust on the tablecloth, till my grandmother, seeing what she was up to, hurriedly scolded her and wiped the spot clean. With nothing to do, bedtime came early. Nana made the children sleep with their coats tented over their faces to filter out the dust.

The next morning, residual dust from the waning storm masked the dawn and powdered the highway as if a brown snow had fallen. Continuing their journey, the family traveled through a war-ravaged land.

In some towns only one building still stood; the rest had been knocked down by the wind. Granddad stuck to the paved road because many of the side roads were blocked by wind-sculpted drifts of dust. As they drove west, gradually leaving behind the devastated plains of the Dust Bowl, conditions improved. Finally, somewhere west of Limon, the Rockies shimmered into view on the horizon. They had journeyed through the maelstrom and come out the other side.

Mom and her family were only observers to the great price paid in human suffering and loss during the Dust Bowl. Many other families in Kansas, Colorado, and adjacent states were not so lucky. More than 10,000 farms were abandoned by destitute families during the Dirty Thirties. What happened to the families who had lived in those ghost houses my mother saw? I doubt there are many records of where those busted farmers ended up. Like their farms, they just blew away with the wind.

Mom, like most who lived through the Dust Bowl, has always blamed "drouth" for the cataclysm, but dry periods are an integral part of shortgrass prairie ecology. Those who study climate cycles say that the drought of the 1930s was not as severe as other dry spells the High Plains has seen in recent centuries, even in recent decades. So what happened differently to create the Dust Bowl?

Environmental historian Donald Worster, author of *Dust Bowl* and *Rivers of Empire*, has thought a lot about the causes of this ecological cataclysm. As with so many passions, there is a story behind his fascination. Worster's parents lived through the Dust Bowl in Kansas, fleeing eventually to California, where he was born.

Worster expands upon the usual suspects of drought and exhaustive farming to name agricultural capitalism—the rush to turn the Western prairies into a vast money-making grain factory with no regard for the ecological consequences—as the true culprit for the Dust Bowl. With invention of the mechanical combine, wheat could be cut and threshed in a fraction of the time needed to do the work manually. After World War I, with Europe in a shambles, the price of wheat boomed. Big dollars could be made on the fruited plains of America. The stage was set for what Worster calls the Great Plow-up. Between the mid-1920s and mid-1930s, 33 million acres of virgin prairie were broken for cropland, turning under drought-resistant native grasses and leaving the soil naked to the wind. To disrupt the network of native vegetation that bound the soil and maintained the integrity of the prairie ecosystem was like crumbling a brick wall and leaving the debris in a pile. The prairie lay crumbled to dust and vulnerable. Like the Devil smelling opportunity, drought arrived, and then catastrophe.

But ultimately it was a spiritual bankruptcy, a loss of connection to the land, he says, that fomented the catastrophe. Agribusiness had emerged to replace individual land ownership. Huge corporate farms and absentee landowners replaced small family farmers, then leased the land to tenants. "In most Dust Bowl counties," writes Worster, "less than half the land was owned by residents." In Colorado's most southeastern county, Baca County, the rate of tenant farmers was only 3 percent in 1910. By 1935, it was 44 percent.

Men who owned the land no longer worked it. Acres and acres of the Great Plains were farmed by tenants who had only a tenuous emotional tie to the land and moved on frequently. Tenants lacked the personal connection of landowners, seeing the soil as a commodity to be worked hard each season, not nurtured for the future. Neither was there much love of the land in company boardrooms. The open country was no longer the cradle of family, home and culture but just one more commodity to be used for maximum profit.

A climatic drought triggered the Dust Bowl, but it was helped out by a second drought: one of heart and spirit, not water.

Finally, instead of understanding the limitations of the land and learning its rhythms, farmers tried to impose their will and their ways on a land that could not withstand the changes. Intensive farming practices used in the East were not appropriate for the shortgrass prairie. In both a physical and a metaphysical sense, the people were out of harmony with the land, upsetting the balance of the prairie ecosystem, and chaos resulted.

Is a bare and blowing prairie still a prairie? In most years, the prairie I visit grows knee-high with pale green grass in May and is studded with wildflowers of one hue or another through the summer. By autumn equinox rabbitbrush paints the land a marvelous gold. But if I ripped the hide of grass and flowers off this prairie it would be just a place. Before the Dust Bowl, the High Plains farmer had an identity, that of a tough, hard-working man of the soil, making a life in a tough land. But in the end, busted, destitute plainsmen were forced to abandon the land. The derisive term "Okies" ironically described them as the people they no longer were. When they stumbled west to California or other places, with gaunt-eyed children and meager belongings, they no longer hailed from Oklahoma or the plains states at all. They were no longer people of the land but itinerants blown away from the land along with the dust. The prairie had defined them, yet their own actions had broken that covenant. Without a relationship to the land, they were landless both physically and spiritually.

Chapter 10:
Nighthawks

I saw a good-sized hawk flying low over one of the fields," reports my friend Rick. We met playing volleyball, on opposing teams, and discovered we shared a love of the Colorado landscape. Rick is dressed in jeans and a cobalt-blue shirt that highlights his Paul Newman eyes. But instead of Paul's cool gaze, Rick's eyes are warm, the color of wild flax. He radiates good health and good nature—muscles and masculinity tempered by a balanced spirit.

"You know, I see those birds a lot." Rick sits on my sofa, rubbing Cody's head absently as he describes what he's seen. "They're different from redtails." He has been roller-skiing at the state park, his off-season training regimen for the cross-country ski racing that is his passion. By chopping the tips and tails off a pair of skinny skis, and fitting them with inline skate wheels front and back, the Nordic racer can train for his sport year-round. Roller-skiing through the state park three times a week spring through fall, Rick has observed a parcel of remnant prairie in all its seasonal guises. I'm impressed with how much wildlife he notices—a roller-skiing naturalist.

Now he is describing in great detail the hawk's behavior: "It was grayish-blue with a white rump, and it was diving up and down." I recognize the bird as a male northern harrier, and Rick as truly intrigued by his sightings on the prairie. My kinda guy.

On an evening in mid-July, Rick and I climb Green Mountain. This isn't much of a mountain, really. It is more of a hill, a treeless mound sitting between Denver and the high mountains, sort of a foothill to the foothills. Green Mountain is really a bit of upthrust prairie, and that's what initially kept it from development. The flatter land to the north, east, and south was more desirable, made better farm and ranch land, and, later, was easier to build houses on.

Green Mountain has been a favorite haunt of Rick's for at least a dozen years. He's spent many hours running the trails here as the clock spun down on the open land surrounding Green Mountain, and he's watched urbanity creep inexorably around this hill. Development would have gone right on up its slopes, too. Only preservation as a county park has saved this place from being overrun by houses and shoppettes.

Not so long ago, Green Mountain was beyond the city, safe, so it seemed, behind a frontier of open land. Now it too is under siege. Suburban sprawl closely encircles the mountain on three sides and an interstate traverses the fourth. Huge new houses encroach on its lower slopes. Like a protective moat surrounding a castle, the curve of Alameda Avenue provides a modicum of protection, guarding the hill's southeast flank and swinging around its south face. Though no development can cross Alameda on the south, due to the park's designation as open space, the land outside the moat has filled in, the houses sprouting like endless fields of thistle. The moat continues along the west in the form of a new connecting state highway, Colorado 470. But to the northeast suburbia jumps the moat near the headquarters for the National Park Service, and monster houses march up the hillside on the north.

We've come to Green Mountain for a picnic with a view. On the High Plains, any elevated spot offers a wonderful vista, and this one, rising more than 1,000 feet above the plain below, gives a view across the city, across the prairie, to the blue east. On a clear day you can see, maybe not forever, but probably to Kansas. On a smoggy day the view is a good deal foreshortened, and discouraging.

We carry our wicker picnic basket along a series of braided trails. The hillsides here are bare of trees, save for an occasional box elder sheltered in a draw. But there are plenty of shrubs, many of them natives that produce edible fruits—buffalo currant, thimbleberry, mulberry, chokecherry, and three-leaf sumac, also called lemonadeberry because sucking on the tart, dry berries relieves thirst. Though these hillsides are higher in elevation than the plains below, they are still home to many prairie plants. In midsummer the wildflowers prove the prairie's ability to blossom seasonally from ugly duckling to multicolored swan. Our progress is slow as we repeatedly set down the picnic basket and move out to greet the flowers. We find purple lupine, red Indian paintbrush, pink fairy trumpets, yellow sunflowers, lavender wild geraniums, white yucca, magenta loco, golden banner, and blue flax. The names of the flowers read like poetry—prairie primrose, larkspur, mariposa lily, prickly poppy. These same flowers bloom every year. We find nothing particularly unusual among them, no endangered orchids or such. Yet discovering summer wildflowers is always a delight. Butterflies, bees, birds, and humans all see and respond to color. Not bad company, I think.

Even with the city's encroachment, there is a variety of wildlife in the park. Coyotes and mule deer leave their scat in the trail as proof of their passage, and there are plenty of birds in evidence—magpies and meadowlarks, robins, goldfinches, western kingbirds. Everywhere we hear the *Drink your teeeee* call of spotted towhees. This handsome black, white, and robin-red bird, with a bold red eye, scuffles in the litter of oakbrush and other shrubs, scaring up insects which it promptly grabs and swallows. The rustling that betrays a towhee's presence always sounds like it is made by a much larger animal. A few years back, this species' official name was changed; it was formerly known as a rufous-sided towhee, an arcane name that conjures wonderful images of stuffy British birdwatchers in pith helmets and sturdy shoes, reciting in upper-crust accents—*Rrrrufous-sided TOE hee*. Alas, those anointed to decide such things prefer the descriptive but decidedly more mundane adjective "spotted."

As dusk gathers we hear the laughing chatter of violet-green swallows and the nighthawks begin their patrol on scimitar wings; at the top of the hill they will fly so close above us we feel the air moved by their passage. A faint whooping begins, the *poo-wee* call of hidden poorwills, nocturnal birds often heard but seldom seen. Passing through a draw we feel the cool air spilling down toward the prairie. It is July but I pull on my jacket as the Colorado air readily gives up the day's heat.

We search for a nice spot on the slope's rounded cap, away from any trails, with a nice view and solitude. We spread the worn plaid blanket, fighting to keep the dogs off it. As soon as the blanket hits the ground, 14-year-old Margo, now a grand dowager, hobbles in to settle herself, always smack in the middle, of course. We must shift her to the edge, ignoring her indignation, so that we have fanny space ourselves. Cody the big retriever is still snuffling and investigating; he will come for his spot on the blanket as the evening grows dark and quiet and cool.

We break out our picnic dinner of homemade chicken and pasta salad, fresh fruit, crusty bread, wine, and brownies. This has become traditional fare, our Green Mountain picnic. We begin by just lying back and sipping wine. Below us the city spreads as if without boundaries, both ghastly and beautiful by turn. In the daylight, the view is of endless houses cluttered upon each other like flotsam washed up on an inland shore, laced insanely together by endless paved roads and highways. But as night comes over the land, myriad lights blossom as if by magic and I cannot deny the beauty of the sparkling carpet below us. The city is a mirror for the sky, the twinkling city lights merely reflections of the stars. As night purifies the city, we sit up here in darkness like eagles. The sense of being above it all, pure and omniscient, is wonderful. We are invisible and anonymous. No one knows we recline here on our blanket throne, surveying the world. We soak in an elegant bath of darkness, unnamed and unknown. Late-departing hikers and mountain bike-riders might pass very close by, yet they would not know we are here, for we sit in silence. Even Cody comes to lie next to us, a mute prince. He is our protector, keeping vigil in the night, alert to every sound and movement. Sometimes he bolts into the darkness—after a passing coyote, I suspect, which is like a utility vehicle pursuing a Ferrari—then returns without a word to take up his watch again.

The sounds of voices and laughter drift up to us from below, the closing strains of a church picnic. We can see the circus-style tent and the rows of picnic tables, looking like dollhouse furnishings from this perspective, on the lawn of the Lutheran church. There is occasional distant traffic noise, sometimes a few discernible bars of a country-western song, but mostly we hear only the poorwills, the leathery passage of a bat (or is that my imagination?), the yips and howls of coyotes.

Green Mountain is a wonderful place to imagine what the prairie was like before there was a city. I can bring the image to my mind quite clearly. I see it in summer and in winter. The grassland rolls slowly downward toward the eastern horizon. The undulations in the landscape are subtle, hiding here and there a few trees in folds creased by Bear Creek. I see the path of the South Platte River, marked by cottonwoods, meandering out of Waterton Canyon, cutting a path across the High Plains. The shadow of a herd of bison lingers like a dark watercolor wash; I imagine them rolling in the fine dust bath of a wallow, sending into the atmosphere as many particulates as today's automobiles contribute. There is no cacophony of metal-, petroleum- or silicon-based sound, only the wind drumming on our ears, and perhaps the cry of a red-tailed hawk. In winter, snow marks the ground in patches like a pinto pony. Even the worst prairie blizzard will break the next day to crystal sky and sunshine, as if to say it was only kidding. The melt proceeds more quickly with no buildings creating artificial shadows.

From our high point, Denver lays its story out before us, the open pages of a history text, chronicling the advance of Western settlement and the retreat of native prairie and America's wild heritage. Any reference to "Denver" usually means the entire metro area encompassing some or all of six counties—Denver, Boulder, Adams, Arapahoe, Jefferson, and Douglas—and about 40 different cities, towns, and metropolitan districts, depending on how you count them. Following the patterns of other metroplexes, this jigsaw puzzle of communities grew slowly into one giant urban area, like dough balls slowly rising together in a pan to form one continuous pastry. And it is still growing. The Denver metro area now covers 4,500 square miles and is home to more than two million people. "Colorado Fifth-Fastest Growing State in Country," trumpeted a headline in the *Denver Post* in 1997. The story also reported that Douglas County, which lies south down the ribbon of C-470 from Green Mountain, is the fastest growing county in the United States. There had been quite a stir the year before when *National Geographic* ran a story about booming development along the Front Range illustrated with a less-than-flattering photo of a vast spread of featureless homes in Highlands Ranch, a planned housing community in Douglas County, which presently sprawls across thousands of acres of what was once rolling, grassy prairie. Once this beast is done devouring open land for human *lebensraum*, it will consume some 22,000 acres and be home to an immense beehive of humanity, some 95,000 residents. Any semblance of prairie will be neatly covered with turf lawns, concrete driveways, and manicured parks touted as valuable "open space."

How much can the prairie bear? As we change the land, what are we losing? The soft amorphous ball that is the ecosystem responds in some way to every poke, prod and punch. The repercussions of ecosystem change are certainly building even now as we alter the landscape. We inherently know the responsive nature of the world. Haven't we institutionalized it within Christian philosophy? "As ye reap so shall ye sow." Physics teaches that for every action there is an equal and opposite reaction. What goes around comes around. (Or maybe it should be reap 'em and weep.)

Between 1990 and 1996, more than 350,000 people moved to the Front Range, the area where the High Plains meet the eastern skirts of the Rockies, crowding into a strip of urban sprawl from Fort Collins 50 miles to the north to Pueblo 80 miles to the south of Denver. At the end of the millennium, Colorado's population was approaching 4.5 million. The 2000 census showed an overall growth rate for the Denver metro area alone of more than 53 percent since 1990; Douglas County grew an astounding 191 percent in that time. Colorado is losing farm and ranch land at the rate of 90,000 acres a year to development, a trend that is rapidly reshaping the character of the state.

The High Plains are semi-arid. Where will the water come from to sustain all these new people and businesses? Wells were reportedly running dry in Douglas County as early as 1990, less than a decade after the first residents moved into Highlands Ranch. In the tract-home twenty-first century, as in the sod-bustin' nineteenth and for 10,000 years before that, water remains the great limiter on the shortgrass, the tyrant that will eventually determine how much life the region can support.

With intermountain and Western Slope water largely spoken for, thirsty eyes are turning toward the Eastern Plains. Water is an enormous question in the West and Colorado water law is a complex and rigid world of its own, a feudal system with rules of primogeniture and the right of the water lords to sell the precious commodity away from local communities. Allocating water rights seems odd to inhabitants of lands where water is abundant. But if you don't have water, you fight to get it, then guard it with strict laws.

Agriculture holds the oldest claims to prairie water. Cattle ranchers and the dryland farmers of the uplands must live within the limits placed on them by the prairie, but irrigators can defy the land and coax miracle crops from the ground. Water drawn from the Arkansas River and carried to once-arid fields by a series of canals and ditches fostered an entire new industry of irrigated agriculture in the late nineteenth century. Cantaloupes from Rocky Ford—50 miles downstream from Pueblo along the Arkansas—are world-famous for their sweetness, but melons are mostly water, not plants that survive on their own on the shortgrass. Those marvelous Rocky Ford 'loupes may soon be a memory as financially strapped farmers sell off their rights to water from the Rocky Ford Ditch. The city of Aurora is the biggest purchaser. It bought more than half the rights to Rocky Ford Ditch water in the mid-1980s, and most of the rest in the fall of 1999 from the remaining ditch shareholders. Instead of cantaloupes, the water will nurture houses and suburbs along the Front Range. What is really drying up is a way of life, farm life on parts of the Eastern Plains. It has only been a bit over a century since irrigation turned the Great American Desert into a garden—three or four generations in human time, the blink of an eye to the prairie. Native prairie doesn't depend on irrigation; it is sustained by rain water. If the loss of irrigation water to booming urban growth makes agriculture untenable in some rural counties, the shortgrass prairie, that patient landlord, will, in its own time, return to its native ways. But what ways will the farmers return to? Will the cities continue to creep eastward, paving over the shortgrass until the water is all tapped out?

Where will we go to learn our lessons when the prairie is gone? I cannot hear the sighing voice of the wind above the clamor of traffic. The graceful curls of blue grama and the gnarly tufts of buffalo grass are gone, replaced by pampered lawns of Kentucky bluegrass, clothed like a huckster in a shiny, too-green suit, dull of mind and spirit, lacking wisdom. This isn't Kentucky, it's Colorado, it's the shortgrass. The turf lawn's caretakers shower it with moisture heedless of water's scarcity. This close-growing, nappy turf is like a spoiled lapdog—mowed, watered, and catered to endlessly—while the native prairie hungrily patrols its well-watered perimeter like a scruffy coyote.

The grasslands that comprise the Great Plains of North America once spread from Illinois west to the Rocky Mountains and from the northern prairies of Alberta and Saskatchewan to the arid Staked Plains, the Llano

Estacado, of eastern New Mexico and west Texas. The Great Plains have been plowed, irrigated, overgrazed, planted with trees, depopulated of native wildlife, and built upon with cities and sprawling development. Though native plants survive in places, no natural prairie, functioning as it evolved to function, still exists. How could it? Two keystone animals have been removed from the system. Bison, the largest vertebrate, whose grazing, trampling, and wallowing had a tremendous impact, have been destroyed as wildlife, and prairie dogs, whose clipping and burrowing aerate the soil and change the composition of plant species in a defined area, have been reduced to an estimated 1 to 2 percent of their pre-settlement range.

When a forest is clear-cut or a wetland is drained of water, the change is dramatic and obvious. But the changes to a prairie are less apparent to the eye. At a glance wheat fields or overgrazed pasture do not seem greatly different than a natural prairie. The High Plains of Colorado look much as we might expect, an expanse of grass and plants, green or gold by season. Yet mere open space, a lack of trees, and vegetation that doesn't rise above the height of a man's head do not make a prairie. High Plains is a geographic term we can use even when the land is covered by cities or farms, airports or shopping malls. But shortgrass prairie refers to a natural community which, like a giant organism, is composed of a multitude, a sum total of its parts. It is a complex ecosystem of grasses, flowering annual and perennial plants, shrubs, a few trees, and a variety of wildlife, from the macro-vertebrate to the microcosmic.

A century ago the grasslands seemed so foreign to Easterners used to dense green forests that they called the High Plains by a far different name. I found it on an old map in a musty book in the Western History section of the Denver Public Library. The map was dated more than 170 years ago. A spider's web of fine lines indicated creeks and tributaries spreading across the land, all eventually draining eastward. Tiers of looping squiggles like the tracks of a beetle denoted the rise of the Rocky Mountains and the swell of the Black Hills. There were no state or county boundaries, no highways, not even any roads, but I could recognize it as a map of the Great Plains. The Platte River was identified, and by following it with my finger to the squiggles of the Rockies I could even pinpoint the site of Denver. But most intriguing was the inscription emblazoned across the swath of mysterious country between the Missouri River and the Rocky Mountains—"Great American Desert–Unexplored."

That map inscription, that "Great Desert" condemnation, stemmed from a summer odyssey made when the United States was less than half a century old. In the summer of 1820, U.S. Army Major Stephen Long led 20 men on an expedition into a brave new world, to a place only a handful of whites had visited. The group journeyed west along the South Platte River to the base of the Rocky Mountains then, splitting up, returned east along the Arkansas and Canadian rivers. The party included numerous men of science whose intent was to bring back a sound record of observations and specimens from this uncharted country. Among them was noted zoologist Thomas Say, known to birdwatchers as the namesake of a sprightly and handsome bird, the Say's Phoebe (of which he made the first recorded sighting). He also gave his name to the genus for the entire group of busy flycatchers known as phoebes—*Sayornis*. Major Long himself is immortalized by Longs Peak, the only 14,000-foot mountain in Rocky Mountain National Park.

If I look north from my post on Green Mountain, I can see the boxy-topped summit of Longs Peak poking up in the distance, standing a head taller than the crowd of peaks around it. Neither Long nor any in his party ascended the mountain, but, in an interesting turnabout, Dr. Edwin James of the Long Expedition made the first documented ascent of Pikes Peak, which Pike and his men had attempted but failed to climb some 15 years earlier. Looking south from Green Mountain, I can see the snowy head of Pikes Peak rising like an elder behind the rounded humps of the intervening Rampart Range. Long honored James' accomplishment by naming the peak for him, but the designation didn't stick. One might argue over which man deserved the honor—the one who first saw it or the one who first climbed it—but my vote goes to Pike because you've just got to love a mountain named Pikes Peak. Of course the peak had been seen before by many people—paleoindians, Native Americans, even early white adventurers—and certainly climbed by some of them, they just hadn't had the presence of mind to write it down and report it to Washington.

The Long Expedition's journal is still in print, and I found a copy at the bookstore. It is delightful reading for a naturalist, a record of a world now vanished—"We saw immense herds of bison, blackening the whole surface of the country through which we passed." I try to imagine this, to ride my horse alongside a vast herd of wild cattle, to come close to these massive, hulk-shouldered mammals, a multitude that are one.

Long's expedition glimpsed a world poised at the very moment of great change, sand grains slipping inexorably through the hourglass. "Turkies (sic) were very numerous. The paroquet, chuck-wills-widow, wood robin, mocking bird, and many other small birds, filled the woods with life and music. The bald eagle, the turkey-buzzard and black vulture, raven, and crow, were seen swarming like the blowing flies. About the river were large flocks of pelicans, with numbers of snowy herons, and the beautiful ardea egretta."

While the bison is gone now from the prairie, it still survives as a species. Not so the "paroquet" seen by Long's party. The Carolina parakeet was a brilliant green and red bird, the only parrot native to North America. On the Western prairies, parakeets lived along the wooded bottomlands of streams and rivers. Prone to descend on orchards and help themselves to the fruit, Carolina parakeets made bitter enemies of farmers, who were unmoved by the birds' beauty. Parakeets were slaughtered in great numbers as agricultural pests, a task made easier by the birds' apparent lack of fear of humans. "They seem entirely unsuspicious of danger," reported naturalist John K. Townsend in 1839, "and after being fired at, only huddle closer together, as if to obtain protection from each other, and as their companions are falling around them, they curve down their necks and look at them fluttering upon the ground, as though perfectly at a loss to account for so unusual an occurrence. It is a most inglorious sort of shooting; down right cold-blooded murder." It didn't help that the parakeet's brilliant feathers were also in demand for the adornment of ladies' hats. The Carolina parakeet was last seen in the wild in 1907; in 1914 the last captive parakeet died at the Cincinnati Zoological Gardens. With its death, the Carolina parakeet was extinct.

On July 5, 1820, the Long party reached the base of the Rocky Mountains, camping at the confluence of the South Platte River and Cherry Creek. If Rick and I had been sitting on this spot atop Green Mountain on that July night, we might have seen the light of Long's campfire to the north. Denver would not be founded for another four decades.

Like everyone who first comes to the mountains, Long's party looked at the looming peaks which seemed so near and thought they could walk up into them in an afternoon. I have to smile when I read in their journal of one abortive attempt to find the source of the South Platte River: "After climbing successively to the summit of several ridges, which they had supposed to be the top of the mountain, they still found others beyond higher and more rugged." Every mountain hiker has made this discovery. I'm reminded of the song lyrics, "First there is a mountain, then there is no mountain, then there is." I long ago learned that climbing mountains is certainly a metaphor for life.

Having reached the great obstacle of the mountains, the party now turned south, following a path that would have taken them around the base of this hill where Rick and I now sit. Perched here like golden eagles, we would have looked down on them, following their progress by the dust kicked up by their horses' shod hooves. The party proceeded along the edge of the Rockies, pausing several days for an arduous climb of Pikes Peak. The men attempted a measurement of the mountain, but the resulting 11,500-foot reading was a bit shy of the true 14,110-foot height, though close enough, I suppose, for 1820-era government work. Riding on, the party turned east near what is now Pueblo. Half the group, under Long, then journeyed south in search of the Red River. The second group continued downstream along the Arkansas River. Today that corridor of the Arkansas, rolling gradually downward and southeastward from Pueblo, is a series of small farming communities, spread out like a string of beads along U.S. Highway 50. Most famous among them, and the spot where the group forded the river, is Rocky Ford, Cantaloupe Capitol of the World.

But in 1820, the valley of the Upper Arkansas was still a wilderness, cantaloupes not yet dreamed of.

On the return, two soldiers of the group deserted, taking along many of the expedition's journals. The only written account that has survived is that of the expedition's physician and naturalist. Dr. James compiled his narrative three years after the party's return based upon the recollections of its members. The Long Expedition actually failed in its main objectives—to find the sources of the Platte and Red rivers. And yet the journey was to have a profound effect on the settlement of the West. It was in James' account that the character of the High Plains was painted for the public as the Great American Desert, ironically delaying settlement of the shortgrass prairie for decades.

Dr. James and I do not see eye-to-eye on the prairie. His geology section is titled, "Of The Great Desert At The Base Of The Rocky Mountains" which "seems to have been designed as a natural barrier between civilized man and the savage." East of this boundary he describes a lush, timbered, well-watered land, but crossing to the "savage side commences those barren and desolate wastes, where but few small streams greet the eye of the traveler, and these are soon swallowed up by the thirsty sands over which they flow."

James continues with this glowing non-recommendation. "In regard to this extensive section of country, I do not hesitate in giving the opinion that it is almost wholly unfit for cultivation, and of course uninhabitable by a people depending upon agriculture for their subsistence." He did see value, though, to this inhospitable desert's role as a natural barrier, "to prevent too great an extension of our population westward, and secure us against the machinations or incursions of an enemy that might otherwise be disposed to annoy us in that part of our frontier." It is unfortunate for the Native Americans who inhabited the area that this arid country was not ultimately inhospitable enough to secure them against the machinations and incursions of American settlers and miners that was to follow.

Prairies are particularly subject to cycles of wet and dry, and it seems likely Long and his men visited the High Plains during a period of drought. Their "inhospitable desert" was described by other travelers as a green and fruited plain. "The grass was the country, as the water is the sea," wrote Willa Cather. The characterization of the prairie as an ocean, its grasses waving in surreal dance, was the most common depiction of this animated landscape. It was always in motion, writhing and humming, so that the land itself seemed alive. The pioneers voyaged across the prairie grass, and called their wagons "prairie schooners."

But the die was cast. For decades after the Long Expedition, maps bore the inscription "Great American Desert" across the region of the High Plains. As a result, in the 1840s, America's western frontier leapt a vast expanse of open country as pioneers risked life and property to make an incredible journey 2,000 miles across the continent. They followed the Oregon Trail across the prairies to reach forested country that more suited their image and experience of land upon which they could make a living.

The Great American Desert was a reprieve that delayed settlement of the Great Plains—much of the shortgrass prairie wasn't settled until the early twentieth century—but inevitably, land-hungry settlers turned their eyes to the prairies. Passage of the Homestead Act in 1862, offering 160 acres to settlers who would "tame" a patch of the public domain and live on it for five years, drew farmers to the fertile land of the tallgrass prairie and then ever westward into the midgrass and shortgrass prairies.

That the prairies faced a formidable barrage of betterment, civilizing and efforts to turn them to "productivity" is aptly summarized in the introduction to *The Plains of the Great West* by Col. Richard I. Dodge, first published in 1877. The introduction was written by Englishman William Blackmore:

> The countless herds of buffalo, which formerly ranged the plains, will be superseded by treble their number of improved American cattle; the sparse herds of the smooth-haired antelope will be replaced by countless flocks of woolly sheep; and the barren prairies, now covered with the short buffalo grass, yellow sunflower, and prickly cactus, barely sufficient to support the wild denizens of the Plains, will under cultivation teem with yellow harvests of wheat and corn, providing food for millions.

Fears of a great desert no longer held off homesteaders eager for free land. "Rain follows the plow" became the mantra of settlers who readily believed the erroneous idea that plowing and cultivating dry ground would stir things up, agitate the air, and cause rain clouds to form. They were convinced if they could only get land of their own, work it with their hands and their backs and sow it with their sweat, they could will that barren country to bear fruit.

But rain didn't follow the plow. Since only fields near natural waterways or canals could be irrigated, much of the farming done in eastern Colorado and Wyoming, western Kansas and the Texas panhandle was dryland farming, limiting the choice of crops to drought-resistant plants like wheat, barley, and oats. Even then farmers might get a crop only three years out of five. Dryland farming required more acreage, meaning shortgrass prairie farms were larger, the people more thinly distributed, and the life lonelier. Ironically, the great despot which had always governed life on the shortgrass prairie—water—now protected it from extensive cultivation. Today a greater share of shortgrass prairie, about 17 percent, survives than either midgrass or tallgrass.

After millennia of seasonal cycles of winter death and spring rebirth, the rhythm of the prairies was broken by the plow and the cow. Plowing broke up the prairie sod, destroying the extensive root networks of the grasses and replacing native plants with crops. As plows pushed through sod for the first time, they opened the prairie like a surgeon's knife, laying it bare. The grassroots were so tough that sodbusters reported the fibers would stretch to the breaking point across the metal blade of the plow, finally snapping with a musical ping. Fiddlegrass, they called it, as it serenaded their plowing, zinging and pinging like the strings of a fiddle.

Just as the Cheyenne and other Plains people found nutritious forage for their pony herds on the shortgrass uplands, now ranchers found pasturage for their livestock. While moderate grazing stimulates the growth of grasses, too much grazing destroys them, allowing invasive, non-native plants— weeds—to move in and set up shop. Unlike the grasses, the weeds are less drought-hardy and their shallow roots don't anchor the soil.

The shortgrass is a harsh master whose rules cannot be broken without consequence. After only about 50 years of agriculture, the Dust Bowl of the 1930s brought this lesson bitterly home. The prairie ecosystem was a hardy organism evolved to absorb and rebound from the toughest punches of weather, climate, and wildlife. Yet it was fragile, too, and the changes brought by settlement proved to be the arrow that found its Achilles' heel. Decades of overgrazing and plowing disrupted the basic integrity of the prairie, killing much of the native grass, depleting the soil and leaving it vulnerable to the elements. To an intact prairie, periodic droughts are part of the family. Like meddling in-laws, they are annoying but endurable. But when the prolonged drought of the 1930s parched the Great Plains, there was no longer a functioning prairie ecosystem to withstand the visit. All that was left was naked soil, and it dried up and blew away.

Personally blaming those who farm and ranch the land for changes made to the prairie is absurd. The truth is closer to Pogo's pronouncement— "We have met the enemy and he is us." All Americans have reaped great benefit from the bounty of American agriculture. The prairies became America's bread basket, providing vast amounts of food that both fed us as a nation and contributed to making the United States powerful and wealthy. I remember the Goddard farm along the banks of the Kansas River, its fields still bearing corn and soybeans. My father's family owned a dairy farm on what had been tallgrass prairie in western Iowa. My people mined the prairie's riches. As a nation we celebrate this abundance. Yet the prairies we panned for agricultural gold were not wasteland turned to productivity only by the industrious hand of man. They were vital communities of plants and animals, nations both wondrous and wild, nations now all but gone. As we celebrate what we have gained shall we not also mourn what has been lost?

The sun has long since headed west beyond Green Mountain to sleep, abdicating her throne in favor of the moon. We must linger here no longer.

We fold the blanket, pack the plates and silverware into the basket, and make our way down the silent hill. We use no flashlight; the moon, even a sliver, shines plenty enough to see. Our feet find the path and there is pleasure in the rhythm of our passage through the night. We rely on foot-feel and the tug of gravity to find our way. The slowly swelling sounds of the city draw us gently back. Our descent is a return to ordinary life, and though we aren't quite gods descending Olympus to the mortal world, we know we leave behind a brief moment of wonder, of having journeyed briefly from our world into another, into a memory.

Chapter 11:
Coyote Willow

I have begun following rivers. It's a natural hunger to need to know more of the landscape, to follow its veins and arteries and see how they form the land and are formed by it. I want to know the texture and contour of the land, how it changes over distance and geography. I want to trace tributaries upstream, discover where the water is born. And I want to follow the water downstream to glimpse its future.

Geologists tell me that 300 million years ago a mountain range even older than my Rocky Mountains stood in their place. I cannot grasp the truth of geologic time. What is a million years to me? I still find the earth's traverse from winter solstice to the first buds of spring a long journey. Understanding the epic world of geologic time requires me to free myself of a human-bounded sense of time, even, perhaps to redefine my idea of living things. To the geologist, rock is an inorganic life form. Rock is born, grows, moves, dies, erodes back to dust, then is reborn.

In that ancient time beyond imagining, when those first ancestral Rockies lifted up their heads, the apron along their eastern flank tilted down, forming a pocket that today we call the Denver Basin. Like an ancient kingdom, those older mountains stood through countless years, slowly giving up bits of themselves to the powerful armies of wind and water, finally falling away, their eroded debris and sediments interred in the sepulchre of the Denver Basin.

Orogeny. The birth of mountains. Between 70 and 40 million years ago—was anyone there keeping count?—the modern Rocky Mountains began the long process of geologic birth, a coming into being known as the Laramide Orogeny. Like a titan rising slowly to full height, an enormous dome including all of Colorado and parts of Kansas and Utah lifted up from the earth. To the east of this uplift lay a plain, called by geologists the Colorado Piedmont—the feet of the mountains. Beckoned by the plain, tugged by gravity, rivers began flowing eastward down the mountains' shoulders and across the Piedmont. Begun on an eastward course with its sister rivers, the South Platte reached the Denver Basin and had its mind changed for it. The basin's contours took charge of the river, routing it northward. Like a younger sibling, Cherry Creek tagged along. Rather than flowing away from the Front Range, these two waterways flow south to north along its skirts.

The South Platte is born along the Continental Divide, in the Mosquito Range, on the slopes of mountain peaks whose names are hopelessly inadequate for their majesty. Mounts Democrat, Lincoln, and Bross belong to the elite class of Colorado mountains rising more than 14,000 feet in elevation. The Platte's waters fall first as snow on these peaks, then traverse the high, treeless valley of South Park. Determinedly they march toward the lowlands, draining onto the prairie at the mouth of Waterton Canyon in the southwestern suburbs of Denver.

Cherry Creek is a waterway with more humble aspirations, carving through grasslands that lie like a blanket across the toes of the Rockies. This vena cava of creeks gathers water from dozens of tributaries that spread across the prairie in a spidery network of capillaries, feeding it their lifeblood of water. While the Platte begins where the continent divides, a high lord paying its liege ultimately to the Gulf of Mexico, Cherry Creek is an underling that pays its tribute to the lordly river. Its headwaters lie along the Palmer Divide, the high ground dividing the valleys of the Platte and Arkansas rivers, south of Denver and north of Pikes Peak.

Denver was born at the joining of waters of Cherry Creek and the South Platte River. Their marriage, five miles from where I live, is a meeting of mountain and plain. It is these, my home waters, that I will follow.

I have stood atop the fourteeners—Lincoln, Democrat, and Bross—and seen where the Platte begins. Now I seek the headwaters of Cherry Creek.

Cherry Creek's path into the Denver metropolitan area is paralleled closely by a well-traveled thoroughfare called Parker Road in the city and suburbs, and called State Highway 83 in the country. I know its course well from Denver to Parker. This town, my former home, is exurbanizing at lightning speed along with the rest of Douglas County. I find it almost unrecognizable, swathed in a stranglehold of tract-home developments. But I am headed on, passing through pine- and grass-covered hills, where handsome horses graze in baize-green pastures and red-tailed hawks stand sentinel on power poles. I reach a marvelous prairie canyon, deep-etched by Cherry Creek's patient waters. Dropping hundreds of feet to the bed of the creek, Castlewood Canyon is a hidden treasure, its inner recesses shaded and cool, haunted by bobcats and canyon wrens. In my Parker days, before much of the canyon was protected within a state park that bears its name, I used to sneak through the fence to explore this wonderland, scrambling down its rocky palisades and wading the creek with never another soul around. On one tricky descent, made by finding secure hand- and footholds, I reached solid ground at the canyon's bottom, my right hand grasping the lip of a tiny crevice hardly bigger than my fist. Peering inside I saw a nest of baby rattlesnakes the size of fat licorice whips.

Beyond Castlewood, the road rises up onto a grassy plateau—high, windswept, treeless. Here is high prairie in its truest sense. Ranching still dominates but there is little cultivation, this ground too high and cold for most crops. I pass occasional high-end developments, gated communities where the wealthy play gentleman farmer amid 35-acre tracts. I understand why those with money would be drawn here, for the view of the Front Range is fine, pegged by Pikes Peak to the south and Longs Peak to the north. The interstate that lies 10 miles to the west is completely hidden by a ridge. Here the path of Cherry Creek still holds the serenity of earlier times.

The creek is a wild and lovely creature beneath this wide sky, at home amid swelling grasslands, unhemmed by concrete or traffic. Unlike the downstream course of the Platte, heavily grown with cottonwoodlands, Cherry Creek is marked by coyote willows, rarely growing taller than the height of a man. In winter the willows shed their demure ways along with their foliage, revealing bark that is a brilliant copper. Lining the stream course, the winter willows paint a river of flame across barren land. Willows are plants with a great power—the ability to relieve pain. Native people have long known the secret the willow carries in its bark. Belonging to the genus Salix, willows contain salicylate, the active ingredient in aspirin. Willow bark tea is an age-old remedy for pain.

Like any organism, this waterway is a one formed from many. With the Palmer Divide, the maker-of-watersheds, still 10 miles off, I come to where waters from the two branches of Cherry Creek come together. If the creek were a two-tined fork, with the tines lying up on the Divide, I have been moving up the handle of the fork, against the flow of the water. The path of East Cherry Creek, the tine on my left, leaves the company of the road to trail cross-country through cattle pasture and high prairie. I stick to the lonesome highway as it accompanies the west fork to its origin on the Palmer Divide. I am surprised when it leads me into an exclusive development of million-dollar homes. Here, in a community incongruously called King's Deer, lies a wet meadow at the edge of ponderosa pine forest—the headwaters of West Cherry Creek. Developers, it seems, pay little attention to the cultural and natural history of the land. I find it absurd that a place so rough-edged and Western is identified with medieval England. The streets bear names like Archer Drive and Trumpeter's Court. I would have opted for a Western theme—High Prairie Homestead, perhaps. But I suppose the cachet of European aristocracy allows a higher price tag.

In this meadow of cattails, rushes, Indian grass, and little bluestem, my prairie creek has its humble beginnings. Just below is a constructed fish pond with a small white pagoda. A paved jogging path winds around the meadow. The surrounding homes are handsome, set on multi-acre lots that at least allow the feel of the country to remain.

I retrace my steps to seek the source of East Cherry Creek. I follow the ribbons of the creek, threading through grasslands too cold and windswept to allow growth of much else. The horizon and the sky offer lessons in space and form, so tangible I feel I could touch them with my outstretched hand. Above the horizon, the pyramidal head of Pikes Peak peers like a voyeur, watching as I visit the mudholes and alkali washes that are the creek's headwaters. Here in this high, lonely place, the creek is born from the earth, like First People emerging into this world through a sipapu in the ground.

I have climbed to the lip of the South Platte basin at 7,500 feet to find a high island of grass backed by a thick ponderosa pine woodlands known as Black Forest. Beyond this border, the land spills over the Palmer Divide into the Arkansas River watershed. South from here in the Arkansas Valley, the vegetation changes, angular cholla cactus becoming dominant. Spanish enters the lexicon in town names like La Junta and Las Animas, counties like El Paso, Pueblo and Huerfano. This high place is a border for more than watersheds. It is here, at the Palmer Divide, that the American Southwest begins.

*   *   *   *   *

On a February morning, with fractured clouds a mosaic above the Indian Peaks, I head north, following the South Platte River downstream from Denver. I seek not its mountain origin but its prairie future. Joined now by the waters of Cherry Creek, the South Platte flows across northeastern Colorado, leaving the state at Julesburg on the way to its marriage with the North Platte River at North Platte, Nebraska. Along the 183 miles between Denver and Julesburg, the South Platte drains some 15,000 square miles of Colorado prairie. After a convoluted journey and extensive appropriation of water by dozens of communities along the way, the waters of my dry prairie find their way from the Platte into the Missouri, then the Mississippi, and finally to the Gulf of Mexico. Those waters are used and reused hundreds of times by communities all along the route. Strange to think of hail fallen amid the yucca and rabbitbrush of the shortgrass finding its way into a Cajun roué in New Orleans.

My journey starts at a place that is distinctly non-prairie—Confluence Park. Here in the shadow of downtown Denver, the waters of the South Platte and Cherry Creek come together. On warm days, suits from downtown high-rises picnic on terraced concrete benches and little kids splash in the water. It's easiest to tour this part of the river by bicycle, following paved paths crowded by walkers, runners, cyclists, and skateboarders. These mingled waters still have a mind of their own, despite our efforts to enslave them as nothing more than channels to transport a resource. They still buck and churn, a bit of their wild character surviving in a crescent of sandy bank and handful of cottonwoods. Great blue herons stalk the river's shallows, kingfishers chatter and bright-plumaged ducks float in a winter regatta. Down river lies a different world from the Yuppie playground of the Cherry Creek bike path. Here shanty towns huddle along the river's edge, offering havens for the homeless. As I pass, a pile of boards and trash trembles then opens like a makeshift cellar door, and a disheveled, bearded man emerges. Under what circumstances, I wonder, might someone need or want to make a home here?

To follow the river beyond the city, I must travel by car. My sister Sally joins me for the trip. The river marches, resolute, through the industrial neighborhoods north of downtown. Smokestacks, factories, the stink of refineries echo the misuse of rivers in Rust Belt cities, though, mercifully, on a far smaller scale. This community's name—Commerce City—proclaims its mission. Soon we are in Brighton, where agriculture is still king, or at least prince, though the area is urbanizing rapidly. We are within the river's floodplain and the soil is dark and rich, so unlike much of the High Plains. Truck-gardening—growing vegetables for the grocery market—has long been important in the area around Brighton and Fort Lupton. On either side of US Highway 85 lie fields that in summer bustle with migrant farm laborers harvesting onions, potatoes, and other crops. The influx of Mexican and Hispanic workers brings a surprising cultural diversity to these white-bread towns. Along the streets of Fort Lupton are little cafes selling burritos, chiles rellenos, pan dulce buns, and fried buñuelos dusted with cinnamon sugar.

I know this route well from the trips to farm stands I make every September for fresh-picked corn, tomatoes, chiles, potatoes, and onions. Now, in winter, the dark fields lie fallow, waiting for the spring planting, the marks of the harrow-like trails drawn in the soil by a giant's fingers. We pass a farmyard where a ferruginous hawk perches regally atop a huge stack of hay bales.

As we move north, Mount Evans drops behind us and Longs Peak slowly draws abreast. To our west, tangled cottonwoods, bare arms held high, mark the river's course, as they will the entire way. Cottonwoods are wedded to the water, making it easy to keep the river course in view. Migrating birds know this too, following these pathways from the sky. When we draw close we see the water studded with ducks.

At the little burg of Gilcrest we cut off on a county road, driving ruler-straight for the river. Frame and stucco farmhouses squat between raw brown fields. The odor from feedlots and fields newly fertilized with manure has Sally gagging. We learn to spot a feedlot from a quarter mile away, identified by swirling clouds of blackbirds, cowbirds, and grackles come to feast on insects living in the warm piles of composting manure. Feedlots are not attractive places, pen after pen of tan, black, brown, and pinto cattle awaiting their fate.

Then the river is right in front of us and the road makes a hard right just in time to save us from colliding with the cottonwoods. Suddenly there are raptors everywhere, seated sentinels atop trees, on fence posts, on the crossbars of power poles. I wonder if the recent harrowing of the fields has stirred up mice and rabbits, attracting the hawks like shoppers to a blue-light special.

We pass the point where the Big Thompson River joins the South Platte. Many times I have hiked and birded along the headwaters of the Big Tom, high in Rocky Mountain National Park. There, at 8,000 feet, it is still a mountain stream, lean and muscular. I think of the eerie winnowing of snipe above its wet meadows on a summer night, the wells drilled by sapsuckers in the willows that line its course, where hummingbirds raise their young in thimble-sized nests. Countless times I have followed its course down the Big Thompson Canyon, through vertical rock walls, past grazing bighorn sheep, to my family's home in Loveland. Now I see it in different guise, transformed into a fat, lazy prairie river.

We have reached Greeley, where the Platte takes an abrupt eastward turn. Just past the river's bend, the Cache la Poudre River ends its journey from the Continental Divide, adding its treasure of mountain water to the South Platte. This agricultural town began life as a farming commune, the Union Colony, one of many Victorian-era experiments in Utopian living, and one of the few to be successful. Named for Horace "Go West, young man" Greeley, editor of the *New York Tribune,* it was founded by Nathan Meeker. Meeker is renowned in Colorado history less for founding Greeley than for meeting his end in the Meeker Massacre. The well-intentioned but naïve Meeker was appointed Indian agent for the Utes of western Colorado. When he tried to force these nomadic warriors to become farmers, they objected. Violently.

East of Greeley we enter country that is intensely agricultural. Cultivated fields contrast with grassy uplands, many overgrown with sagebrush and yucca from past overgrazing. Like avian cattle, Canada geese graze on waste grain in the winter stubblefields. Between the dried stalks, the earth ripples with their milling bodies. All along the route, flocks of geese boil up from the fields, honking like a bubbling pot, the mass of bodies constantly shifting shape, as amorphous as clouds of steam.

We reach Dearfield, once a model African-American farming community founded in 1910 by O.T. Jackson, a black man inspired by Booker T. Washington's *Up From Slavery*. At one time 60 families lived at Dearfield, where they owned the farms and businesses and had to lower their eyes to no man. But bad times did not elude them. Crop failures and lack of capital gradually busted most of the farm families, and today the town is little more than a name on a highway sign.

Just north of here lies Riverside Reservoir, a lake I know best from the air. A large island within Riverside is home to Colorado's largest nesting colony of American white pelicans, with more than 2,000 active nests. A pilot friend flew me over the colony in a small plane one summer evening. The sight below us was like the Serengeti, with huge white birds in place of zebras and wildebeest. The island was polka-dotted with white forms and all around us pelicans flew like air boats. Pelicans are unwieldy on land but masters of the air. I've stood on the shore as they came in low over my head. With a wingspan of nine feet, they cast the shadow of a small aircraft.

I have a great affection for these marvelous, goofy, amazing water birds, memorialized in Dixon Merritt's limerick as one whose "bill will hold more than his belican." Pelicans must have started life in the military. They fly in formation like an air force squadron, executing precise turns. They fish together cooperatively, dip-netting in synch like a chorus line of hoofers—dip together, dip. I may bemoan the great changes we've wrought to the prairie, but I have to bite my tongue when it comes to the wildlife habitat we've created with irrigation reservoirs. Before settlement, pelicans only turned up on the Great Plains on large bodies of water, which were few and far between. Lewis and Clark recorded them near the confluence of the Platte and Missouri Rivers in 1804. They shot one and measured how much water its bill could hold—five gallons. Now more than 10,000 white pelicans summer here, attracted by those myriad prairie-altering reservoirs dotting eastern Colorado.

We leave the highway to cross the Platte on the county road. I relish the chance to get up close and personal with the river and glimpse its intrigues. Murky water flows wide and shallow between low banks, sandbars lurking at every bend like bandits. Fallen trees lie prone upon these beaches, white as bone. The arthritic fingers of living cottonwoods claw the sky, the pouches of last summer's oriole nests hanging from their limbs. I'm curious to see the town of Orchard. Southern Cheyenne first clashed with whites moving along the Platte River Trail, possibly over camping rights, near here in the 1860s, at a place called Fremont's Orchard. After a long prairie journey, the thick cottonwood forest seemed like an orchard to explorer John C. Fremont. Today Orchard is a cluster of houses built among what is still an impressive cottonwoodland right at the river.

Now we follow the two-lane state highway, keeping pace along the river's north bank, the interstate coming up to ride herd along the south. From here these twin thoroughfares escort the river out of the state. We pass through the farming center of Fort Morgan—boyhood home of big band leader Glenn Miller, the town's sign tells us. Northeast of here, along a quiet creek where the local rancher rides a four-wheel ATV with a white miniature poodle perched up behind, is the Summit Springs battlefield.

After the Sand Creek massacre in 1864, the Dog Soldiers, a warrior society, became the primary fighting force of the Southern Cheyenne, raiding up and down the Platte Valley. Unlike the U.S. Cavalry, the Dog Soldiers were not just a group of fighting men. They were a community, a traveling town, with moms, kids, old folks, tepees, household goods. In July 1869, the cavalry finally tracked the Dog Soldiers to this campsite, known as White Buttes, where a freshwater spring bubbled from the prairie.

Today we call it Summit Springs. I visited the site on a Colorado Historical Society field trip one hot July day, with yellow prairie coneflowers blooming and the ground nests of lark buntings still holding downy young. A steep bluff topped by a lone tree, in which sat a lone kingbird, loomed above a bend of the creek where the tired Cheyenne camped, wrongly thinking themselves safe from the pursuing cavalry and their Pawnee scouts. But the Army found their trail and attacked the village, killing 52 warriors and an unknown number of women and children. The surviving Cheyenne escaped across the prairie with their lives, leaving behind all their possessions, all the things they needed to live on the land. The soldiers inventoried the contents of the 84 lodges. In addition to lots of weapons and ammunition, there were 9,300 pounds of dried meat, 690 buffalo robes, 200 tin coffee pots; then the soldiers set fire to this mobile village, and burned everything these people owned.

Summit Springs is a place of historical interest to people of European heritage, but to the Southern Cheyenne, it is a sacred site, where their heroes and their people died, a monument to the destruction of their way of life. Three elders of the Southern Cheyenne, Laird Cometsevah, his wife Colleen and her brother, Arlie Rhoads, accompanied our group that day. They are handsome people, the men over six feet tall, with barrel chests and round faces. Laird's big hand engulfed mine when I shook hands with him. They are reserved and soft-spoken, willing to answer my questions about contemporary life of the Southern Cheyenne. There are 10,000 people on the tribal rolls of the combined Cheyenne and Arapaho Tribes of Oklahoma, Laird said. Most of them live around Clinton, Oklahoma. The Cheyenne lost most of their reservation in the 1890s, he explained, when the Dawes Act allotted each tribal member 160 acres of land, freeing up the "surplus" reservation land for white settlement. How does the prairie figure in modern Cheyenne life? I wondered. Some Cheyenne women still use chokecherries to make traditional foods, but they must have them shipped in because none grow where they live in Oklahoma. Buffalo are still sacred animals, though they have no buffalo skull for use in their ceremonies. After this trip, my good friends Harold and Betty Oliver give the Cometsevahs a buffalo skull they had found years ago in an eroded wash on the Pawnee Grassland.

Laird drives a Cadillac, watches cable television, but his heritage is strong with him. Moving away from the rest of us, Laird and Arlie solemnly performed a sacred ritual honoring their ancestors. In silence I watched them from a distance, glad to have met these people whose ancestors once lived on the Colorado prairie and glimpse just a bit of their relationship with the land.

Sally and I continue east, stopping now at Prewitt Reservoir. When two bald eagles fly over I can't resist setting up my spotting scope for a better look. I slowly troll with the scope, scanning more than 180 degrees of shoreline and trees. Eagles are everywhere. Several stand on the ice like dogs waiting for a bone. In a single old cottonwood I count 13 birds, their white heads dotting the limbs like Christmas ornaments. Or perhaps they are more like enormous, predatory finches clustered in backyard shrubs around a feeder. But here the reservoir is the feeder and its fish and waterfowl the seeds. While human action brought bald eagles to the edge of extinction, it is human action that benefits them here. The eagles hang out on man-made reservoirs where fish, and ducks crippled by hunters, offer easy meals.

Alaska's famous Chilkat River Eagle Preserve has nothing on the humble and homely Platte. I count 44 eagles, of all age classes. Bald eagles don't get their characteristic white heads until they are four or five years old. Until then young birds are dark brown or mottled, often looking scruffy compared to the adults. Up to 1,000 bald eagles winter in Colorado, many attracted to the open water, fish, and waterfowl of these prairie reservoirs.

From my spot on the shore I'm treated to a morning in the life of bald eagles. A young bird flies along the shoreline, repeatedly assaulted by other eagles trying to pirate the prey it carries in its talons. I feel like the air-traffic controller at an eagle airport. When I follow one bird flying right to left, more eagles cross my field of vision left to right. An eagle flies directly overhead, sun glinting off the scales of a newly caught fish in its talons. Is it my imagination or does the triangular tail flap in its death throes?

Back at the car, as I pack the tripod, musical honking sounds overhead. A ragged V of snow geese glitters like twinkling lights against the blue, their black-tipped wings painting the sky in powerful strokes. Unlike the regimented flight of Canada geese, snow geese spread out like a ragtag army. I estimate more than 200 birds in this passing corps. Among the crisp white birds are five blue geese—gray-blue with bright white heads. Blue geese were classified as a separate species until biologists discovered that white- and blue-phase snow geese freely interbreed. Like bald eagles, snow geese are winter visitors to the Colorado prairie. Tens of thousands of them gather on eastern reservoirs where there is open water and food.

Once again on the highway, I stop at a dark shape on the pavement—a cock pheasant hit recently by a passing vehicle. The remains of animals killed by vehicles offer an irresistible meal for raptors—bald and golden eagles, hawks of all kinds. The birds don't know that it's dangerous to stop and eat in the middle of a road, where gas-powered predators roar down at 65 miles per hour. Sigrid Ueblacker, who rescues and heals raptors at her Birds of Prey Rehabilitation Center in Broomfield, blames roadkill for the high number of raptors killed and injured by vehicles. I can't help the pheasant but I can prevent injury to other animals that might feed on him by pushing his remains off the road. The pheasant's body is cool but still supple, largely undamaged. I grasp the lizard-skinned leg, noticing the sharp cockspur on his heel. Even in death he is beautiful, emerald and copper, changing color in the light. I can't resist plucking his handsome tail feathers to carry home as talismans. Then I lay him in the snowy field beside the road. With so many raptors in the area, it will not be long before some hawk-eyed predator spots him from the air and drops down to feed.

It has been a long day and we're glad to reach Julesburg, where we will turn the horses' heads toward home. The river flows on without us, across the state line into Nebraska and its rendezvous with the Missouri. Sally and I opt for the interstate, glad for the quick return journey. The winter afternoon has turned soft. Floury clouds sift past distant cobalt mountains in a late afternoon promenade as we travel against the river's flow, back toward the Rockies.

*   *   *   *   *

Cherry Creek and the South Platte together etch a wide V, shaped like a wedge of geese, across the map of the Platte Valley. Between their wide-flung arms lie millions of acres of dry uplands fractured by creeks and seasonal drainages. Old US Highway 36, a two-lane thoroughfare dating from the Depression, travels eastward straight and true through this big country. It is autumn now and I abandon the waterways to explore the uplands. The terrain carries me like a ship, rising on upland swells, dipping into the troughs cut by watercourses.

My sister is with me again, the mate for my prairie voyages. We launch from the eastern edge of suburban Aurora, quickly entering open land and prairie dog towns that will not long survive the bulldozer. We cross dry creeks with names evocative of the land—Box Elder, Kiowa, Sand, Wolf. Gullies and washouts gouge the landscape as if made by strokes from an angry sculptor. The October vegetation is finely spun gold, spiked with green yucca. No smooth green pastures of gentle grass here, but a place scruffy and textured that makes me want to reach out my hand and touch its fuzziness. The prairie birds are busy. I see meadowlarks studding fence posts, kingbirds with yellow bellies, clouds of horned larks. The bloated carcass of a mule deer lies in a gully to the side of the road.

The landscape out here is a delight, not flat and dull but sculpted, holding mysteries. The undulating dips and rises tickle our stomachs. In winter these steep dips can fill treacherously with snow, engulfing cars, people, and animals. There is nothing out here to break the prairie wind when it blows up in a temper.

We pass ranks of brown sunflowers, standing like soldiers at parade rest, their round faces bowed as if in prayer. Other fields hold wheat, milo, corn. White alkali salts line seasonal drainages. It's past haying time and hay rolls big as elephants dot the fields as if giants were playing marbles. Our view is horizon to horizon, far and free, and I revel in it.

We clock our descent of the prairie by the elevations posted on town signs. Other states post a town's population, Colorado posts its elevation. We reach the town of Last Chance where the sign reads 4,780 feet. If ever a town name conjures images of busted Okies and desolate prairie it is Last Chance. In 1926, Essa Harbert and Archie Chapman opened a gas station and store at the crossroads of two highways, US 36 and Colorado 71. It was miles to anywhere from there—35 miles, to be exact. The spot was equidistant from the towns of Brush, Strasburg, and Limon. The two entrepreneurs put up a sign reading "Last Chance For Gas And Water For Thirty-Five Miles."

I went to college with a boy from Last Chance. The other kids whooped when they learned the name of his hometown, good-naturedly nicknaming him L.C. But Last Chance isn't at all what I expected. Rather than a barren crossroads in the middle of endless plains, it is a pleasant little spot in a wooded dip along Plum Bush Creek. The only sign of life is at the Dairy King. Crossroads is still a good description of this collection of buildings at the junction of the two highways. This was once a spot along the Texas-Montana cattle trail, says a stone monument at the intersection. Like the characters in Larry McMurtry's novel *Lonesome Dove,* Texas cowboys drove their cattle past here on the way to the XIT ranch north of Miles City, Montana, a journey of 1,300 miles. Those millions of acres of free prairie grass must have been rich and nourishing to make such an endeavor worthwhile.

Now we climb up out of Last Chance onto the dry uplands. The land grows flatter, there's more distance between the dips, we see further across open ground. Broken country along drainages is best suited to cattle grazing, but this land, more easily plowed, is home to vast cultivated fields. Sugar beets became king of northeastern Colorado but they require irrigation. Where irrigation is unfeasible, farmers engage in dryland farming, their crops and their livelihood living and dying by the rains. The wheat fields we see owe their existence to a Russian immigrant—drought-resistant dryland wheat.

It is mid-October, harvest time, and combines lurk in the fields like great dinosaurs, accompanied by the balloon-tired trucks that will receive their bounty. Huge trucks loaded with sugar beets pass us on the highway. There is no evidence of prairie amid this cultivated land, except for the weedy road edge and an occasional fallow field.

Eventually native vegetation reasserts itself, but it is different from the familiar rabbitbrush and blue-green sage. These shrubs are grayish, their foliage a lacy fountain. I stop to take a look and confirm my suspicions. It is sand sagebrush, dominant shrub of a grassland community known as sand prairie. We have reached the sand hills of northeastern Colorado.

We sail upon a prehistoric inland sea, these sand hills the remnants of ancient dunes. I've been in this country before, to see the courtship dance of greater prairie chickens. Prairie chickens once roamed all over eastern Colorado, nesting on the ground, scurrying with their plump chicks through the prairie grasses. But cultivation is their enemy, and the plow destroyed land they needed for shelter and food. Prairie chickens are creatures of tradition. Each spring these plump ground birds gather on ancient dancing grounds, called leks, following the songs of their ancestors and the irresistible urge of spring. Here the males strut and pirouette, inflating yellow air sacs on their throats and expelling the air with a hollow pop. The hens wander among the displaying cocks, called boomers, evaluating their performance, deciding who would make the optimal mate. As the ancestral dancing grounds were plowed under, the prairie chickens died off. Only in the sand hill country, which takes poorly to the plow, did some leks survive.

Yuma County became the bastion of survival for Colorado's prairie chickens. The surviving leks were all on private land but far-sighted ranchers who loved the prairie and its wheezing wild chickens agreed to allow public viewing trips on their land. Soon scores of visitors crowded the Division of Wildlife's viewing blinds, enduring predawn visits to watch the chickens strut. The little town of Wray saw an economic boom with the arrival of the chicken-watchers. Today the Wray Chamber of Commerce sponsors chicken-viewing trips on weekends throughout April. The locals benefit from the motel, restaurant and shopping dollars the tourists spend, and the prairie-chicken population, now a part of the rural economy, is bouncing back.

We come to the Arikaree River, named for a once-powerful Plains tribe that is little remembered now. The Arikaree is dry as we cross its bed, but the cottonwoods grow along it in a thick woodland. The Arikaree drains the edge of the sand hills and carries its water to our destination, the Republican River.

Ten miles from the Kansas border, our route makes a 90-degree turn south, to keep us in the state, I suppose. As the landscape begins to buck and roll, the prairie's layers once more laid bare by the eroding knife of flowing water, I know we are approaching the river that challenges the South Platte for the waters of the northeastern prairie. Two stories are told of how the Republican River got its name. The first is tied to the Pawnee, a tribe organized into a loose federation of related villages, what seemed like a de facto republic to early white visitors. The Republican was an important water source for the vast bison herds when they migrated across western Kansas and eastern Colorado. The buffalo waded and wallowed in the river in great numbers, relieving themselves in it, which fouled the water downstream. Thus the Pawnee called it the Shit River, this being the source, so it is said, for the expression, "up Shit Creek." White settlers didn't think this a very attractive name, so they changed it to Republican in honor of the republic-minded Pawnee. The other story says the Republican was named for political reasons, because it is shallow and crooked. I guess the story you favor depends on your political affiliation.

We drop down high bluffs to the river and are delighted to find it flowing full, its water a welcome sight after hours of traversing high, dry land. A side trip brings us to the big waters of Bonny Reservoir, known for its warmwater fishing, boating, waterfowl hunting and, in the circles I run in, birding. This great expanse of water and woodlands amid vast dry prairie draws migrating birds like kids on a long car trip spotting a Dairy Queen in Dumas.

The town sign for Burlington tells us its elevation is 4,163 feet. In 160 crow-fly miles we've dropped more than 1,000 feet from Denver, the Mile High City. Burlington has changed from the tired town where my mother's family found refuge from a Dust Bowl storm nearly 70 years ago. Burlington isn't a big place, its population only 3,054, but it has a vibrancy that surprises me. So many small towns have a feeling of being left behind, their empty streets and shuttered storefronts like yellowed pages in a musty book. But Burlington sits on one of America's mighty automobile rivers. The flow of Interstate 70 may have brought Burlington the crass development of fast-food restaurants and convenience store gas stations but it also now throbs with the energy and urgency of people, goods, and vehicles all on the way somewhere.

A sign points us to the county fairgrounds and the crown jewel of Burlington, the Kit Carson County Carousel. The carousel is closed for the season but we are lucky. Will Morton, the artisan who restored the carousel in the 1970s and is now its conservator, is here working on this marvelous artifact of Victoriana. Purchased by the county in 1928 from Elitch Gardens amusement park in Denver, the carousel's hand-carved wooden animals fell into disrepair over the years. In 1976, Kit Carson County made the commitment to restore it.

Will invites us into the 12-sided wooden cupola within which a fantastic menagerie surges in frozen motion. Elaborately painted horses, writhing sea monsters, tigers, monkeys, dogs, and zebras gallop and prance. The deer heads bear real antlers, the horsetails are real horsehair. A gnome hides beneath a zebra's saddle and a snake curls up the neck of a giraffe.

The carousel's purchase for $1,250 in the 1920s was thought to be so frivolous, Will tells us, that two of the county commissioners didn't dare run for re-election. When he was called in to restore the carousel, mice had destroyed the band organ and the animals were badly chipped and discolored. Will's eyes glow as he describes his work on this marvelous carousel he has nursed back to health and beauty. Watching him, the phrase "lovingly restored" comes to my mind. Sally and I promise each other to return after Memorial Day when the carousel opens to ride these magnificent beasts for the full admission price of 25 cents a ride.

Now we direct our car onto the interstate, joining the flow westward to Denver. Here on the Kansas border we have long since lost sight of the mountains. At Exit 370 we come up a rise and have our first view of Pikes Peak. We're headed home.

Chapter 12:
Sand Sagebrush

W ho would be crazy enough to come out on the prairie in winter, if you didn't have to?" Rick asks me with a dubious look. It's early December, and we're driving east along the Arkansas River through a bleak winter landscape. "Oh yeah—me," he says, taking one hand from the steering wheel to point at himself with an exaggerated gesture, "following after my crazy wife." Rick is not the prairie-lover I am, but since we were married last spring, he's come along on some of my prairie explorations.

Our banter passes the hours as we drive out along the Arkansas, but I carry with me on this trip a vague feeling of sorrow. We are heading for a place of great tragedy, the site of the Sand Creek Massacre. On what is now a ranch in a remote part of southeastern Colorado, on November 29, 1864, Colorado Militia attacked a village of Cheyenne and Arapaho and killed more than 100 peaceful people, mostly women, kids, and old folks. I have been enthralled with this event since I first read about it as a child. November 29 is a date that holds special significance for me, since it's also my birthday. I can't explain why that coincidence should matter, but it does, giving me an undefined sense of connection to the events at Sand

Creek. For years I would scan Colorado maps looking for the Sand Creek site. It wasn't until interest in Native American culture became fashionable in the 1980s that it began to show up on maps, sometimes labeled as the site of the Battle of Sand Creek. Its namesake stream is actually known as Big Sandy Creek.

"Indian troubles" were growing on the prairie in the 1860s. After the 1859 gold strikes in Cherry Creek, whites flooded into the western reaches of what was then the Kansas territory across Indian lands. They saw the open country as vacant and free for the taking rather than the home of nomadic peoples. How could the Indians own the land when they obviously weren't making use of it, had no permanent dwellings, and were usually nowhere to be seen? Plains Indians saw it otherwise and resented the increasing incursions onto their lands. Warriors sporadically raided isolated settlements and wagon trains. Whites particularly feared the Cheyenne, who were the dominant native people on the Colorado prairie. Hatred of Indians grew, inflamed by rhetoric from William Byers, editor of Denver's leading newspaper, the *Rocky Mountain News*. What was needed was "a few months of active extermination against the red devils," the paper proclaimed. Then in June 1864 a German immigrant family, the Hungates, were killed and mutilated by Arapaho warriors. The victims included a two-year-old girl and six-month-old baby. While such raids were the acts of small groups of warriors, sentiment flared against all Indians and in favor of their complete annihilation.

Territorial Governor John Evans raised a regiment of Colorado volunteers and put them under the command of U.S. Army Col. John Chivington. Chivington was a sometime Methodist minister, aspiring politician, and the hero of the Civil War battle of Glorieta Pass, which halted the Confederate Army's western advance and thwarted their attempt to grab control of the Colorado gold fields.

Despite his role as a clergyman, Chivington had no trouble seeing the solution to the troubles with the Cheyenne—"I am fully satisfied that to kill them is the only way to have peace and quiet." He felt no qualms about also killing Indian children and babies. "Nits make lice," he said.

The peace chief of the Southern Cheyenne, Black Kettle, seeing the growing presence of white soldiers in Cheyenne lands, knew his people were vulnerable. He led them to camp along the dry bed of Big Sandy Creek after being directed there by an officer at nearby Fort Lyon. Black Kettle thought his people were now safe under the protection of the U.S. Army.

Attacking the Indian village before dawn on a bitter winter morning was no haphazard choice for Chivington. Winter on the prairie was harsh, even for those who knew the land. Plains Indians spent the cold months sheltered inside their tepees most of the time. Unlike the horses of whites,

Indian ponies had to live on natural forage unsupplemented by corn or grain and in winter were weakened from poor food. Attacking in winter caught the Cheyenne at their most vulnerable.

Chivington's militia were "hundred-day men," meaning they had joined up for 100 days, and their enlistment was nearing its end. Many were unemployed miners or fortune-seekers who had come West with no plans and few resources. Many had been recruited out of saloons with inflammatory rhetoric. Chivington led what has been described as little better than a mob out from Denver for the long ride onto the prairie. Once in the Arkansas Valley, Chivington forced the renowned black mountain man James Beckwourth to guide him to the Cheyenne camp. Beckwourth, known as Medicine Calf by the Cheyenne, had lived as a member of the tribe and had a Cheyenne wife. He came along only at gunpoint. But Beckwourth was nearly 70 and the night ride drained him. Needing another guide, Chivington stopped at a ranch along the Arkansas and dragged the rancher from his bed. Robert Bent was the half-breed eldest son of trader William Bent of Bent's Fort. He was now forced to guide the attack on his mother's people. In the Cheyenne village were his two brothers, Charlie and George.

At dawn the militia, many of them having drunk heavily on the long night ride, thundered down on the sleeping village. Most of the men of fighting age were miles away, hunting buffalo along the Republican River. At home, asleep in their lodges, were old folks, women, kids, and babies. The mounted soldiers rode through the village, firing at everyone. Stunned and desperate, Black Kettle called to his people to gather around the American flag he flew on a lodgepole above his tepee. The old chief White Antelope, who was in his seventies, had worked for peace, telling his people the whites were good. Now, as he saw white soldiers killing his people, he decided not to live any longer. The old man, who had been a famous warrior, crossed his arms and began to sing the traditional Cheyenne death song, "Nothing lives long, only the earth and the mountains."

White Antelope was shot down but Black Kettle escaped on his pony, pulling his wounded wife up behind him. After Sand Creek, Black Kettle lost the allegiance of most Cheyenne warriors and was considered weak and ineffectual. He was killed almost four years later to the day in a nightmarish replaying of Sand Creek. At dawn on November 27, 1868, U.S. soldiers under the command of Col. George Armstrong Custer attacked Black Kettle's camp along the Washita River in what is now western Oklahoma, once again killing Cheyenne noncombatants. Ironically, this site is now part of the Black Kettle National Grassland.

The Sand Creek site sits along the Big Sandy north of Lamar near the town of Chivington, on the Dawson ranch. Rick and I arrive at the ranch with the wind blowing hard as steel, after driving 40 miles in the dark on country roads from our motel in Lamar. We won't visit the massacre site until tomorrow morning at dawn, but I'm eager to interview Bill Dawson first, as much to talk about his life ranching the prairie as for information on this historic site.

Dawson is a big man, appears fit, and runs a tidy ranch. I judge his age at about 58. Bill is an interesting character, a mix of well-read, articulate, thinking man and hard-headed redneck. Though a local county judge, he's butted heads with the law himself more than once. He's been arrested for harassing trespassers who come on his property without respecting his posted rules. His anger seems justified, though his means of dealing with interlopers may not be. Visitors making pilgrimages to the Sand Creek site have built campfires on his land, let their dogs run loose to chase his cattle, refused to pay the very nominal $2 per car fee at the entrance, and left the gates open so that his cows wander out. A military history buff, Dawson has a collection of antique and contemporary firearms and has been known to threaten trespassers with them. But instead of a gun-toting wacko I find Dawson to be an intelligent, analytical man. He is a confirmed conservative about land-use, property rights, and the environment. He doesn't seem a man you'd want to cross, but he is honest with me about who he is and what he thinks. We may disagree but I respect his viewpoint. He also reminds me of my own hard-headed, opinionated father. I can't help but like Bill Dawson.

Dawson's paternal grandfather came to eastern Colorado in 1904. "He said he wouldn't stay here for love, money, or marbles," Bill explains, "but he never went back." His mother's people came even earlier, about 1886, moving West in a covered wagon pulled by oxen. The ox yoke still hangs over the mantle in his mother's home. Dawson bought his present ranch in 1964, seeding the cultivated land with grass for cattle "when my wife got too lazy to run the tractor," he says with a grin.

Dawson has begun following a system of rotational grazing. By fencing his land into small pastures and moving his cattle frequently among them, he's already seen positive results after just two years. "We've found less disease problems because the cattle are rotated onto fresh pasture; less fly problem because we move them before the larvae hatch," he explains. The down side is the 15 miles of costly two-wire electric fence he had to install. "I hate electric fence," he says. "I think it's a good way to ruin a horse and just teaches a cow to jump higher."

As we move to discussion of the history of the Sand Creek massacre, Dawson reveals a practical man's perplexity over the reaction of many visitors to this patch of ground along the Big Sandy. "The crazy tourists show up and stare off into the North Pasture," he says with a wry grin. Yet he respects what he considers legitimate interest in the Sand Creek site. Though basically a Chivington man—"I don't consider it a massacre because both sides were armed," he explains—Dawson allows the Southern Cheyenne to use the site for sacred ceremonies.

"I've felt some responsibility for the site," he continues. "As a historian, I'd like to see the site open. It's important to a lot of people. But as a landowner, I'll tell you some of these people can be a real pain in the neck." Many visitors refuse to pay the entry fee, a self-pay coin box at the gate. "Nighthorse Campbell said it's like charging Catholics to go to Mass," he says with disgust, speaking of Colorado's senator who is of Northern Cheyenne heritage and has proposed purchase of the Sand Creek site as a national park.[1] "I don't see the parallel, and I don't like him taking cheap shots at me."

Dawson has a good working relationship with the Southern Cheyenne. We had been unable to visit on the anniversary of the massacre because Dawson closed the site to the public so the Descendants of Sand Creek Survivors group, including the Cometsevahs, would have privacy for religious observances. Two years ago, Laird and Colleen invited Dawson and several historians from the Colorado Historical Society to witness the ceremonies, explaining each step and what it symbolized. "Lots of people don't understand about the Cheyenne," Dawson says. "They had a society that was very admirable in a lot of respects, it just couldn't survive with our white culture, so they were relegated to a reservation." His next comment surprises me. "It's really sad. White Europeans have a history of barging into someone else's culture and straightening it out for them. This is nothing new. The Cheyenne weren't the first and won't be the last."

Dawson sees a parallel between Sand Creek and the My Lai massacre during the Vietnam War. "Lt. Calley went by that village every day and drew fire. One day something snapped and he went in and took care of the problem. I guess the people in Colorado felt the same way about the Indians," Dawson explains. "The opposition to Sand Creek at the time came from the East, not from Colorado. Those people who were so shocked had already taken care of their Indian problems in ways not that different. It's easier to have sympathy for Indians when they're 1,500 miles away from you."

As we talk, Dawson slowly thaws, beginning to enjoy sharing stories of his life and family. He shows us some of the firearms in his collection, including an antique Sharps cavalry carbine. I'm intrigued by the uniform tunic of a Colorado militiaman that stands on a form in the corner. Dawson is a history reenactor and belongs to a group that re-creates military episodes on the Colorado frontier. The irony isn't lost on me.

*   *   *   *   *

We're standing at dawn on a prairie that chills me to the bone. To the east, the waking sun paints the sky with vermilion. This should be an eerie

---

1. In 2002 a private donor purchased the Sand Creek site and deeded it to the Cheyenne and Arapaho tribes. It is being developed as a national historic site by the National Park Service.

place, this patch of ground at a quiet bend of the dry Big Sandy Creek, but it doesn't feel eerie to me. Just still and peaceful, one creek oxbow that's not much different from the next except when viewed with the knowledge of what happened here.

Atop the bluff overlooking the creek, I feel the northwest wind even through my down jacket. A granite marker adorned with the stylized head of an Indian chief with a war bonnet reads "Sand Creek Battleground, November 29 and 30, 1864."

A steep trail cut deeply into the bank leads us down the bluff to the wide creek bed and its cluster of bare cottonwoods. The soil is sandy and loose and I realize we're in sand hills country. It's a pretty spot down among the cottonwoods, silent except for the rattle of dead leaves. The air is warmer here, in the shelter of the bluff. Across the creek is a wide, open area, the creek's floodplain. This was where the Cheyenne village lay, a sheltered campsite near the water.

Like a stone carving, the sleeping prairie is beautiful but cold, brutally cold. My face grows numb. Despite my gloves I lose feeling in my hands. The western horizon reflects the first light, swelling slowly to pale blue. The clouds blush pink. I think of tepees silent in the dawn, women not yet ready to leave their warm beds to build the breakfast fires.

The sun is just below the horizon now, making black skeletons of the cottonwoods. Dry leaves crunch beneath our footsteps. An owl flies low and silent from the grove. This is the time the horror started, soldiers riding through camp waking people, shooting them as they ran from their lodges, sleep still in their faces.

A meadowlark startles from the grass, spooked by our passage. The nest of an oriole lies fallen from a cottonwood branch to the ground. From the trees blackbirds gabble like crones. I peer through the shrouded light, imagining the figures of mounted soldiers riding at me across the open ground. Do I hear the jingle of tack, the firing of rifles, the thumping of shod hooves on the hard ground? What would it be like to be awakened in your bed by the shouts of armed men and the firing of weapons, your children frightened and calling out to you?

The sun breaks free of the horizon, a floating orange sphere. The air of this newborn morning is so clear I feel my throat scraped with each breath by its sharp-edged crystals. I see the plumes of my own expelled breath and think of the hard-ridden cavalry horses blowing clouds of steam in winter air.

The blue grama grows thick here, knee-high. The hill is covered with sand sagebrush, its foliage tipping gently over like a fountain. The soldiers galloped toward the village, crushing the sage beneath their horses' hooves. The air would have been heavy with the fragrance of sagebrush, until overpowered by the acrid smell of gunsmoke.

We come to a large, mowed area where two tall posts with crossbars rise like Christian crosses. This must be where the Cheyenne conduct their ceremonies. I wonder what they use these posts for. Colleen Cometsevah is a direct descendant of Black Kettle. The memory of Sand Creek has been kept alive among Cheyenne families, Colleen explained to me when I met her at Summit Springs, handed down through stories told by the grandmothers. Her face revealed little, but I remember the emotion in her lilting voice.

I stop in the center of the open area, ringed by cottonwoods. A flicker flies tree-to-tree, its white rump flashing. Juncos flutter in the branches, goldfinches feed in the thistles. The low sun casts long, long shadows, and I see my image lying on the ground, 15 feet tall. The sun's light is bright now but hard, the air still bitter cold. The people ran from the soldiers. Some hid in ravines. The blood from their wounds froze on their skin.

I see deer tracks in the sand of the creek bottom and leading up one of the steep gullies. Some of the Cheyenne dug rifle pits below the bluff and hid until nightfall. Many others managed to escape onto the prairie, making their way to the warriors' hunting camp along the Republican River. About 600 people were asleep in the village at dawn. After the shooting ended nearly 150 lay dead, many of them the easy targets, the children, the women carrying babies.

I expected the horror of what happened here, the emotional fingerprint of the people so violated, to hang heavy on this spot. But I sense no ghosts here, only a stillness, a winter-quiet prairie. Perhaps the tragic events of human lives are an overlay on the land that blows away like smoke. The prairie was before, and continues afterward, unmoved by human tears.

*   *   *   *   *

The town of Chivington is a desolate place. I feel more ghosts here than on the prairie. There isn't much to this town, which lies a few miles from the Sand Creek Massacre site, just a few buildings—the roofless Chivington School, a Chivington Friends Church(ironic considering Quakers are pacifists), a mobile home, a few scattered houses. Perhaps in a deserved fate, Chivington is almost a ghost town. Its eight residents include the preacher and his wife, the postmaster, a few other couples. Chivington boomed in the 1880s when it was the end of the Missouri-Pacific railroad. The locomotive turntable was here and the population grew to 2,800. It was said to have 21 saloons in a row. It's not quite so grand now.

By 8:20 the sun is well up, dazzling in brightness as we drive toward home. Grain silos line the main street of the town of Eads. We stop at the Country Kitchen for coffee. Twenty-five cents buys a huge cup of java. In the café's parking lot are four pickups. Inside four coats and four caps bearing the logos of seed companies hang on the coat rack. At one table four farmers joke and chat. The waitress calls each by name as she refills their cups. The menu offers pork chops and gravy and homemade pies—sour-cream lemon, chocolate-chip cream.

I have just come from the Sand Creek site, walked in out of the sunny cold morning into the warmth and small-town charm of this little café. My mind turns on the ironies of history, how the present grows from the past and its events, both benign and tragic. Eastern Colorado and its small towns are the home of American agriculture, of the life sung about in country songs. Sand Creek opened the way for this, drove the native people from the prairie, gave the land over to farmers and ranchers and city developers. The truth I face is that I benefited from Sand Creek as much as those who live out here. My little farmhouse in Denver lies on what was once Indian land and I am the descendant, culturally if not by blood, of the people who drove out the native people.

Back in the car, we drive on to the next county. Cheyenne County. The Beautiful People live now in Colorado only in the names of places.

A few days after our trip to Sand Creek I make another sojourn. I visit Fairmount Cemetery, a lovely, peaceful place, one of Denver's oldest cemeteries. Blue spruces, oaks, ashes, and maples shelter quiet rows of headstones, an urban forest so lovely that the cemetery hosts arbor tours. To the west Mount Evans lies mantled in new snow white as marble.

I roam this cemetery in search of a monument, not to the death of a man but to the passing of the native prairie. I'm seeking the end of the Sand Creek story, the grave of Col. John Chivington. It's fitting that Chivington lies buried in a place so unlike the prairie, a landscape he worked to alter. He lies beneath mountain spruces and shade trees that could not grow here without irrigation and the active attention of urban gardeners.

Fairmount is the resting place of many of Colorado's notables— politicians, tycoons, city fathers. My own parents will lie here one day. Chivington's grave is the first listing in the self-guided tour pamphlet available at the cemetery office. I find the grave quickly. It is marked by a simple granite headstone with CHIVINGTON carved in bold letters. I read the few lines below the name: John M. Chivington, 1821 to 1894, Colonel First Colorado Cavalry, First Grand Master of Masons in Colorado, 1861.

Two Canada geese fly close overhead, their honks hanging in the cold air like crystal. I look up as they pass, hearing the *whoosh* of their wings, seeing the strong working of their wing muscles as they row the air. Their wingtips almost touch the tops of the trees. Rabbit trails braid the snow around the headstones, wild things living in a forest of granite.

Also buried here, very close to Chivington, are the Hungates, the settler family whose killing and mutilation was the catalyst for Sand Creek. A four-foot-tall obelisk bears the name Hungate across its base: Nathan W

Hungate born January 18, 1835. Ellen his wife born August 31, 1838, and their children Laura V born November 3, 1861 and Florence V born January 18, 1864. Killed by Indians June 11, 1864.

Here too is the grave of William Byers, founder of the *Rocky Mountain News*. Byers was a land speculator who stood to lose a great deal of money if Indian raids kept immigrants from Colorado. Eliminating the Cheyenne benefited his pocketbook. In 1996, the publisher and editors of the *Rocky Mountain News* arranged a meeting with Native American leaders to find out how better the newspaper might serve that community's needs. Representatives from the Southern Cheyenne had only one request—an apology for the encouragement of anti-Indian public sentiment which led up to the Sand Creek Massacre, and subsequent support of those events. Editor Bob Burdick refused, saying he could not know the thoughts, feelings and motivations of William Byers and would therefore not apologize for them. The meeting between the newspaper and the Indians went no further; after 130 years, a gulf of pain, misunderstanding, firm opinion and intractability still separated them.

"But sad as the fate of the Red Man is, yet, even as philanthropists, we must not forget that, under what appears to be one of the immutable laws of progress, the savage is giving place to a higher and more civilised race," wrote William Blackmore in the introduction to *The Plains of the Great West*, published in 1877. A Britisher, Blackmore yet expressed perfectly the unequivocal sense of moral right and duty white America felt in settling the West:

> Three hundred thousand Red Men at the present time require the entire occupation of a continent as large as Europe, in order that they may obtain an uncertain and scanty subsistence by the chase. Ought we, then, to regret if in the course of a few generations their wigwams, tepees, and mud lodges, rarely numbering more than one hundred in a village, are replaced by new cities of the West, each equaling, perhaps, in magnificence, in stately structures, and in population (exceeding that of all the Indians), either St. Louis or Chicago? Or if in supplanting less than 300,000 wandering, debased, and half-naked savages we can people the self-same district with a population of many tens of millions of prosperous and highly civilised whites?

Blackmore's closing pronouncement is chillingly prophetic: "In a few years the only reminiscence of the Red Men will be the preservation of the names of some of the extinct tribes and dead chiefs in the nomenclature of the leading cities, counties, and States of the Great West."

What is the meaning of Sand Creek? While the massacre didn't destroy the Cheyenne, it was the death song of their life on Colorado's High Plains. Sand Creek signaled the end of Native Americans as the dominant people of the shortgrass prairie and the ascendance of Europeans. The change in human culture brought with it vastly different ways of using and managing the land. It was followed by immense ecosystem change. The new Coloradans replaced native vegetation with foreign species, including tenacious weedy plants that rode the coattails of introduced crops and set up housekeeping for the long haul. Even today Coloradans continue to force out native wildlife and appropriate the prairie's resources as huge numbers of people move to the Front Range urban corridor. Ultimately, Sand Creek signaled the loss of the native prairie itself.

Chapter 13:
Longspurs

It's the first of November and Rick and I are on the highway heading onto the Eastern Plains. It's been nearly a year since our last journey into the Arkansas Valley, on our pilgrimage to the Sand Creek massacre site. Now we're on our way to visit an 8,000-acre ranch near Hugo in Lincoln County that's been in one family for 100 years. Gene and Judy Vick are people of the land, earning their living on the Colorado prairie. They're ranchers, grass farmers as some say, managing the range grasses to graze their cattle. Their daily lives and their livelihood are connected to the prairie directly and I'm eager to hear their story.

We're heading east out Interstate 70. As we leave Denver behind we pass Watkins, Bennett, Strasburg, Byers—farming towns being slowly gentrified and swallowed up by the metropolitan area. We cross small drainages and dry creeks flowing north to the South Platte River. But we're heading out of the Platte Valley, crossing over the lip of the Platte watershed into the Arkansas drainage at Limon. From the landscape you'd never notice that the creeks now flow south to the Arkansas instead of north to the Platte. We're following the Big Sandy Creek now, heading toward the ranch town of Hugo. The Big Sandy flows on past our destination. Seventy miles south is the Dawson Ranch and the Sand Creek site. Twenty-five miles beyond that the Big Sandy joins the Arkansas River, which carries prairie water across Kansas, Oklahoma, and Arkansas to the mighty Mississippi.

A week ago Rick and I would have risked our lives driving this route. Last weekend a record-breaking blizzard swept the High Plains, shutting down the airport, stranding travelers in their cars, closing highways all across eastern Colorado. A curtain of white transformed the High Plains into a frightening world. Snow fell three feet deep, reaching to the car windows of drivers foolish or frantic enough to try to travel through it and smothering and freezing more than 25,000 cattle beneath its mantle. A century of settlement and civilization hasn't changed the dénouement of such stories. Human life was lost too. Near Rocky Ford, a grandmother in her seventies drove off the road in the blizzard. Her car stuck in a snowdrift. The elderly woman got out and tried to walk home through the storm. Stumbling through deep snow she became disoriented, and was found frozen to death in a snow-filled field, 600 yards from her car.

I read the newspaper article in passing, felt a moment of sadness for her family and her fate, this country woman who had lived nearly eight decades in this land only to be killed by the prairie. Then I looked more closely at her name—May Householder Hunter. I know her, I realized with a start, or rather, I recognize her name. Mrs. Hunter was raised on a farm at what is now the Rocky Mountain Arsenal National Wildlife Refuge just north of Denver. I knew May's name from my research into Arsenal history, and I remembered it because I thought it a charming name. After Pearl Harbor, the U.S. Army moved the farmers out and took over their land to build the Rocky Mountain Arsenal. May's family home, the Householder house, is one of only two homes still standing at the Refuge, the only remaining evidence of the families who lived and farmed there.

I call Ernie Maurer, a volunteer at the Refuge who grew up on a farm there before the war. Yes, he confirms, that is the same May Householder. May was a brilliant girl, Ernie remembers, winning every state title in contests for typing, bookkeeping, shorthand, and other such skills. After the war she went to Rocky Ford to become a clerk of the county court, married, raised a family there. "The news stories said May was a lifelong resident of Rocky Ford," Ernie said with a snort, "but she grew up with us on the Arsenal."

In contrast to last weekend's tragic weather, the sky today is impossibly blue, the sun blazing as if to say all is forgotten. A week ago we huddled, shell-shocked, inside our little wood house in Denver, watching the snow pile up outside while the TV news reported accidents, strandings, and eye-popping meteorological data. Now those many feet of snow are almost all melted, leaving mud, standing water, and patches of white hopscotching across brown. The sun coming in the car windows is so warm that we take off our jackets and sweaters for the two-hour drive out onto the Eastern Plains.

In the fields on either side of the highway I see prairie dogs busy in the sunshine. During the blizzard their behavior would have paralleled ours, staying snug inside the relative warmth and darkness of their burrows, all cuddled together. The prairie dogs will not long inhabit this open ground. On the east side of the Denver metro area, development is booming in response to the opening of Denver International Airport. Looming above the grazing cattle and prairie dogs are signs advertising 35- and 60-acre tracts of land for sale, most of the signs crossed with enormous letters—SOLD. Soon the cattle will be moved or sold and the prairie dogs poisoned to make room for housing developments, hotels, and retail business strips.

We pass through the town of Deer Trail, which welcomes us with a sign claiming to be the home of the world's first rodeo. Tumbleweeds blow across the highway. Long lines of cottonwoods mark the course of Bijou Creek, keeping pace with us to the south. Patches of snow, enduring despite the sun, contrast with bare ground, painting the land like the hide of a Hereford cow. We're riding across low rolling hills, treeless and bleak on this winter morning despite the cheery sunshine. They remind Rick of the ocean—whitecaps rising to a peak, falling over only to rise again to the next peak. The total absence of trees bothers him. It feels foreign, he says, it's disconcerting with no points of reference. He finds the barrenness surreal. "I want more texture to the landscape," he says. "I couldn't spend too much time out here," he adds with a sidewise look at me as if I might be offended. Then we come over a rise and the cottonwoods along Bijou Creek come again into view. His tension at too much openness abates and he feels reassured again.

Just off the highway, atop a small rise, we see a forlorn little graveyard surrounded by a small fence and shaded by one lone pine. Planted on this open plain, fiercely nurtured by someone against the wind and the dry, that single tree bears witness—to memory, to kinship, to love. Even more, it is someone's mark, a statement of humanity persisting in a land that used people up and still tolerates only a few souls per square mile. Like the people who planted it, the tree is out of place in open country, lonely, but still surviving.

From Hugo we count the miles south to the turnoff for the Vick ranch. Now that we can't see the mountains I realize what a sense of reassurance I feel when those peaks are visible to the west. Then we're turning off the pavement onto a gravel county road, scanning mailboxes as we pass in search of the right name, then turning again. To our right a cluster of cottonwoods marks an old farmstead. On the upland to our left is the turn-in for the Vicks' place. An iron cutout of a cowboy welcomes us at the driveway.

The Vicks' house is trim and modern, shaded by a few trees. Behind the house are a barn, outbuildings, and corrals where men are working with cattle—neighbors, it turns out, borrowing the corrals to hold their animals awaiting pick-up. A friendly, aged border collie ambles over on stiff legs to greet us. Judy Vick opens the door and invites us in with a smile. She's a slim, pretty woman with a perky wedge haircut. I estimate her to be in her late forties. Gene is out mending a windbreak in one of the pastures, she says, and invites us to ride along to meet him and call him back in to the house. We load into the front seat of her pickup and head off across cow pasture to find him. The land is open and treeless, a wash of browns and grays offset by a sky of purest blue. The sense of flatness is deceptive. Arroyos and rises give contour to the land. The pastures are a treacherous mix of persistent snow patches, standing water, and mud. Judy picks our route carefully, never knowing if a benign patch of white might hide a snow-filled hole. "One little old sagebrush can cause a huge drift to form behind it," Judy says. The pickup fishtails frantically as she spins the wheel right then left, navigating around mud-slick tracks and patches of snow, keeping the truck moving forward. We drive past herds of black cattle that seem unconcerned by our passage. The Vicks have been lucky, or perhaps more accurately, prepared. They only lost 10 head in the blizzard.

We find Gene working with his hired man on a framework of wood and corrugated metal braced against the prevailing wind. He waves and comes over to the truck to meet us. Leaning in the window, he reaches across Judy to shake hands with me, sitting in the middle, and then Rick, who is riding shotgun. Gene's large hand swallows mine, the grip firm, the skin rough. We chat for a moment, then he promises to come right up to the house as soon as he gets the hired man working on the job. As we drive back to the house we scare up clouds of gray-brown birds feeding in the grass, as busy and vigorous as the men working in the next pasture. They settle again to the ground as we pass.

The Vicks' home is neat and comfortable, decorated with a Western flavor—a drawing of worn cowboy boots framed in barn wood, a photo of a pronghorn, a watercolor of snow geese. Between the living room and breakfast nook stands a drum-shaped woodstove. We gather at the kitchen table and as Judy plies us with frosted homemade brownies, cider, and hot coffee, Gene comes in, his face ruddy from the cold. He is an amiable man in his late fifties, burly of build with a handsome, weathered face and twinkling eyes. He settles in a chair at the table and we make small talk. I remind him of the mutual acquaintance who has put me in touch with him, explain my book project, my interest in finding out what life is like out here on the plains. Judy pours Gene a mug of hot coffee and he begins the story of his life on the land.

"Grandpa Vick came here in 1903 on horseback from Junction City, Kansas, at the age of 14," he says. Gene is intelligent and articulate, but his speech carries the casual phrasing and inflection of a country man. Gene's grandfather homesteaded south of the present ranch, near the town of Boyero, which at one time was a large community with a hotel, livery, lumber yard, section houses for the railroad, stock yards, a high school, and a grocery store. But the passage of humans on the prairie is often brief and the evidence disappears quickly. Today Boyero is mostly a ghost town, with only two resident families. Boyero died when the highway was altered to follow a straight line from Hugo to Wild Horse. The residents left, the businesses closed down, and even the church was carted off to another town and reborn as a filling station.

Eastern Colorado was still wide open prairie when Grandpa Vick arrived to stake his claim. Decades of earlier pioneers had passed through this country on the way further west. The remains of a stage stop, still bearing the ruts of countless wagons and coaches, marks where the Smoky Hill Trail passed through the north end of the Vick ranch. Gene gets up and goes to his desk, comes back and puts into my hand several rusty cartridge shells that he has picked up over the years at the ruined stage stop. "That one there is a center fire," he explains, pointing out the location of the firing pin, "and that one is a rimfire. It strikes on the edge." Rimfire. It makes me think of a town in a B-Western, with dusty streets and false-fronted buildings. Then he shows us stone arrowheads he's found on his land. Though I don't know geology very well, I recognize one as obsidian, likely bartered for or carried here from far away. Another point is of iron, fashioned after whites brought metal items to the plains.

Like Bill Dawson's grandfather, Gene's came to the shortgrass in the early 1900s, to the last unclaimed land in the West. There were reasons why the remote and austere shortgrass was the last place to be settled. Time would prove that a homestead of 160 acres was not enough land on which to make a living here. "They couldn't raise enough feed to sustain 10 or 12 head of cows on no more acres than they could farm with a horse," Gene explains.

While the fortunes of others dried up, Gene's granddad was savvy enough to hang on, acquiring more parcels of land as others gave up and sold out, often for as little as 50 cents an acre. Some busted farmers who owed a bill to the grocer or money to a neighbor just signed their land over for what they owed and walked off. At one time the Vick name held title to nearly 10,000 acres of Colorado prairie.

Today the Vicks ranch about 8,000 acres, three-quarters of it deeded and another quarter leased. Gene runs what's called a cow-calf operation. He maintains a herd of about 300 breeding beef cows—"momma cows," he calls them—that produce calves in the late winter or spring. By fall Gene sells off the calves to a feeder operation that will put them out on wheat and corn stubblefields after the crop has been cut. Later, when about a year and a half old, the calves will be sold to a feedlot for intense feeding and fattening in preparation for slaughter. "It takes a lot of land out here to run cattle," Gene explains. Each cow needs about 30 acres of grass to sustain herself and her calf for one year. Parsimonious with its grass and its water, the prairie dictates the lifestyle for Eastern Plains ranchers. With individual ranches covering thousands of acres, neighbors are spread thin, and even with automobiles to shrink the miles, the Vicks' home is remote, though it doesn't seem lonely.

The remoteness of shortgrass farms and ranches held back the area's development. Gene's stories of growing up here in the 1940s and 1950s sound more like a nineteenth-century pioneer lifestyle than post-World War II America. "Our house was built of 'dobe block," he continues. I ask him if what sounds like "dough-bee" is the same thing as what sod houses were made of, but I don't quite understand his answer. Somewhere between true Southwestern adobe—bricks made of mud and straw and baked in the sun—and sod cut from the ground, 'dobe block seems to be sod mortared with a mix of mud and straw.

Built by an early homesteader, the Vick family home was on a half-section of land his father bought when Gene was two years old. What was it like growing up in a house from another era, one that was pretty primitive for the mid-twentieth century, even on the prairie? "It was natural," Gene says. "We didn't think we were abused." The dirt walls were plastered on the inside, covered with stucco on the outside. Glancing around his modern, comfortable home, Gene gauges the size of the little sod house he grew up in. "The whole house was about the size of our living room and kitchen in this house," Gene explains, "with six of us living there." I'm reminded of the sod house I helped build at the Plains Conservation Center, which was about that size. With a single door and small windows, it was dark, low-ceilinged, and definitely cozy. With rugs on the floor and the walls whitewashed, it could be homey enough, but Gene's life still seems like a page out of Willa Cather.

Electricity didn't reach some rural areas of eastern Colorado until the 1960s. The Vicks' 'dobe block house was lit by coal-oil lamps. In the late 1940s the family got a wind-charger, which harnessed a windmill to recharge electric batteries in the house. "Wind is one resource we've got plenty of," Gene says, smiling. Not that it provided brilliant illumination. The 32-volt batteries powered bulbs about as bright as Christmas lights, but they were still brighter than the kerosene lamps. I try to imagine studying and reading by the light of a Christmas tree. "We thought we was real uptown 'cause now we had electric lights," Gene adds.

A world without electric lights. I've known that only when camping far from towns or high in the mountains or canyons. I love to see the stars, with no interference from city lights, but living out here on this cold prairie I would feel, I think, a sense of supreme isolation on a winter night. The nights of midwinter are long and dark, affording no warmth from the pale glow of a cold moon. The sun sets by 4:30 in the evening and doesn't rise again until 7:30 the next morning. On these lonely plains the hours between dusk and dawn are a long tunnel, the lights of neighboring ranches too far away to be seen. In a city where lights burn brightly around the clock, the reassurance of streetlights and the neighbor's porch light offers a sense of protection and orientation. On the prairie, the lights you see are the lights of your own home. Beyond that is the dark.

The 'dobe house was warmed by a small stove in the center of the living room, and Gene's mother cooked on a wood-burning range in the kitchen. But wood was scarce, so the ranch family turned to a fuel source plains dwellers have long used. "I can remember hauling cow chips in for the cookstove," says Gene. "They burn pretty good."

Gene recalls some of his best friends from childhood—*The Lone Ranger* and *Fibber McGee and Molly*. In these days of lowbrow, tell-all programs like *The Jerry Springer Show,* such radio programs seem almost naïve. We consider ourselves more worldly, but perhaps all we are is jaded and desensitized.

"I can't remember being without a radio," Gene says. "In the evenings we kids'd read and do our homework by the kerosene light at the kitchen table." They would move the one kerosene lamp from room to room. After their homework was done, the kids could listen to the radio. The radio was an essential part of family life. Before the luxury of the wind-charged battery, the family ran their radio on six-volt car batteries. Gene's folks listened to the *Grand Ole Opry* and station KOA for news.

Rick and I smile at that. KOA is still an important AM radio station broadcast out of Denver reaching throughout the West. Talk shows, news, and sports are its mainstays today, as they must have been when Gene was a boy. KOA's all-night radio shows still bring news and companionship to long-haul truckers, night owls, mothers up with sick children, and lonelyhearts from Kansas to California. And KOA brought the world to the lonely ranch house on the Colorado prairie. "We'd all just sit there and listen to the radio—Mom and Dad and the kids," Gene continues, "just like a family'd sit and watch TV now." I imagine the little family clustered around the radio in their tiny earthen house as the night wind howled outside, their faces lit by the dim glow of a coal-oil lamp, listening to the sounds of people and laughter, to the stories and adventures about places far away and very different from their home on the plains. When an actor standing at a microphone in New York read the lines for a character named Fibber McGee, and the sound effects man imitated the creaking of a closet door then banged pots and crates, a young boy on a ranch in Colorado saw shoes and boxes and baseballs crashing out on the floor from inside an overstuffed closet.

Gene continues to surprise us with stories about his austere boyhood. "We had a big round bathtub and we all took turns taking a bath, using the same water, of course." He gives a big grin, "The littlest of us would take a bath and it graduated up like that till Dad was the last one. He'd just add a little more water." Gene, who was born in 1938, recently hosted a visitor on a tour of the county. After listening to him describe his childhood, she commented, "Gene, there's not many 60-year-olds that lived like you did. Most would be more like a hundred." To which Gene replied, "Sometimes I sure feel that old." He laughs heartily at his joke.

Ranch life was all about making a living, which meant producing food. Milk came from a cow, not the grocery store, requiring twice-daily milking. Without refrigeration, the milk was cooled in a water barrel down by the windmill. The cream they skimmed off the top and sold every Saturday in town for grocery money, along with eggs from the hens Gene's mother kept. A cream station in Hugo bought milk and cream from local farmers then shipped it by rail to Denver.

When things got really bad, Gene's father and uncle took their rifles out on the prairie in search of skunks, badgers, and coyotes; they'd skin them and sell the hides to get extra cash. In those days, before the Colorado Department of Game, Fish and Parks was renamed the Division of Wildlife, such animals were considered varmints—worthless nuisances. "The statutes of the state of Colorado," says the 1969 reference *Wild Mammals of Colorado,* "classify the striped skunk (and badger, bobcat, lynx, gray wolf, coyote and others) as a predator and afford it no protection." Mountain lions, wolves, and coyotes were persecuted under a bounty system, the goal to rid the state of these "obnoxious mammals."

In the early fifties, an explosion of the jackrabbit population opened up another cash source for the Vicks when Lincoln County put a 20-cent bounty on them. Locals organized rabbit drives—armed with clubs, a large group of people would form a big circle to drive rabbits into the center, then club them to death. People even came out from the city to join in the sport.

On cold days like today, the rabbits would hunker down under a sagebrush. Gene and his father would climb in their 1938 pickup with their .22-caliber rifles and drive out across the ranch hunting rabbits. The men would shoot the rabbits, toss them in the back of the truck and take them to town. To claim the bounty, they just had to present the ears—a pair to be sure someone wasn't paid twice for the same rabbit. "All you had to do was cut the ears off," explains Gene, "so you'd string these ears on a piece of baling wire and take in this whole string of rabbit ears." The county man would count the pairs of ears like beads on an abacus—"one rabbit, two rabbits, three rabbits."

Considered nuisances, jackrabbits were not protected by state game laws. "The carcasses of jack rabbits are sold to dealers who utilize them for fur and for food of domestic animals," states *Wild Mammals of Colorado.* "The white-tailed species may sell for from $.25 to $.75 per individual at certain times in certain areas. The meat of jack rabbits is not unpalatable and is certainly fit for human consumption." Though the family supplemented their food with cottontails, Gene doesn't recall ever eating jackrabbits.

In summer, with no way to preserve meat, fresh chicken was often the main course. Cornering one of her birds in the henhouse, Gene's mother would wring its neck, pluck the feathers and stew it for dinner. Come the cool weather of October, when meat could be kept outside without spoiling, Gene's father would butcher a cow. Hauled up with a pulley, a whole side of beef hung on the north side of the house in the shade where it would keep cool. "When we wanted meat, Dad would just go out and cut off a hunk and Mom would cook it." Gene's mother also canned beef, putting pieces of meat in Mason jars, sprinkling them liberally with salt, then cooking the jars in a pressure cooker.

While the beef took the family through winter, cured pork gave them an alternative to chicken in the warm months. "Come close to spring, I can remember us butchering hogs. We'd shoot them hogs and lower 'em with a pulley from a tripod over a 55-gallon drum full of water." They'd build a fire underneath the drum to heat the water, then lower in the hog to soften the skin before scraping off the hair. But that was just the beginning of the work. They made their own bacon and cured their own hams with salt and brown sugar or molasses, injecting salt along the bone with a big needle. Gene's mother made sausage patties of pork fat and meat, storing them in a big crock sealed with lard. As she needed the patties, she'd dig down through the lard and fish out the sausages, then fry them up in a skillet.

While the rest of the country had changed drastically after World War II, the week still revolved around Saturday, for this rural Colorado family. On this big day the family went to town—Hugo—to do business and socialize. The women did their shopping then sat and visited while the men played pool and drank beer in the pool hall. For the kids, it was the chance to play with other kids in the park and get to know the neighbors they saw only occasionally.

One Saturday the man who ran the county road maintainer came into the pool hall reporting a tornado northeast of town. Gene's father didn't believe him. But when the family returned home they found that the tornado had blown down the chicken house and killed the 150 chickens Gene's mother had been about to butcher. The 'dobe block house was still standing but the tornado had raised the roof up on one corner. The kids ran inside and by standing on their bunk beds could look outside over the top of the wall.

I was curious to hear how you put the roof back on a 'dobe block house. "Dad got up there with a sledgehammer," Gene continued, "one of those 15-pound hammers they used to drive the spikes with on the railroad. He mixed him up some mud and wet that down really good and let that mud dry around the wood rafters again and then he pounded our roof back down." Home repair at its essence.

Before the twister hit their place, Gene's family had been planning a vacation to visit his grandparents. "Soon as the chickens are butchered we'll go to Wisconsin," his mother had said for several weeks. Then the tornado killed all the chickens, "so we gathered up the dead chickens, pounded down the roof, got in the car and went to Wisconsin for a month," Gene says with a grin. "The tornado let us go on vacation!"

Judy had been listening to Gene's stories but now she had one to tell. Judy's grandmother homesteaded in the southern end of the county in the early part of the century. In 1918, the year of the influenza epidemic that killed half a million people in the United States, she was living in a little sod house with her husband and two babies. Judy's aunt was two years old and her father only three months old. Around Thanksgiving, Judy's grandfather came down with the flu just as a big blizzard hit, trapping the family in their sod house. The young husband became delirious, thrashing around until his wife tied him to the bed with the harness reins to keep him from injuring himself. "She was snowbound in a raging blizzard with two babies and her husband dying," Judy says, her eyes intense, "and she didn't have anybody to help her and no therapist except God."

We all listen to Judy but no one says a word. In the background I hear the howling of the wind, the groaning of cattle. "The blizzard lasted two days and my grandpa died during the storm. When it was over, grandma hitched the team to a sled. She bundled up her babies and somehow got my grandpa into this sled and she drove through the snow into town." I think of how I stayed inside and snug during last week's storm, watching the news and baking cinnamon rolls while the snow piled up outside, my greatest worry for my husband was that he might strain his back shoveling the front sidewalk.

Talk of the blizzard turns our thoughts to the effects of a much more recent storm. Because of such freakish prairie weather, the Vicks try to sell their calves each year by the tenth of October. This allows the mother cows, who have been nursing their calves all summer, to gain weight and recover body conditioning so they can better withstand the harsh winter weather. This plan kept the Vicks' losses in the recent storm to only 10 animals. Still, the loss of their cattle is no easy thing. "I took pictures of them after the storm," says Judy quietly and I can tell the memory of the dead animals bothers her. "The ice was hanging all over them. It freezes their eyes shut and they're blind and they can't see where they're going."

Mired down in deep snow, the cattle exhaust themselves struggling. They can't draw a clear breath and they breathe in snow until their lungs fill with moisture and they drown, a bizarre fate on the dry prairie. "The wetter the snow, the worse," says Gene. "This last storm the chill factor was 30 below zero." He shows us a gruesome picture of one cow completely covered with snow except for her head, her nose pointed up trying to breathe.

How did bison survive such fierce weather? During storms, bison face into the prevailing wind, rather than away from it as cattle do, shielded perhaps by the thick hair on their heads and shoulders. To reach their food supply after a deep snow, bison swing their heavy heads back and forth, brushing the snow aside to reveal the grass. In a 1974 study, researchers found that in late fall, winter, and early spring, buffalo make more effective use of low-protein diets than domestic cattle do; in other words, bison can get by on poorer food.

Cattle can take just about anything for 24 hours, explains Judy, but then their stamina runs out, they lose body heat, they can't eat or drink, and they don't have the energy to hold out against hard conditions. "It's like you hear of people getting lost in a storm and stumbling into a drift," she says. "Like that lady in Otero County." She's speaking of May Householder Hunter. Her death has made headlines all over the state and, although they didn't know her, to these ranchers her death is especially significant, since but for the grace of God her fate could have been theirs.

Judy points to a clothesline post outside the window, "Sometimes we can't see that pole in a blizzard." The post is only about 12 feet from the house. "Before they had all these fences, you could get out there and get disoriented. The wind made you think you were walking in the right direction and you just wandered around on the prairie blind till you died."

At least in this age ranchers have weather warnings they didn't have a century ago. Gene prepared for this storm by putting his cattle in the pasture with the large windbreak. A windbreak doesn't kill all the wind, Gene explains, and it changes the wind pattern, creating a vortex out in front of it that some of the cattle don't like. "We lost four of them in the windbreak and six of them what wasn't in the windbreak, so we're wondering how effective is a windbreak!"

Gene made sure to move his cows out of one pasture that is cut by deep ravines. In 1946 his dad lost 40 newly purchased calves in that pasture when a sudden storm hit. He didn't find the calves till spring, buried by snow in one of the rugged draws.

Gene is thankful this hard storm came so early in the season, followed by warm weather that is melting the snow and uncovering the grass. "If this happened in January, we'd be feeding them cows every day," he explains. He goes across the room and reaches into a large bag lying in the corner, comes back and lays a pellet about the size of my thumb in my hand. It's a cattle feed called range cubes, a concentrated, high-protein mix of compressed hay and cottonseed or soybean meal. "They call it cake," Gene says and I tell him I'll stick with Judy's frosted brownies.

In 1977 a March storm devastated the Vicks' herd. Gene had put all his animals behind windbreaks and in corrals ("cor-RELLs" Gene calls them) and still lost 80 head of cattle. After that he got blizzard insurance, not a common practice among ranchers.

The Vicks' cattle are a cross between Angus and a French breed called Gelbvieh. I've never heard of this breed of cattle, so Gene has to spell it for me. Crossbred cattle are desired by the packing companies because they put on weight faster than Herefords or Angus and go from calf to market quicker. When I ask how they decide what breeds of cattle to raise, Judy answers with a snort of disgust. "It's the trends," she says. "Trends can break you."

"I think we're about done chasing trends," Gene interjects with the note of a man tired of dancing to someone else's tune. "By the time you've invested in a certain type of bull, they want something else." The economics of ranching keep ranchers walking a financial tightrope. While life on this prairie may not be as physically hard nor as lonely as it was in earlier days, making a living here is still tough.

In 1950, Gene says, he could sell a dozen calves and buy a new pickup with the money they brought him. Today it would take 65 calves to buy a new truck. "It still takes as many acres to run that cow on as it did then," he laments. "Everybody says ranchers are land barons, but don't you have to be a land baron to keep up with that?"

Three years ago the Vicks sold their calves at the same price Gene's dad sold them for in 1954, though, Judy is quick to add, meat does not sell for the 1954 retail price in the grocery store. Gene blames the middlemen— four major meat packing companies in the United States—for controlling prices. The rancher's price for cattle goes down or up daily, but the price at the retail level is slow to change. Ranchers must dance a quick-step to stay on top of the quicksilver beef market, gambling on what route might bring the best price.

"There's three ways to sell your cows," says Gene, holding up three work-worn fingers. "One, a rancher can take his cows to the sale barn and get the price cattle will sell for at that moment. Two, he can go to private individuals who will contract for these calves to be delivered on a certain date, say the tenth of October." The buyers visit the ranch in August and agree on a price. While ensuring the rancher a market, if the price goes up in the intervening months, he must still sell for the lower price. And what is the third way? I ask. "He can sell his cows on the satellite," Gene answers. On the satellite? My ears prick up at that comment. Video of the cattle are broadcast via satellite across the continent so a buyer in Tennessee can look at them on television while sitting in his living room, then place an order by phone without ever seeing the animals, or the rancher, in person.

The irony of this isn't lost on all of us. Gene is a man straddling two eras, a rancher who grew up in a sod house lighted by coal-oil lamps who today sells his cattle via satellite link to buyers across the country. But he still goes out every morning in coveralls and boots to care for his cattle; he still loses animals to fierce weather and factors he can't control. His livelihood is governed by the bitter or benign whim of the prairie.

The Vicks have most of their land in native grasses—buffalo grass and blue grama. "It has a lot of food value to it," Gene continues. "For shortgrass country, you can't ask for better grass to put weight on animals in the summertime, because it's so high in nutrition." He sees the value of the grass directly in how it affects his livelihood—how well his cattle fatten up, how their calves grow and thrive. "Our ranch still has good integrity of grass since we've never plowed."

Unlike Bill Dawson, Gene isn't yet using the intense management of rotational grazing, which involves moving cattle every three or four days between fenced pastures of 160 acre each to keep the range clipped and the grass vigorous. The ranches doing that are successful, though, he says. "It keeps fresh grass for your cattle and gives the grass time to recover. It's like mowing your lawn. If you cut off that much every week," Gene holds up his hand with finger and thumb an inch apart, "and add all that up, you've grown a lot of grass." I like hearing this grass farmer talk about what he knows best. I can't help but smile because I've had different versions of this same conversation with grassland ecologists and native plant specialists, people who might be viewed as on the other side of the fence from a cattle rancher concerning range management. When it comes to grass, we all sing the praises of Colorado's blue grama.

Gene no longer uses horses much to work cattle. "We used to," he answers, shifting in his seat, "but the older you get, the less amount of horse you use." He pauses for effect, then laughs. He is replacing his horse with a four-wheel ATV—all terrain vehicle. "My dog rides on the four-wheeler with me. Now every time that four-wheeler starts up she hops up behind me." I laugh at this new version of the pickup dog and tell Gene about the rancher at Summit Springs who rode around on his four-wheeler with a white toy poodle riding up behind like a reverse hood ornament.

The romance of the cowboy on horseback is appealing, but it's obvious today's rancher must do what is most practical. Most ranchers hold down some other kind of job to make ends meet. Gene earns a salary as a county commissioner. "I'm not a politician," he is quick to say but was motivated to get involved when a developer proposed a 1,800-acre landfill for Lincoln County. "I can straddle a horse but can't force myself to straddle the fence," was his campaign slogan. Through Gene's efforts, the county adopted the same stringent landfill regulations required in New York state—effectively halting the landfill, at least for now. "Lincoln County doesn't need to be the national dumping ground," he adds.

I wonder how much prairie wildlife remains on this ranch. Land that hasn't been plowed has fewer invasive weeds, unless it's been overgrazed and eroded, and maintains more native plants, offering better habitat for wildlife than cultivated land. But ranchers are selective in what animals they allow to share the land. I know I can't talk easily with the Vicks about prairie dogs; we have views of this animal that are completely opposite. They have no use for prairie dogs since, as grazers of rangeland, these communal rodents are direct competitors with ranchers for the resources of the prairie. And I know the Vicks and I will face each other across a void if we talk about coyotes. I decide to start on safer ground and ask generally about what wildlife they have on their ranch. Gene easily ticks off the animals living around him.

"We've got antelope, jackrabbits, some deer—muleys and a few whitetails. We used to be strictly mule deer in Colorado but the whitetails come up here from Kansas along water drainages like the Big Sandy, the Arikaree, and the Arkansas. They start cross-breeding with mule deer till pretty soon they breed mule deer plumb out." I'm not sure this is biologically accurate—there is occasional hybridization between the two species, but nothing significant—but I don't say anything. A few wild turkeys live along the creek outside of Hugo, he says, transplanted from Kansas in a trade for pronghorn. Some of the pronghorn sent to Kansas were captured on the Vick ranch.

I can tell Gene has a fondness for the tawny pronghorn with the soft, dark eyes. "A few years ago the antelope came through in herds and they congregated down there near Wild Horse. The wildlife people estimated 4,000 to 5,000 antelope in that one herd." In the spring, the animals dispersed in groups. "You'd see 30 or 40 going that-a-way and 30 or 40 going that-a-way." He motions off to his right, then off to his left.

Swift foxes sometimes wake Gene and Judy up at night with high-pitched barking. Gene mimics the foxes' *yip, yip, yip.* "They come right into the yard chasing a cottontail. They'll lay out there by their holes and we can see the little pups around in the spring." He doesn't mind the little prairie foxes, which are smaller than red foxes, because they don't bother his livestock. In other parts of the Great Plains, swift foxes have become so scarce they are being proposed for listing as a threatened species with the U.S. Fish and Wildlife Service. But according to Dr. Jim Fitzgerald, a retired biology professor from the University of Northern Colorado who has studied shortgrass prairie ecology extensively, Colorado's swift fox populations are doing fine.

The Vicks' pastures are full of the songs of meadowlarks. Killdeer, small shorebirds that nest on the bare ground of the prairie, are abundant. The ranch is on a natural flyway for migrating birds, Judy explains, and they often see Canada and snow geese, ducks, and sandhill cranes.

Mockingbirds drop by to visit early in the morning in spring and once in a while they'll see bluebirds and orioles. Lark buntings come through and at times the trees are black with migrating flocks of red-winged blackbirds.

In mid-October this year the skies were filled with the primordial silhouettes of thousands of birds, probably pushed ahead of the pending storm. "I stepped outside and watched flight after flight after flight of sandhill cranes come over," Judy says. The migration that usually occurs over about two weeks happened instead in two days. "There were thousands upon thousands of them. They were down in a pasture and the ground was just black with those cranes."

About the time Judy was watching the flights of cranes above her ranch I had received a call from a friend who lives on a two-acre mini-farm near Elizabeth, less than 60 miles from Hugo as the crow, or crane, flies. My phone rang in early evening and I heard Deanna's excited voice, "Mary! I'm out by the barn. Can you hear those birds?" Over her portable phone, which she was obviously holding up to the sky, I couldn't hear anything but rustling and breathing. "Oh, you can't hear them!" she said, disappointed. "These big flocks of birds have been flying over for the last few days"—blackbirds and grackles was my first thought—"and they have the most beautiful voices." Definitely not blackbirds and grackles, I thought. "But they're not geese..." Oh, I said to myself, big birds, not songbirds as I had assumed. "Are their calls a kind of trilling *karooo, karooo*?" I asked, rolling my r's musically. "Yes, that's it!" Deanna answered. "It's beautiful!" Now I had no doubt to the birds' identity. "They're cranes, Deanna, sandhill cranes."

Some 20,000 sandhill cranes that nest in Montana, Wyoming, and northwestern Colorado move south along the Rockies in fall, heading for farm fields and wet meadows along the Rio Grande River in New Mexico. A much larger group—half a million cranes—moves along a more easterly flyway, down through Nebraska to the Gulf of Mexico. I'm not sure to which group the birds passing over eastern Colorado belong.

Flying overhead, the cranes seem reptilian in form and design, their snake-like necks balanced by long, trailing legs. Their large wings slowly feather the air in measured brushstrokes. Like a line of ballerinas, a gathering of cranes dances across the sky, performing pliés.

It's time to ask Gene and Judy about prairie dogs, animals I've learned rural people have a hard time tolerating favorable opinions about. "Oh, you just think they're so cute with those big eyes," said one family friend from eastern Colorado. I could almost lip-synch his next comment as he repeated the old litany, "If they'd called them prairie rats instead of prairie dogs you wouldn't think they were so great."

Still, I'm interested in the Vicks' perspective. "In Lincoln County, pretty much if anyone finds a prairie dog hole, we go out and get rid of them before they get started," says Judy. Then she adds the usual filthy vermin comment, "They're very disease-prone."

But Gene breaks in with the real reason ranchers object to prairie dogs. "They ruin your grass," he says matter-of-factly. For this reason, ranchers have exterminated prairie dogs wherever they could. "I bet we don't have prairie dogs within 20 miles of here." At its basis, the conflict between ranchers and prairie dogs is a competition for resources. For the same reasons some hunters shoot mountain lions to "protect" the deer population, anglers will kill pelicans and herons to keep them from catching fish the anglers want to hook for themselves, and urban developers poison prairie dog colonies on vacant real estate—the animals utilize resources people want.

Rather than competition for resources, the case against coyotes is a fear of the animals directly taking the rancher's livestock. "We do have a coyote problem," Gene adds. "They'll kill baby calves in the spring when you're calving. Three years ago they tried to catch three calves, bit them in the loin area, and the calves got huge abscesses on them." He has horror stories of coyote predation on cows giving birth. "If there's a cow down calving with a calf half out of her and she can't get up, the coyotes will go and start eating the rear end off the cow." I've heard such tales before. Not all coyotes prey on livestock, but the potential always exists and the rancher, branding coyote as Enemy Number One, is in no mood to quibble over the culpability of one animal versus another. Better to get rid of as many as possible and be done with it.

"We still have ways to control coyotes," Gene says, referring to tighter state restrictions on coyote control. "But we don't trap them, 'cause we all have dogs—cow dogs and pets—and your dogs will get in the traps." Judy adds, "Every year I've shot some right here at the house. I've looked up from work and seen them here and I've gone out and shot them." Judy does income taxes to supplement their income from ranching. I imagine her glancing up from her tax forms to see a coyote coming into the yard, leaving her desk to grab up a rifle, open the door, and draw a bead on the scavenging animal. Accounting on the range.

Gene has another coyote story for us, "The day right after the storm there was a dead antelope and there was six coyotes eating on it and they ate it in one day." For me his anecdote is a simple illustration of the cycle of life—the death and devastation left by the blizzard offer food, and therefore life, to those who survived. But I know Gene doesn't see it that way; his voice registers disgust as he tells of the coyotes feeding on blizzard casualties. "The hog-raisers over here say they're eating a dead hog a night—the carcasses from the storm. They gorge themselves." The coyotes that are a constant threat to Gene's livelihood benefited from the storm that hurt him.

We've talked about family history, about the economics and logistics of ranching, but what I most want to know is what the prairie means to Gene and Judy, how it touches their hearts and their spirits. Our lives are very different. I am a city girl who escapes to the prairie, or what of it remains around the city, as often as I can to explore and bring the natural world into my life. The Vicks live on the land; they deal with the whims and moods of the prairie daily. It shapes their days and their lives. We come from such different places yet we share a kinship in the way this austere landscape influences us. But I can't ask these ranchers about the spirituality of the prairie, if they feel connected to the earth—such talk would sound to them like New Age blather. Instead, I ask them what it is about living in the open country that keeps them here and working so hard instead of selling out and moving to Florida.

Judy is eager to share her feelings about the land and speaks first. "This country has absolutely the most beautiful sunrises and sunsets in the whole world. The cloud formations coming off the mountains give us magnificent colors."

She praises the clear and sunny weather. "Ninety-three percent of the time you couldn't ask for better weather. The other seven percent, well, it's hell. When it's bad, it's really bad." Like people everywhere, Judy likes to talk about the weather, and like people everywhere, I like to join in. I'm no stranger to the extremes of prairie weather and I still tell stories that start out, "I remember the Blizzard of '82."

"Like the girl with the curl," I say. Judy chimes in, "When the weather's good it's very, very good, but when it's bad it's horrid." Judy and I laugh at our cleverness, but Gene has grown pensive. "That probably don't keep me here," he says quietly. He pauses, then, "It's love of the land. My ranch is not for sale. It's not for sale. Absolutely. You could come in here and offer me almost anything and I'd have to say, 'I'm sorry, my ranch is not for sale.'"

Judy is touched by his emotion. "Roots," she says, and Gene agrees. "It is, it's got to be, roots. It upsets you when you see an oil company want to come in here and dig an oil well and make a trail on your land. If I want to make a trail, I'll make my own trail." Judy looks at her husband with affection. "I remember when we tried to talk him into selling the cows and just renting the place out. He said, 'But Judy, when the calves come, it's just like Christmas.' See, when it's calving, they're all new and all different. There's the excitement of buying a new bull and seeing what kind of calves you'll have next year." Judy pauses. "Then the disappointment if they're not so good." Gene gives a rueful smile, "Used to be the excitement of riding a different horse, training a new horse."

I notice Gene grow very quiet, suddenly overcome with emotion. Gene is not a hard man; indeed, his manner and spirit are gentle. But he lives a hard life, dealing daily with life and death, harsh cold or baking heat and, always, demanding physical labor and the constant risk of disabling injury. This talk of the land has touched a deep chord within him. His eyes tear up a bit. He turns his face away, unable to talk. The prairie is rooted deep within this plainsman, a part of his soul. I turn my attention to Judy and we carry on.

"The serenity of the prairie," she says, "but then there's unforgiving Mother Nature. You don't fight it. You can't fight it. Mother Nature can be very, very cruel and very, very beautiful." She talks about the violence of the prairie and the haunting sound of geese passing overhead, the cruelty of coyotes eating a newborn calf and the music of their lonely calls at dusk. Coyotes are the enemy, yet a part of the landscape that defines these ranchers.

Gene is composed now, joins in again: "You don't hate the prairie or the weather. You forgive it once the sun shines." He describes heading out to feed the cows the morning after the big blizzard, using the tractors because of the heavy snow. "We just stopped for a while and looked around, and it was beautiful. It just stole ten of our cows, yet it was beautiful."

The ranch will soon pass its one hundredth year in the Vick name and Gene's greatest hope is that in another century it will still carry his family name. The land is who Gene is. He talks then about his two sons, and his young grandson, how his kids will have to buy the ranch from him, as he is buying it from his parents, to assure each older generation an income in their later years. But as with so many rural families, economics will dictate whether the Vick family stays on the land. "We're changing with the times, but there's only so much we can change," Gene says, acknowledging the force that has always been the ultimate master for those deriving their living from the land. "It still comes down to the amount of rain we're going to get, the number of blizzards we get. It still comes down to what the prairie's going to give us."

Gene walks us to our car, then points towards a ridge to the north. "That marks the boundary of the ranch," he says. "My father's ashes are scattered on that ridge, and I suppose mine probably will be, too."

Rick and I drive back out the Vicks' driveway, turn right and head past rangeland clipped short from grazing and flattened by the recent snows. A flock of gray-brown birds—horned larks, identifiable by the black bar across the brow and black bib on the chest—swirls up from the ground, flashing black tails with white edges. The birds move a short way ahead of us then light again as we slow down for a look. Among the larks we spot a handful of smaller, darker birds—Lapland longspurs. These ground-dwelling cousins of sparrows gain their name from the exceptionally long claw on their hind toe—the long spur—a balance aid, perhaps, when running over open ground. In breeding plumage, the male longspur is a handsome bird, with black cap, face, and breast contrasting with a broad patch of chestnut-red on the nape of his neck. Few humans see his summertime finery, however, for the Lapland longspur breeds in the far north, on the barren ground of the Arctic tundra a world away from humans. In summer, longspurs feast on the insects and grubs of lush Arctic meadows, lining their nests, hidden among the tundra grass, with the hairs of lemmings and caribou.

Two other longspur species, the chestnut-collared and the McCown's, call the Colorado prairie home. These birds, more southerly in their range and less intrepid perhaps than the Arctic-nesting Lapland, visit primarily in summer. Only the Laplander, a bird of the polar north, considers the shortgrass a milder winter environment. At home in open and treeless lands, longspurs migrate in fall 2,500 miles south to pass the winter on our hard prairie. Here the longspur contents itself with a monastic diet of grass and weed seeds, the only food available, and finds what cover it can among the shrubs and dried grasses. Moulted now to a nondescript brown, longspurs are such a part of the winter prairie that few visitors notice them.

We often think wildlife is somehow magically impervious to the ravages of nature, but harsh weather takes a toll on wildlife, sometimes a very costly toll. A fierce storm in March 1904 killed an estimated five million longspurs on the Great Plains. Many longspurs, I am sure, did not survive last week's blizzard. But that storm is over. This morning the survivors are out feeding in the grass. Why do the longspurs choose to pass winter here, on the prairie? Why don't they migrate further south, to warmer places? Why does the rancher stay on in this land of extremes? These small drab birds find what they need in this hard land, making their living on the open country just as the rancher who calls these pastures his own. Kindred spirits share this prairie. For the longspurs as much as for the rancher, it still comes down to what the prairie will give.

Chapter 14:
Blue Grama

On an afternoon in late May, I drive out onto the 27 square miles of the Rocky Mountain Arsenal National Wildlife Refuge, just north of Denver. The Refuge has a bizarre and ironic history, with more incarnations than a Hindu god. Once shortgrass prairie, homesteaded into farms and cattle range, it was the site of a chemical weapons plant during World War II where the U.S. Army produced napalm, incendiary bombs, and nerve gas. The Army manufactured weapons here for two more wars—Korean and Cold—ceasing production in 1969. Fortunately, none of these weapons was ever used. Eventually stockpiles of napalm, lewisite, chlorine and mustard gas, phosgene, arsenic chloride, and other chemicals were destroyed at the site.

Even after the Army shut down its portion of the Arsenal, toxins continued to be produced there. In the late 1940s the Army had leased part of the Arsenal facilities to private companies. Shell Chemical Company made agricultural pesticides, herbicides, and other chemicals until the early 1980s. The list of products is a deadly roll call of toxic chemicals—DDT, dieldrin, chlordane, parathion. The activities at the Arsenal, and especially its toxic products, figured in Rachel Carson's landmark environmental work, *Silent Spring*.

But the Arsenal story gets curiouser and curiouser. As these activities were going on in the center of the Arsenal, a surprising variety of wildlife was fleeing into the buffer zone of open land around the core. Prairie wildlife on the run from ranching, farming, and the growing Denver metropolitan area found an island of habitat where they could live relatively free of disturbance.

The greatest surprise came when bald eagles, at that time an endangered species, were found to be using the site as a quiet wintering area. Eagles are primarily fish-eaters but the Arsenal population was marching to a different drummer—they were dining on that plump rodent, fruit of the prairie, the prairie dog.

The bald eagle, our national symbol, the poster child of endangered species recovery, was living happily at one of the most contaminated hazardous wastelands in the country. As it turned out, eagles were just the headliners. Mule deer, coyotes, jackrabbits, badgers, burrowing owls, golden eagles, ferruginous hawks, soft-shelled turtles, white pelicans, lark buntings—the list of wildlife species inhabiting the Arsenal sounds endless. Research found that for the most part the wildlife, at least those that didn't enter the core of the site, were relatively unaffected by the contamination (though through the 1950s and 1960s, waterfowl that landed on the open surface of the waste ponds had died by the thousands). Life serves up some wonderful ironies. In this place dedicated to producing instruments of death, wildlife was thriving. So the Rocky Mountain Arsenal, an EPA Superfund cleanup site, became a national wildlife refuge. The Refuge, still known as the Arsenal to locals, is the focus of one of the largest prairie restorations in the West. Protected from the plow and the cow for nearly 60 years, the northern half of the site remains a fairly good stand-in for shortgrass prairie. As the cleanup progresses, disturbed areas will be returned as close as possible to native Colorado prairie.

I'm riding with the Refuge's plant ecologist, Carl Mackey. Carl and I have known each other for several years, as a result of my writing for and about the Arsenal and its wildlife. Carl is a great resource person, an expert on the ecology of the shortgrass prairie community, and I call him when I have questions about native vegetation or prairie restoration. We are friends, too, both sharing a spiritual connection to prairie.

Carl takes me on a tour of the sites where grassland restoration is underway, and we talk about the mechanics of returning this site to native prairie: the merits of mowing and disking, the challenge of using fire as a grasslands management tool at a hazardous-waste site where the sight of smoke would have some people calling the haz-mat team, the governor, and the National Guard. We've been riding around in the truck all morning, banging down dusty roads, pausing to let a hognose snake cross in front of us, stopping to look across the prairie restoration plots. As works-in-progress, they don't look like much yet. "That will be sand prairie," Carl points out, and later, "at this one we're trying to establish a mix of grama and western wheatgrass." I gaze across the dusty patch that is mostly plowed earth and invasive weeds, not my image of a lovely prairie. I raise my eyebrows and look at Carl skeptically and we both break out laughing. "Well," he says, "restoration is still more art than science and we're learning as we go. There are native plants growing underneath the cheatgrass." I'll accept that. Like the prairie, we all must be patient.

But there are places on the Arsenal where shortgrass prairie has survived all the years of abuse, and I am eager to revisit them. "Let's go look at my favorite spot," says Carl. "I think this place is most like native prairie of anywhere on the Arsenal." I don't need to be told that no true prairie like that which existed 200 years ago exists now. Even land that has escaped the plow lacks the input of a key element—herds of grazing, trampling, wallowing buffalo.

We aren't biologists now; we're not professionals discussing the technology of native habitat restoration. We're two kids on an adventure; we're going to see the secret cave where the treasure lies hidden. The prairie is Carl's work, he lives with it daily, sees it in all its moods and guises. Yet I know without him telling me that the prairie speaks strongly to him. When he plucks a long stem of blue grama grass and rests the seedhead gently against the open palm of one hand, when he squints as he explains the habitat requirements of a particular plant species, looking to the horizon as if relating it all within the context of the landscape, I see in his face the same sense of attachment, of being drawn to this landscape that I feel.

We stride through bristling grasses and flowering plants, the vegetation greeting us with a soft *whish-whish* against the legs of our jeans. Carl is a scout, his hawk-eyes scanning for familiar plants. A healthy prairie can contain a dozen different plant species within one square yard. Even for me, a prairie-lover, it is a wonderful journey of enlightenment, to scan this wide plain and have my eyes opened again, to be reminded to look close and read the grasslands' cryptic messages. As Carl calls my attention here to a purple spiderwort (an unlovely name for a lovely flower) and there to a sand verbena, the smear of green prairie resolves, as if twisting the focus ring on binoculars, into a mosaic of unique life forms. We crouch down and examine a tall stalk with spiky leaves. It isn't in flower yet, but Carl's knowledgeable eyes recognize the gestalt of each species and he gives it a name—plains penstemon. I feel as if I'm peeking through a window on the past as we find one native shortgrass plant after another. "I don't think this area was ever plowed," Carl is saying, "that's why there's such a good representation of natives here." Among these plants I feel myself in the company of elders, ones who have survived through all the moons of change. The prairie is teaching me—*Stop, get down, look close, seek a perspective beyond your own. Be patient, evaluate before judging, appreciate hidden beauties. You cannot see if you do not look.* The prairie is not a land to offer up its secrets easily.

We come upon a plant that represents the havoc non-natives can wreak on original landscapes—a thistle. In the West, thistles are the poster children for the devastating effects of invasive weeds. Like mounted marauders, they take root in disturbed or overworked soil, blasting across rangeland hell-bent-for-leather, choking out natives and desirable cultivated plants alike, blanketing the land with fierce and prickly stalks. Musk and Scotch thistle can grow eight feet high, one plant producing tens of thousands of seeds annually. Spreading quickly, thistles choke out plants that offer forage for cattle and wildlife and form impenetrable, spiny thickets that restrict the movements of grazing animals. Thistles are bad guys, we all know that; they are scorned and hated. Just as I am prepared to condemn this purple scourge and yank it up, dirt-clodded roots dangling, Carl says, "Well, actually, this little thistle belongs here."

About 15 species of native thistle grow in prairie habitats of the Rocky Mountain region. This one is wavy-leaf thistle, *Cirsium undulatum.* Growing one to three feet high, with the wicked spines of its family bristling from particularly curly leaves, the wavy-leaf thistle has pretty purple flowers that bloom throughout the summer. Its tiny seeds provide food for songbirds like goldfinches. In fact all parts of the thistle are edible except the spines. Native prairie people ate them when other food sources were scarce, roasting the seeds, peeling and boiling the roots and stems. Thistles saved the life of Truman Everts, one of the first whites to explore Yellowstone. Separated from his party, thrown from his horse, his spectacles broken, Everts was slowly starving until he dug up and ate the roots of thistles, which he found growing abundantly. For nearly a month he survived mainly on thistle roots until he was finally rescued. My horse loves to eat thistle flowers—I suppose they are sweet since I have often seen bees and butterflies sipping from them. Thunder plucks the fibrous purple flowers from their stalks, his thick horse lips never seeming bothered by the sharp spines just below the blossom. Thistles are composites, members of the sunflower family. While the wavy-leaf thistle is a native, it has the same bad habits of its Attila-the-Hun Eurasian cousins and will spread rapidly on disturbed or overgrazed soil. But kept in balance with other plants and with appropriate grazing pressure from animals, this thistle is a component of a diverse prairie. *Evaluate before judging.* I will never look at a thistle the same way again.

As we linger on the prairie, the day subtly shifts. It is classic High Plains—the open land, the shaggy vegetation in its rough coat of gray-green, the backdrop of purple mountains providing a border, a sense of boundary, to the west. The clouds amble in, their movements the silent padding of a bobcat. The breeze sidles up and tousles my hair. The light alters as if passing through a polarizing lens, enriching and saturating the colors—gunbarrel blue, sage, smoke. It is a magnificent scene, a prairie scene, which dissolves the last century or more of change.

In the game of weather, the prairie is a poor poker player, showing its hand in the mirror of the sky—tranquillity in a morning sky the color of old denim, anger in the gathering evening clouds of inky cobalt and billowing gray. The sky boils now with clouds turned suddenly dark and angry. In moments the friendly breeze blows cold and stern. Carl and I have continued to talk, to look at plants, to enjoy the dance of the cloud formations, but now we give each other knowing looks. As we turn to head back to the truck, the rain starts, as quick as flipping a switch. There are no warm rains here. Cold drops hit my head and shoulders, leaving wet circles the size of quarters on my bare arms. We're running now. Forty steps from the truck the hail begins. I reach the vehicle, fumble with the door, tear it open, throw myself in, slam the door as the drumming hail pelts the metal. The din of the hail on the truck's cab is deafening as we drive as quickly as possible back to Refuge headquarters, though driving on hail is like driving on marbles. Like a snowshoe hare moulting to winter plumage, the prairie transforms gradually to white. The pinging stones bounce as they hit the ground, sending other hailstones jouncing, trapping us inside a popcorn popper.

The hailstorm's power leaves me wide-eyed. Then, after berating us for 20 minutes, it suddenly stops, like a drummer reaching the end of his solo. The clouds fracture and the sun peeks out again, blinding me with the dazzle of its smile.

Carl and I don't say much, both a little humbled, I think, by the storm's power and fury. At the parking lot I thank him and get in my car. As I drive out I stop in a quiet spot to look again at the open country, my ears still ringing from the pelting of hail on the truck's metal cab. The sky is almost virginal in its purity, its blue face lacking in malice or intent. It's beautiful, I think, realizing my words echo those of Gene and Judy Vick after the big blizzard—"It just stole ten of our cows, yet it was beautiful." Like them, I have come to love this place, this intemperate prairie.

This land is like a wild child, brown-skinned and barefoot, its tangled hair sun-bleached and snagged with bits of grass and feathers. It is impervious to blizzards, fierce winds and sun. Indeed, the prairie is born of these things. The prairie is neither boy nor girl, but sometimes one and at other times, the other, by turn rowdy or gentle, nurturing or destructive. The prairie laughs with pleasure at the gifts of spring, watches with wide eyes the marvel of autumn. It weeps, and laughs, and sings with many voices—calling as a pair of geese pass overhead, hissing with the dry grass in a winter wind, winnowing eerily to the courting snipe, or howling the querulous, heartfelt song of the coyote.

Like any child, the prairie is capricious. It awakened on this tender spring day in a tantrum, pelting the earth with iceballs, then abruptly smiling again like a toddler offered a new toy. I have come to know this land, to value both its dramas and its subtleties. Like the Vicks, I can forgive its rages in the healing wonder of its smile.

*   *   *   *   *

"Hey, I can see two people sitting over there in lawn chairs," Rick calls to me. He's holding his binoculars to his eyes as he scans the prairie. I sit up with surprise from where I am slouching in my own lawn chair, enjoying the cool evening. Then he flashes me a big "gotcha" grin. I can't help but laugh at the preposterous idea that anyone else might be out here. It is an evening in late May and we are camping on the Comanche National Grassland in the wide open spaces of southeastern Colorado, a place more often called The Middle of Nowhere. Cows undoubtedly outnumber humans in this county.

I take a sip of my Bailey's Irish Cream. Rick and I are communing with the prairie, sitting in our lawn chairs in the cool evening admiring the rolling grassland like the leisure class reclining in deck chairs on an ocean liner. Before us spreads a visual feast, a palette of blue-grays and dusky greens, of buff and gold, richly textured like brocade. No smooth turf lawns here, but a landscape of textural dissonance—fuzzy sagebrush, scruffy rabbitbrush, spiky yucca. Like the jarring rhythms of Stravinsky, its discord is somehow pleasing.

May is the best time to camp on the prairie; in a month the days will be oppressively hot. In this moon comes the greening of the grasses, their blades emerging strong and fresh, giving the prairie once again its defining character. Around us the leaves of blue grama poke above the ground. Grass is the key to life on the prairie—for wildlife, livestock, and people. High in protein, blue grama, *Bouteloua gracilis*, is the nutritious jewel in the crown.

Sleeping within its roots much of the year, blue grama awakens only with the warming soil of late spring. Nudged above ground in late May, coaxed by the moisture of a late spring storm, its new leaves and shoots emerge green and fresh among the dead hay of last year's growth. Blue grama is a bunch grass, growing in clumps very unlike the familiar turf of cultivated lawns. Up to a hundred seed-bearing stalks can bristle from one clump of grama, the one-inch seedheads, with seeds arranged on the underneath side of the head, waving like flags. The heads curve gently as the flags dry, marking the grassland like long-handled sickles.

I realize I have come, like a rancher, to an appreciation of grass. I love the subtlety of the hues, the gradation of shading, the movement in the landscape when stroked by the wind. Grass is an acquired taste, I think. Friends have given me those skeptical looks when I've stopped at a patch of open range and exclaimed, "Isn't it beautiful?" Maybe if they got down on their bellies and saw the world from an ant's perspective, felt the waving seedheads close above them like a limber forest, learned of brave new worlds below knee height, they'd come around. So far, I've had few takers.

I feel at home out here on the Comanche Grassland, just a cow-pie chuck from Kansas, except for one thing. I cannot see the mountains. I miss my view of them, realizing I am not completely an open-country dweller but rather the resident of a borderland. My home lies between mountain and plain. To the west the Rocky Mountains rise, a constant presence. At times they huddle low and indistinct beneath the clouds, the rounded shapes of bison. At others they stand out stark and sharp, etched with such clarity they sting my eyes with their brightness, their ridgetops the frozen crests of an alpine ocean.

The mountains and the plains are like two sisters, siblings as different from one another as earth and sky, and equally joined. The Rockies stand ornamented in silk and pearls, while the prairie sits at their feet, dressed in a cotton shift and sensible shoes. But the prairie abides in infinite patience, for it is as much mother as sister. The Rockies don't spring into the world but rise up from the High Plains, rearing upward still in remembered passions of geologic birth. My life in Colorado began as a journey to the mountains, but now it is to the prairie I most often turn.

I think it does not come easily to us to love such a land. It is easy to love a mountain, with its inherent grandeur, handsome profile and aristocratic air. But the prairie's charms take more looking. The prairie doesn't run off with your heart the way a mountain does. Its charms are subtle, rooted in the hues of the grasses, the undulations of the land, the infinite sky. The prairie is a girl whose beauty lies in her smile.

I've come to see the grassland as a place of magic, of transformations and world-wise creatures. A coyote drifts from a fold in the landscape, catching me with wise green eyes, the wary, weary eyes of a survivor. Sometime around Easter, the sand lilies appear like stars fallen from the sky in the night. White, six-petalled and perfectly formed, with stems so short the blossoms lie upon the earth, the spring lilies transform a gray and sleeping landscape, carpeting it with jewels.

It is easy to name a mountain. Mountains demand a name. Sometimes we name them for a physical feature, such as Mount Massive or Lizard Head Peak. But most often we name them for one of our own—Longs Peak, Mount Evans, Pikes Peak. I find an arrogance in that, but an admission of weakness, too, as if by naming a mountain for ourselves we hope somehow to conquer it.

How do you name a prairie? A prairie is elusive, its boundaries not easily defined. A prairie flows. Its edges expand and retreat. Its surface moves like water. A prairie dodges definition. It is a wiry colt that bends and twists and dances away from the bridle. For while a mountain is a landscape feature, a prairie is a community of living things. A mountain offers externalized spirituality, a place of pilgrimage. A prairie, lacking in dramatic edifices, is more of a window. It requires that you look through, not just at, to see what lies within.

A sojourn in open country brings me close to God. There is no forest's mantle of organic mass to shelter me, no canyon wall of mineral rock to deflect the full brunt of the world. People who live in the forest find spirits in the trees. Those in canyon country see ancient ones in the rock. On the prairie there is only myself and the sky. It watches me, night or day, listening, speaking to me directly. There is no choice but to confront the elements, the natural world, and, inevitably, myself.

Finding the beauty of the prairie is like a meditation. I must sit still, release present concerns, pace my breathing to the wind. The prairie reveals its power over time. It is felt rather than seen.

It is so easy to travel the open country and see nothing but emptiness. The prairie and its space can be overwhelming, exhausting, defeating. Eyes used to woodlands and hills, tall buildings and houses, look across open country and feel a sense of exposure and vulnerability. A prairie is not empty, but its vitality projects downward into the earth instead of up. The life of a grassland dwells in an enormous network of roots and the galleries of prairie dog towns. It embraces the land, growing over and covering sharp rocks and hard places, softening them, making them its bones. The prairie turns its life force inward. To look beyond the open space, to truly know a prairie and its secrets, I must look inward also, see with other than my eyes. I must look with my spirit. In this lies the prairie's greatest lesson.

Afterword

It's hard to write about a landscape that's disappearing. This book grew out of a journal kept over a 15-year period. Many of the special places I tramped and explored, my "secret" places, are gone now or so altered they have lost their character, victims of rampant development. My house in Parker is hemmed in by dozens of other homes. The rangeland where I raced pronghorn has disappeared beneath houses, lawns and streets. The golf-course prairie fell to the bulldozer a few years back, the prairie dogs poisoned. I am sure its Texas-based developer has little interest in the spiritual value of a damaged landscape. Someday perhaps a homeowner will excavate in her backyard and find the deeply buried bones of long-dead 'dogs, and perhaps alongside them one of the golf balls Cody dropped down a prairie dog burrow.

Cody and Margo, my dogs that kept me such close and excellent company in my years exploring the prairie, have both died from old age, as has Thunder, the wonder horse. Things change and special friends and places pass away. New ones come into your life. Rick and I have a wonderful daughter, Olivia, who comes with me now on my adventures outdoors. In time she may learn the lessons of the prairie, wisdom that lives beyond changes to the landscape. Look close, appreciate subtlety, see with your spirit not just your eyes.

Enduring despite decades of change, the prairie yet has much to teach us. Seeing beauty and joy in the commonplace is part of accepting ourselves as we are, others as they are. Few, few of us will be movie stars or super-models, presidents or champion athletes. To judge by narrow extremes of appearance or accomplishment is to blind ourselves to the truly sublime—the wonders of our daily lives and daily selves. As I learned to see the beauty and wisdom of the prairie, this ugly duckling land, I grew to appreciate the simple beauties within myself. Inside we both are swans.

—*Mary Taylor Young*
Castle Rock, Colorado
April 2002

EarthTales Press

"Listen to the Earth and the tales it has to tell..."

Since 1981, Westcliffe Publishers has produced quality guidebooks, coffee-table books, and calendars—works that celebrate nature's wonders through full-color scenic photography. Westcliffe's EarthTales Press imprint views the natural world through a different lens: the compelling words of acclaimed wilderness writers. EarthTales Press explores the human relationship with the environment and encourages readers to develop both physical and spiritual connections with our treasured wildlands.

Other EarthTales Press titles include:

Living on the Spine
A Woman's Life in the Sangre de Cristo Mountains
by Christina Nealson

Through journal-style passages that follow the movement of the seasons, Christina Nealson chronicles her courageous five-year journey into solitude at the foot of Colorado's Sangre de Cristo range. Her stirring descriptions of the landscape paint a clear picture of life in the high desert, and her captivating story blends the simplicity of her lifestyle with the intricacy of the human spirit. By living gently, honestly, and passionately, Nealson cuts life to the core to discover the truths of a woman's soul. ISBN 1-56579-471-0

People of the Mesa Verde Country
An Archaeological Remembrance
by Ian M. Thompson

In this book the late author—well remembered in the Southwest's Four Corners region as a newspaper editor, town mayor, and the executive director of Crow Canyon Archaeological Center in Cortez, Colorado—puts a human face on the study of archaeology. His lyrical meditations reveal a deep connection with the land, legacy, and people of the Great Sage Plain, from ancient Puebloans and early homesteaders to the archaeologists who shared his passion for working in the field. ISBN 1-56579-474-5

PrueHeart the Wanderer
From Western Wilderness to Concrete Canyons
by Lynna Howard

Idaho-based Lynna Howard—alias PrueHeart the Wanderer—discovers wildness in the heart of New York City just as easily as she does in the fringes of her home state. PrueHeart's urban adventures juxtapose her witty, insightful travel diary entries and poetry written on wilderness treks throughout the American West. The interplay she creates between urban and backcountry experiences reveals much about the connection of the two "wilds" and redefines exploration as anything that stretches the spirit and inspires the soul. ISBN 1-56579-432-X

Stone Desert
A Naturalist's Exploration of Canyonlands National Park
by Craig Childs

For the length of a winter, author and National Public Radio commentator Craig Childs traveled the mysterious and desolate Canyonlands National Park in Utah—a region full of shadows and surreal sandstone shapes. Within this landscape, geology becomes a language of poetry. Botany turns to the taste of a leaf on the tongue. The author followed paths of rivers, chasms, and sensual backs of stone to emerge the following spring with a journal in his hands. Its drawings and text became this book, a search for order and understanding in an enigmatic desert. ISBN-56579-473-7